DEFENSE LOGISTICS FOR THE 21ST CENTURY

AN ASSOCIATION OF THE U.S. ARMY BOOK

DEFENSE LOGISTICS FOR THE 21ST CENTURY

GEN. WILLIAM G. T. TUTTLE JR.,
U.S. ARMY (RET.)

NAVAL INSTITUTE PRESS
ANNAPOLIS, MARYLAND

Naval Institute Press
291 Wood Road
Annapolis, MD 21402

Library of Congress Cataloging-in-Publication Data

Tuttle, William G. T.
  Defense logistics for the 21ˢᵗ century / William G. T. Tuttle, Jr.
    p. cm.
Includes index.
ISBN 1-59114-883-9 (alk. paper)
  1. Logistics. 2. United States—Armed Forces—Procurement. 3. United States—Armed
    Forces—Supplies and stores. I. Title.
U168.T88 2005
355.6′21′0973—dc22

                                                                                2005007917

Printed in the United States of America on acid-free paper ∞
12 11 10 09 08 07 06   9 8 7 6 5 4 3 2

Contents

PREFACE

This book comes from my more than forty years of working with the defense logistics system of the Department of Defense (DoD). That experience began from the vantage point of a rifle platoon leader in the Eighty-second Airborne Division as a customer of support for forty-four paratroopers and custodian of the platoon's weapons and equipment. It extends through nearly thirty-four years in the Army as a commander and staff officer at all levels, occasionally outside—but never far from—logistics organizations, culminating as commanding general of the Army Materiel Command during Operation Just Cause in Panama and Operations Desert Shield and Desert Storm in 1990–91. That experience has been enriched by a ten-year association with the Logistics Management Institute in support of logisticians in the Office of the Secretary of Defense, Organization of the Joint Chiefs of Staff (hereafter Joint Staff), the armed services, and the defense agencies. During that period I also participated in several defense advisory panels examining logistics issues for the DoD.

This book is written for defense logistics leaders—those currently coping with the challenges and those logisticians aspiring to lead—and for those responsible for the numerous logistics educational and training courses taught in DoD institutions of learning. It is my hope that the military and civilian leaders of all the armed services, the DoD staff, and the defense agencies will find something useful here. The book is intended as a comprehensive treatment of defense logistics that could become a supplemental resource for many courses of instruction, from senior service college to junior staff and command schools.[1] The book also will help American industry, which is so critical to America's defense capabilities, to better understand the complexities of projecting and sustaining defense forces around the world—the enduring tasks of defense logistics.

---

[1] An initial tour experience of 3–4 years in logistics practices probably is necessary for understanding this book.

WHY A BOOK ON DEFENSE LOGISTICS NOW?

Many military logisticians will recall two excellent books, for their times, on military logistics: *Logistics in the National Defense*, by Rear Adm. Henry Eccles, USN (Ret.) published in 1959; and *Supplying War: Logistics from Wallenstein to Patton*, by Martin Van Creveld, published in 1977. Both volumes offered reliable insights in their times. However, in the intervening years revolutionary change, enabled by the information revolution, has swept the field of commercial logistics. And the nature of the post–Cold War national strategy, whose outline emerged as early as the Vietnam War, has mandated new principles of logistics support.

My aim here is to update the understanding of logistics as what Van Creveld defined as the "practical art of moving armies and keeping them supplied."[2] While we might agree that this definition, adapted from the military theoretician G. H. Jomini, remains descriptive, it is inadequate to describe 21st-century reality—both in the variety of operations to be supported and in the technological and management innovations in logistics. On the other hand, a great deal has been written and spoken about both the "revolution in military strategy" and the "revolution in military logistics." These terms and the more recent term of art, "transformation," have variously described the new environment and the technologies that can enable the logistics processes to meet new demands. However, it seems like the revolution in military logistics has become a list of technology "enablers," useful perhaps, but lacking a conceptual framework to help decide where scarce resources could do the most good. At the very least, this book offers that conceptual framework, with a set of objectives and supporting principles and consideration of the influence of culture and politics on logistics outcomes.

I have attempted to stay away from using most of the conceptual names applied to the various logistics initiatives over the past decade, principally because the concepts they have represented change frequently, and their meanings are somewhat elastic. Instead, with only a few exceptions, I have preferred to describe the processes without assigning names so that the reader may understand the processes' workings and intended results. Where I have named a process, I have provided a definition of the term. Therefore, those who have been involved with the changes in logistics may be disappointed

---

[2] Martin Van Creveld, *Supplying War: Logistics from Wallenstein to Patton* (Cambridge and New York: Cambridge University Press, 1977), p. 1.

in not finding a familiar name, such as "Focused Logistics," "Future Logistics Enterprise," or its successor. I apologize and hope they will understand my purpose in this omission.

FRAMEWORK OF THE BOOK

Twenty-first-century defense logistics must meet two objectives in order to support the national military strategy: (1) timely delivery of forces and sustainment to the combatant commanders and (2) minimization of the logistics "footprint" in the battle spaces.[3] These objectives are central to the conceptual framework that begins *Defense Logistics for the 21st Century*. There I address both the nature of defense logistics and the role it plays in the nation's military strategy. From this part of the book the reader can gain a holistic appreciation of the totality of defense logistics before embarking on a journey through the processes, issues, and policy choices that constitute this vital part of the nation's national security capabilities.

Within the conceptual framework, this book also proposes five supporting principles that, if applied to the logistics processes, will produce more effective performance of defense logistics tasks.

Throughout the book I will also treat explicitly two sets of "soft" influences on defense logistics: cultural and political. Cultural issues have to do with the people who lead and operate or influence the defense logistics processes: their beliefs and values, attitudes and behaviors—all of which cannot help but affect the operation of the logistics system. Political influences arise because defense logistics is part of the government—involving several hundred thousand military, civilian, and contractor personnel and over a hundred billion dollars a year of public expenditure. In our democratic society these stakeholders' interests affect executive and legislative policies and practices that heavily influence defense logistics processes and outcomes. Therefore, no project to deepen understanding of defense logistics would be complete without a realistic treatment of both cultural and political influences.

---

[3] The logistics footprint is the collective set of people, equipment, stocks of supplies, facilities, and other components of the resources necessary to provide support to the combat organizations. The term "footprint" has become a useful way of thinking about the so-called logistics tail.

A recurring theme in logistics studies by many groups inside and outside the defense establishment over the last couple of decades has been reducing logistics costs. To achieve such reductions, the defense establishment has structured reorganizations, reduced inventories, and made various efforts to adopt industry best practices. Thus the reader familiar with previous studies might ask, "Why is there no *cost reduction* objective in the conceptual framework?"

I believe that in order to support the nation's military strategy in the 21st century, the DoD must swing its pendulum of focus toward *effectiveness* as the primary goal. A number of policies and practices implemented during that period in the name of efficiency have had unfortunate consequences when the time came to support military campaigns. Efforts to achieve short-term savings by arbitrary inventory reductions and denial of funding for spare parts acquisition, training, and equipment systems have wasted resources when major operations overloaded ineffective management processes and resources.

Logistics cannot be allowed to fail in support of the nation's military campaigns. Yet that does not mean that efficiency, cost control, and other instruments of responsible public sector management should be neglected. And they are not neglected here. Pursuing this book's twin logistics objectives and employing the five proposed principles for operating logistics processes will produce responsible cost control and perhaps even reductions.

Not only do we need a new conceptual framework to understand how defense logistics processes can better support the national strategy, but we also need to become better stewards of the billions of taxpayer dollars that fund logistics work. *Effectiveness* of defense logistics processes must be paramount in ensuring the success of military operations, but their *efficient* employment is important because resources are limited. Waste of resources in one activity means that some other useful activity (such as modernization of weapons systems) goes begging. Defense logistics activities consumed over $84 billion a year in fiscal year (FY) 2000[4]—a level that was destined to rise as DoD dealt with the higher costs of sustaining aged systems and increased its operations in the aftermath of the terrorist attack of September 11, 2001. Operation Enduring Freedom in Afghanistan since 2001 and Operation Iraqi

---

[4] Office of the Undersecretary of Defense Acquisition, Technology, and Logistics, "Product Support for the 21st Century," Report of the Product Support Reengineering Implementation Team, July 1999.

Freedom since 2003 illustrate the dramatically increased operational tempo. Much of that cost is for the people who operate the logistics processes. And therein lies the opportunity for containing cost growth, if not reducing some of the resource demands, as has been done in commercial logistics processes.

Appendix A contains an analysis of DoD's logistics costs. Logisticians who understand the nature of those costs and seek opportunities for leveraging technological and management innovation to improve both effectiveness and efficiency will be heroes in their services.

Because of the transformational changes taking place in the logistics profession and because of the critical demands of the nation's military strategy, this book will examine the need for and development of the *professional* defense logistician of the 21st century. Uniformed defense logisticians already are members of the military profession. I will examine their identity as a subprofession and their civil service counterparts' inclusion in that subprofession.

Finally, I will summarize the major proposals that come from the examination of the processes, the systems, and logisticians' professional development. This "way ahead" chapter paints a picture of how defense logistics could provide even more effective support for combatant commanders in the 21st century's first couple of decades.

WHAT IS NOT COVERED

The book does not examine two sets of processes considered to be part of "logistics" in the Joint Chiefs of Staff definition: mobilization and combat engineering. The JCS definition also encompasses "force generation," a term I have not used but have incorporated into the discussion in chapters 2 and 3 of the "preparation for deployment" phase of force projection.

The nation has long since adopted the "come as you are" policy, reserving mobilization processes for instances of national emergency requiring the reinstitution of the draft and the large-scale industrial mobilization needed in the remote possibility of major conflict with a "near peer" adversary. The mobilization process most certainly involves the major logistics objective—timely delivery of support—and would benefit from the five principles laid out in the next chapter. But logistics is only a small part of the mobilization process; other functions play equally important parts in successful mobilization. Acquisition of weapons systems and support equipment, industrial base development, reinstitution of the draft and personnel accessions, and individual and unit training are all critical. Grappling with the complex issues required to be addressed in national mobilization deserves a separate volume.

While there is a case to be made for including in the logistics realm the kinds of construction required to facilitate both operations and support—e.g., air and naval bases, ports, storage facilities, pipelines, and the like—these processes are outside the historical definitions of "logistics." Engineering, like combat operations, depends upon the traditional logistics processes for the successful completion of projects. Timely delivery of forces and support (equipment, supplies, people) is as important to the engineering function as it is to combat operations. Yet it deserves its own comprehensive treatment. Writing about the adaptation of traditional logistics processes to the demands of the nation's defense strategy in the 21st century is already a "full plate." The pressing needs to understand and improve the processes of force projection and sustainment of weapons systems and people are a sufficient challenge for author and reader in this book.

Acknowledgments

This has been a three-year writing and publication effort, preceded by several years of thought and discussions about the simple concepts of moving armies (and navies and air forces) and keeping them supplied. I owe a debt of gratitude to numerous former colleagues in all the services for educating me in their own logistics processes. My colleagues at LMI contributed much to my critical thinking about these issues and were willing to debate my notions of how to improve the processes. Several colleagues read drafts of various chapters and gave me perceptive comments that improved my thinking. I am grateful to the members of the several Defense Science Board task forces in which I participated who were willing to "think outside the box" on many of these issues and influenced my own willingness to take on traditional concepts. They contributed to launching the early stages of some of the ideas put forward in this book. I am especially grateful to my brother-in-law, Howard Warren, whose encouragement, writing skill, and considerable knowledge of weapons system support contributed greatly to this effort. Of course, the responsibility for errors, omissions, and the raising of controversial issues is entirely mine.

I want to acknowledge the extraordinary help of my copy editor, Carol Kennedy. Her changes significantly improved the clarity and readability of the text. I also appreciate the confidence that both Roger Cirillo of the Association of the U.S. Army and the Naval Institute Press have shown in a first-time author proposing a book on the arcane subject of logistics. They must have become believers in the Army Transportation Corps motto, "Nothing happens until something moves."

Finally, I could not have produced this book without the patient and understanding support of my wife, Helen. She accepted our postponement of the normal activities of retired couples with grace—and my promise that we would have time for those activities when the book was completed.

Defense Logistics for the 21st Century

CHAPTER 1

OVERVIEW OF DEFENSE LOGISTICS—
A CONCEPTUAL FRAMEWORK

This chapter lays the groundwork for understanding defense logistics of the 21st century: its anatomy, the critical role of information in its processes, its linkages to national military strategy, and some principles to consider for critical evaluation of its processes. These are the constituents of the conceptual framework for understanding defense logistics and its component parts.

Defense logistics, as treated in this book, has two major components (succeeding chapters will cover each in detail):

1. *Force projection ("moving armies . . .").* The set of processes involved in moving forces in connection with whatever mission is to be accomplished. By "forces," we mean generally armed services' units, whether Army battalions, Air Force fighter squadrons, Navy ships, or Marine Corps battalions/air squadrons. Another term used to describe this component is "strategic (or operational) deployment of forces."

2. *Sustainment of forces (". . . and supplying them").* This component includes the processes used to enable the deployed force to continuously maintain its readiness to accomplish its missions. While the principal focus here is on the *deployed* forces, I also will discuss the processes that are necessary to sustain the forces at their pre-deployment bases. I divide force sustainment into the components of forces—sustainment of people and sustainment of weapons systems and support equipment—reflecting the different processes central to each:

   ▸ *Sustainment of people.* These logistics processes assure that the fighting (and supporting) capabilities of the members of the forces are maintained in top condition to deploy and accomplish their missions. The processes involve provision of water, food, health care, environmental protection, and other goods—and services—that contribute to "personal readiness." The importance of this set of sustainment processes is nearly self-evident. People operate or support complex weapons systems best when they are healthy, well fed, properly clothed, and equipped to function in harsh environmental conditions. Degradation in these aspects of "people readiness" leads to degradation in the expected performance of combat and support tasks.

➤ *Sustainment of weapons systems and support equipment.* These processes include the whole gamut of activities designed to keep the weapons and support systems operating at their designed levels of effectiveness. Each force unit has designated levels of ready systems required for it to be considered "effective." The set of processes—to be covered in detail in chapter 6—ranges from preventive maintenance through complete overhaul/rebuilding and/or system modification to eventual removal from the force. We sometimes term this component of defense logistics "product support" to show its parallel with the commercial sector. Understandably, airlines need to have their aircraft performing at the levels of effectiveness that they purchased—e.g., "98% availability at the gate"—so they can meet the schedules that justify their investment. Both the airlines and the aircraft builders engage in product support activities to attain the desired results from these expensive investments in the airplane systems. So it is with the armed forces.

THE GEOGRAPHIC DIMENSION OF DEFENSE LOGISTICS

The geographic setting of defense logistics components is significant because the processes used are partly contingent upon *where* they take place. I use the term "battle spaces" to denote areas of active combat or potential combat, places where—generally—only U.S. or coalition military forces will operate. In battle spaces, substantial force protection is needed continuously during the conduct of major operations from whatever threats are foreseen. For that reason force commanders limit or deny access to U.S. or coalition noncombatant civilians who may be supporting the force. Thus the expectation is that logistics activities that take place in battle spaces normally are carried out by the military, with only occasional use of civilians when threat and force protection conditions permit. For example, the character of the Iraqi battle space changed sufficiently following cessation of major operations and the beginning of stability and support operations for the commander CENTCOM (Central Command) to allow civilians to enter. While insurgency and terrorist threats persisted, they were not of the same level as existed during the major combat operations. There certainly is no "bright line" between battle spaces from which civilians would be excluded and those in which they are allowed. It is a situational judgment for the combatant command or coalition force.

Typically in some parts of a theater or area of operations the threat conditions do not require sole use of military to perform logistics tasks. These areas can contribute to both force projection and sustainment tasks through siting of *intermediate staging or support bases* (ISBs). These ISBs can be ashore or afloat. Kuwait, Qatar, and Bahrain have been robust ISBs supporting coalition forces in Operation Iraqi Freedom. A Navy-Marine amphibious ready group (ARG) is an example of an ISB (albeit limited) afloat. Generally, such ISBs should be close enough to the battle spaces to allow responsive support—perhaps one thousand nautical miles at the outside. They should be far enough away to minimize expensive force protection requirements and allow for efficient logistics operations.

The third geographical area we will include is the location of sources of the various supplies and forces—generally the continental United States (CONUS) or the already forward stationed force locations, e.g., Europe, Japan, and Okinawa. For the most part, we will use the term "CONUS" to depict the supply and force sources, but the term can equally apply to other geographic areas outside the ISBs and battle spaces, for example, the Sigonella, Italy naval station. CONUS itself is the location of most defense manufacturing and major system overhaul activities.

Linkage of Logistics and National Military Strategy

The relationship between strategy and logistics is perhaps the most important criterion in evaluating alternative force projection and sustainment policies and processes. The primary metric of defense logistics effectiveness must be how well those policies and processes support the strategy.

At the most basic level the aim of logistics—in fact, its reason for existence—is to *enable* the execution of campaign plans for military operations. Logistics is, of course, not the only enabler; communications, intelligence and the combat forces themselves are all critical enablers. But logistics, which encompasses both the deployment of forces in support of campaign plans and the sustainment of those forces in the prosecution of the mission of the campaigns, is of central importance.

The national military strategy sets the objectives and creates the framework for the military operations that are the means of attaining the objectives. Military operations are executed through *campaigns*. The campaigns are carried out by the nation's combatant commands—Pacific, Central, European, and Southern commands abroad and Space and Northern commands in the CONUS. The gamut of military operations within the campaigns can range from the day-to-day training activities with other nations' forces, sometimes called "peacetime engagement," through humanitarian operations and "dissuasion" operations such as placing a carrier battle group in the Taiwan Straits, through the counterterrorism operations in Afghanistan, to operations such as Desert Shield/Desert Storm and Iraqi Freedom with their large force deployments and intense combat. Simultaneous campaigns are also possible, e.g., major combat in Iraqi Freedom, stability operations in Afghanistan and Bosnia/Kosovo, and counterterrorism operations in the Philippines, including overlapping major conflicts. Logistics, from deploying the forces to sustaining them, provides an important ingredient in enabling the successful execution of the missions in the operations supporting the campaigns and, hence, the national military strategy.

Each of the operations mentioned above includes vital logistics components. One operation could be a training exercise (part of the combatant command's peacetime engagement campaign) calling for the strategic deployment—and simulated forcible entry—of a battalion task force of the Army's Eighty-second Airborne Division transported and dropped by the U.S. TRANSCOM's (Transportation Command) Air Mobility Command C-17s, guided to the drop zone in Uzbekistan by Air Force combat controllers. Arrangements for the sustainment of the paratroopers of that task force and their weapons systems, equipment, and direct support elements are clearly necessary. Likewise, the deployment several years ago of a carrier battle group to the Taiwan Straits in support of the "dissuasion" campaign exercised both the commander PACOM's (Pacific Command) force projection component (the routine for deployed carrier battle groups) and the Pacific fleet's arrangements for sustaining the people and the battle group's systems. In both instances, these campaigns could not have achieved success without the successful execution of deployment and sustainment logistics operations.

In fact, the demonstrated capability to deploy the airborne force halfway around the world, to air-drop it on its objective, and to sustain its people and systems contributes to the strength of the national military strategy. It is one thing for a nation to discuss and even to plan that kind of operation in strategy forums. It is quite another thing to execute it—with full press coverage and observation by all the political actors whose behavior our political leaders wish to influence.

Deployment of the carrier battle group to the Taiwan Straits to help defuse a potential crisis drives home the image of overwhelming military power in a manner not likely to be forgotten by the actors in the Western Pacific for some time. Few look at that deployment and the brief operations as "logistics" exercises. But the logisticians of that battle group and the Navy's Pacific fleet who had to replan the battle group's activities to accommodate the deployment directive had no doubts about how much the reputation of the United States in the Western Pacific depended on their planning and execution of the deployment and sustainment operations.

In these two cases—as well as in the two Gulf Wars and the Afghanistan operation—logistics has clearly been a critical enabler of the campaign's prosecution. And that is an important message for military logisticians, operational commanders and planners, and even the contractors who build and help sustain systems. Those who plan and operate the deployment and sustainment processes should understand *how* the campaign plans they must support are developed and what risks are ingrained in those plans because of planners' assumptions about the performance of deployment and sustainment processes. Logisticians must examine the *draft* plans carefully for such assumptions and analyze the risks that might accompany them. In other words, logisticians must be involved in the initial campaign planning and remain involved through campaign operations.

Unfortunately, lessons taken (although not necessarily "learned") from operations and exercises tell many sad stories about unexamined assumptions. Tactical plans that assumed there would be no need to refuel a counterattack task force or that assumed the adequacy of what proved to be a disastrously small beach landing area for the British force at Gallipoli in World War I: such "assumptions" brought—or almost brought—mission failure. Both the airborne training operation and the projection of the carrier battle group described above required very complex, detailed planning both for the deployment and for the sustainment operations. Because mission failure of either the operation in the Taiwan Straits or the battalion air drop into Uzbekistan would have had embarrassing—if not worse—consequences, the logisticians planned in infinite detail, incorporating redundancy for the riskier parts: backup C-17s, air tankers, and en route bases, for example. The fact that both operations were hugely successful was due in no small part to the thoroughness of the joint operation and logistics planning and oversight.

While military logisticians frequently are given—and earn—the appellation "bean counters," such attention to the myriad of details involved in deployment and sustainment operations is a necessity if risks are to be managed. To be practical, who bears the responsibility if needed fuel is not available or there is no backup for a broken aircraft? The stakes are high: mission success or failure, and certainly the reputation of the military organization—indeed, sometimes of the nation.

When we look back on the successful role played by the nation's strategy of deterrence during the Cold War, logistics doesn't immediately appear as a star. But the policy makers on both sides knew full well that the United States' ability to deploy and sustain both nuclear and conventional forces in conflict areas, and its ability to sustain a high rate of readiness of the strategic land- and sea-based intercontinental missile and bomber forces, gave substance to "deterrent" policy. Those capabilities were enabled by the defense logistics processes we will examine.

Role of Information in Defense Logistics

It should be clear from the discussion about planning for the myriad of details surrounding complex deployment and sustainment operations that information is the "coin of the realm." It is often stated both in the commercial world and in defense that "logistics *IS* information." For example, without knowledge of the status of deployment assets, the characteristics of the units to be deployed, the en route support required, and capabilities of air and seaports, the operation might not even get off the ground.

Similarly, since one can expect the unexpected, e.g., something will go awry, or the deployment plan will undergo last minute change, there must be a way to gain knowledge of deviations from the plan so that those in charge can replan and make the necessary changes to the deployment operation. Obviously, the shorter the time lag between the event that forces change and its realization by the planner-operators, and in turn their ability to replan and get the operation on to another track, the better the deployment operation will proceed.

Information, of course, comes from *data* that must be entered into the "information process" either manually by a human or automatically when captured by a sensor, or by some combination similar to a person's using a bar-code reader at a supermarket. Those data show something about the status of an asset when linked to the date, time, location, and identities of the asset and the data-capturing agent.

The aggregation of those data into a database with other similar data might describe the status of a process such as movement of a unit through an aerial port to board its aircraft or the loading of a container.[1] That aggregated data becomes useful information to the managers of those logistics processes in their efforts to maintain the operations within time parameters, for example.

Through the information processes, that information becomes *knowledge* of the state of the processes when it has been evaluated by the managers or by comparison to previously directed standards, e.g., on schedule, behind schedule, and so on.

The linkage between the seemingly mundane efforts of data entry and the output of knowledge about such critical processes as deployment of the airborne task force or carrier battle group described earlier becomes clearer. It is easy to understand how poor-quality data at the departure airfield can have serious consequences in the deploying aircraft's ability to meet politically negotiated schedules of overflight and airdrop. That linkage demonstrates that poor data can be the root cause of less than successful mission execution and the strategic and political consequences that accompany it. It is a modern variation of the old saw, "For want of a nail, the campaign was lost." Through this example it is easy to see why logisticians regard information in the form of "actionable knowledge" as indispensable to their planning and management of logistics operations.

Objectives and Principles

We have now examined

> - the two major components of defense logistics—force projection and force sustainment

---

[1] The database might be loaded with the "planned" data—number of people and equipments, scheduled time of arrival at the ramp, etc. Then the data captured as the unit arrives at the ramp is entered into the database to permit comparison of actual against scheduled arrival, producing "actionable knowledge."

- ▸ the three major locations of logistics activities—battle spaces, intermediate staging/support bases, and the CONUS and related sources of forces and materiel
- ▸ the linkages between logistics and the national military strategy through the concept of "enabling campaign execution"
- ▸ the critical role of information in the form of "actionable knowledge" as the sinews that facilitate logistics planning and operations that are synchronized with the campaign planning and execution they support.

We turn now to establish a means for assessing the effectiveness of deployment and sustainment processes—an evaluation approach that relates directly to the potential for effective logistics support of campaigns.

The two principal objectives and the supporting principles together lead to the metrics for measuring the "goodness" of the processes and proposed changes to them. Any set of such objectives and principles must first and foremost contribute to the central purpose of logistics, enabling campaign execution. In succeeding chapters, I will elaborate on each objective and principle and its own application to the force projection and force sustainment processes. The two objectives can be considered to be the *major results* of the logistics processes and the critical tests of their effectiveness in supporting campaign operations. The five principles are crucial supporting, or enabling, principles. To the extent that processes follow these supporting principles, the two objectives will be more easily achieved.

LOGISTICS OBJECTIVES:

1. timely delivery of forces and support to the customers
2. minimized "footprint" of logistics activities in battle spaces

SUPPORTING PRINCIPLES:

1. accountability for process performance
2. continuously shared knowledge of asset status, requirements of the campaign, "customer" status, process barriers
3. maximized commercial contracting of logistics activities in CONUS, forward bases, and intermediate staging and support bases
4. use of the "comparative advantage" concept for allocation of logistics tasks to coalition partners

5. simplicity in planning and operations (application of a "principle of war")

Timely Delivery of Forces and Support to Customers

The discussion of the linkages between logistics and the national military strategy makes evident the importance of the first logistics objective. Campaign execution depends upon a complex sequencing of insertion of forces into battle spaces and intermediate staging and support bases. Twenty-first-century operations place an even greater premium than heretofore on the timely delivery of forces in order to achieve the desired *effects* on the enemy's ability and will to resist. The logistics part of these operations ranges from the physical transport of land and air components to enabling the self-deploying force projection elements such as long-range bombers and naval carrier and expeditionary strike groups. The careful orchestration of the joint "effects-based" operations creates the conditions that lead to quickly achieved battle space dominance and rapid conclusion of major combat operations.

Logistics operations historically have oscillated between delivering sustainment supplies "too much, too soon" or "not enough, too late." With long lead times for ordering supplies and having them pass in-transit through many bottlenecks from factory to customer unit, it is no wonder that such variation in delivery times occurs. And, of course, in many operations the customer unit's situation can change several times within the order-receipt cycle, compounding the challenge of providing the needed logistics support not too early—and certainly, not too late.

This phenomenon and the logistics management dilemma is endemic to both the force projection and sustainment components processes. The decisive term "Hurry up and wait!" has been a common complaint of military units, probably for eons. Those who have studied these processes involved, beginning with the famous "Quality Guru," W. Edward Deming, in the early post–World War II years, developed the concept of reducing the "variability" of the processes through process control—and plain disciplined management of the details of manufacturing and distribution processes.[2] This

---

[2] W. Edwards Deming, *The New Economics for Government, Education, and Industry* (Potomac, MD: W. Edward Demings Institute, 1994), chs. 6–10.

work provided the major Japanese auto manufacturers with the ability to both raise quality and reduce both manufacturing and distribution costs over the last couple of decades.

They developed "just-in-time" strategies for components to arrive at assembly line stations to cut waste, and they adopted the discipline to follow through on those strategies. Their watch words were *"Reduce the variability of the processes."* Their successes have shown up in their dominance of the quality ratings, huge gains in U.S. market share, and a large coterie of loyal owners.

While pure "just-in-time" may carry too much risk for deploying and sustaining forces, the concept is useful since it is based on removing as much variability in the processes as possible and requires disciplined design and management of the processes, using the *continuously shared knowledge* principle described below. Having too many forces pile up at an airfield is the same as having too many engines pile up at the engine installation station on an assembly line—except that the forces may create an attractive target for the enemy. Likewise, having aviation fuel arrive late for a carrier can disrupt carefully choreographed strike missions, just as late arrival of engines could stop an auto assembly process. Thus this measure of logistics effectiveness is labeled "timely." The processes that result in timely delivery must be designed *and managed* to reduce variability. As we shall see in later chapters, the achievement of this measure literally depends upon *continuously shared knowledge* of the deployment and sustainment processes.

Minimized Footprint of Logistics Activities in Battle Spaces

New technology and logistics management innovation now makes feasible what has long been desired—reducing the "iron mountains" of supplies and equipment that used to be required to support deployed forces. Throughout the last sixty years U.S. defense logistics practices resulted in building an echelonment of depots from the battle spaces to CONUS. The philosophy was to stock items "just-in-case." At the same time, the commercial practice was to have inventory of finished and intermediate products echeloned behind the retail outlets and manufacturers. It's an expensive practice for both commercial enterprises and the Defense Department; it can undermine effective logistics support for either, and pose major force protection problems for force commanders.

The relatively new thinking about supply chain management in the commercial world revealed this echeloned inventory to be a lucrative cost reduction target. Technology—and disciplined management—now allowed the substitution of information for inventory. Huge cuts subsequently have been made in these distribution channels, converting the inventory investments and distribution costs to profit. The analogue in defense logistics is that the same kind of substitution of knowledge and disciplined management can streamline the distribution processes, also reducing inventory requirements and investment and improving customer wait time. The operational benefits come from the smaller logistics force necessary to store, move, and protect those "iron mountains." That makes the whole force, especially in the battle spaces, far more agile and free of the large logistics tail that must be protected from disruption by the enemy and dragged behind combat forces. The other attractive advantage of a small footprint is the same as that which has motivated the commercial sector: huge savings in costs from fewer people, less equipment, fewer facilities, and lower inventories.

Reduced footprint, like timely delivery, also depends upon *continuously shared knowledge* and the disciplined management of the order-receipt cycle. With robust processes for timely delivery from CONUS sources, the requirement for intermediate storage activities lessens. Some obviously are necessary, but the depth of stockage (and, therefore, the sheer amount of supplies) is greatly reduced. This logic—and the measure of effectiveness—applies equally to deployment processes, as we shall explore later. One illustration comes from Operation Enduring Freedom in Afghanistan in late 2001. The Air Force loaded B-2 bombers with munitions in Missouri for deployment to Afghanistan and carried them directly to their targets with no need for a buildup of expensive inventory, intermediate storage, and distribution. The result was a tightly managed supply chain from factory—to air base storage—to aircraft and delivery to the ultimate customer (in this case the targets). While few other items of combat power can be deployed so efficiently, the objective increasingly should be to deliver combat power directly to battle spaces. The concept of direct delivery of supplies, equipment, and services to battle space customers must be a central ingredient of the logistics process in order to achieve a minimum footprint in the battle spaces.

The Supporting Principles

Accountability for Process Performance

The *accountability* principle gets first place because it is crucial to achieving the process performance standards necessary for both timely delivery and minimum footprint. Achieving both of those logistics objectives requires significant improvements in process performance over past and present practices. In order to achieve those improvements, the logisticians' "culture" must change. The process and organization fragmentation that has so long characterized defense logistics processes ensured that no one person or organization could be held accountable for performance—whether for weapons system support or a timely deployment process. Multiple organizations from different services, and even within a service, unified command, or agency, have had—and continue to have—only partial responsibility for most processes. The result has been a lack of accountability for results within the logistics community (although the combat unit bears the ultimate accountability even though most logistics processes are beyond its influence). As we will discover, both the supply chain and the weapons systems management processes lend themselves to having "process owners." Each weapons system *can* have a program manager who *can* (if given the authority and adequate resources) provide the parts and technical support for combat-ready weapons systems to the combat unit customer. Each joint task force (JTF) commander *can* have a logistics organization commanded by one officer—of any service—who can direct common supplies and services to the customers, assuring timely delivery without a large footprint. Those are the beginnings of achieving the principle of *accountability*. But they require culture change in the services and the willingness of the chairman of the Joint Chiefs of Staff (JCS) and the secretary of defense to mandate these *unity-of-command-over-processes* organization and culture adjustments. And they require the services to put some of their so-called Title 10 and organization protection claims aside.

Continuously Shared Knowledge

Continuously shared knowledge in the following areas is essential:

> ➤ asset status
> ➤ "customer" status
> ➤ campaign requirements
> ➤ process barriers

This principle derives from our earlier discussion about the critical role of actionable knowledge to the planning and management of logistics operations. Note the characteristics of the knowledge we seek: first, "continuously." For example, as force projection processes unfold, the information processes must be able to assemble information continuously on the ever-changing status of forces being deployed; on the infrastructure (rail, highway, ports) through which they must deploy; on the lift assets—trucks, railcars, aircraft, ships; and so on. Also to keep the process "on track," the managers must be aware of proposed changes to the set of forces to be deployed (so they can assess consequences) and must adjust the movement schedules and the myriad of other plans that require change.

The term "shared" reflects the necessity for all the participants in the force projection and sustainment processes to have a common picture (continuously updated) of the status elements, requirements, and barriers, to assure that participants don't act on old or erroneous information and disrupt the processes. The war fighting communities also seek what they term a "common relevant operating picture" of enemy and friendly forces and their activities. That requirement is the same for logisticians.

In order for the deployment and sustainment processes to meet even more demanding time standards where margins of acceptable performance have been narrowed, there must be less friction in those processes. Continuously shared knowledge "lubricates" those processes so that all participants from process owners to force unit "customers" know how their deployment or sustainment processes are developing. They then can anticipate problems more easily and jointly assess appropriate actions, or they can together see the almost inevitable appearance of barriers (such as lift asset breakdown, enemy action, or budget reductions) and react jointly. We will return to this principle in our discussions of force projection and sustainment in subsequent chapters and discuss specific ways for achieving and managing the information processes required by this principle.

Maximized Commercial Contracting of Logistics Activities Outside the Battle Spaces: In CONUS, at Forward Bases, and at Intermediate Staging and Support Bases

This principle results from experiences in both government and industry that suggest that organizations do best when they stick to their "core competencies": those competencies for which they must develop skills and focus in order to survive. High-performing organizations pay other organizations to perform tasks outside those core competencies—organizations whose own core competencies cover the high-performing organization's "non-core" tasks. Such is the practice of "outsourcing."

Clearly defense tasks center around war fighting, the tasks immediately related to war fighting, and its included missions, e.g., operations in threatening environments of battle spaces. Logistics tasks that are not directly related (in battle spaces) to war fighting *could* therefore be candidates for performance by organizations with logistics core competencies. Firms such as FedEx and UPS in distribution and supply chain management; Boeing, Northrop Grumman, and Lockheed in product support; and airlines and ship-operating firms in long-haul transportation all offer world-class logistics services. Logistics **is** their core competency. They have made major investments in information technology; they operate globally—successfully—with management teams whose road to career success lies in those logistics tasks. One can thus argue that the armed services should look to those world-class firms to perform the logistics tasks within their core competencies so that the services and defense commands and agencies can focus their leadership on developing the war-fighting skills necessary to carrying out the national military strategy. And, in fact, the services and defense agencies do outsource some of the tasks. Most sealift is done commercially; most passenger airlift (into safe airports) is commercial: Boeing provides product support of the C-17; Lockheed supports the Trident submarine force; the Army's newly fielded Stryker combat vehicles are supported by a General Dynamics-led contractor team, and Defense Logistics Agency has outsourced the order fulfillment of most food, medical/pharmaceutical items, fuels, and some clothing to private sector firms in those distribution businesses.

These defense organizations have determined that they should refocus their management talent on managing the *outcomes* of transportation, order fulfillment, and product support processes rather than performing the process tasks themselves. They have contracted competitively with firms with the requisite core competencies to perform the tasks. The defense organizations' role has been to form contractual agreements and oversee the firms' process *results*, employing incentives such as profit and continued work. Rather than worry about acquiring the performance skills, the technology, and the unique management talents demanded by the commercial-like logistics tasks, these defense organizations have focused on developing requirements management and acquisition skills—a set of tasks crucial to achieving the required performance results. In effect, these defense organizations have found a way to also fix *accountability* for process results through contractors—accountability they were unable to achieve when operating the processes themselves.

However, taking advantage of private sector core competencies is NOT the prevailing practice; it is a glacially slow evolving trend, bitterly opposed—understandably—by those who have been performing those tasks for years. The Defense Department's depot maintenance activities and shipyards, distribution depots, and commodity management centers are the residuals of a structure that the nation was forced to invest in during World War II. Like many government programs, once established, populated with well-meaning, patriotic people who believe in what they are doing and who are supported by their representatives and senators, they are difficult to end. Arguments about core competencies, efficiency, even effectiveness, do not stand well against congressional loyalty to constituents whose jobs are threatened by change.

This principle of *accountability*, then, directly confronts the cultural and political components of decision making. While in the private sector outsourcing actions impelled by the recognition of organizational core competencies can be carried out in short periods of time, in government long-drawn-out political battles ensue, and even military leaders are loath to take on the difficult tasks of change—no matter what the projected gains might be.

At the same time, military and civilian leaders cannot ignore the resource and effectiveness costs of continuing practices long out of date. In defense logistics, it has been estimated that costs could be reduced by 10–20 percent (a figure that many feel is quite conservative) through competitive outsourcing of product support tasks outside battle spaces. Savings generated could yield $12–15 billion from the costs shown in Appendix A for modernization or other uses. But the far more important benefit would lie in increased effectiveness of processes: more highly skilled technicians to produce better diagnoses and repairs of systems or better delivery of a variety of products and services. We will go more deeply into the discussion of the application of this principle in succeeding chapters.

"Comparative Advantage" Allocation of Logistics Activities to Coalition Partners

The first question the reader will have is "Why even bring up logistics activities and coalition partners as one of your five supporting principles?" The rationale for offering a principle for coalition logistics management starts with the proposition that the purpose of the logistics activities is to support the execution of the campaign plans of the combatant commands. The United States' experience in warfare since the beginning of World War II has been to engage in campaigns with allies in coalitions. The natural concomitant of this engagement has been to extend it to forms of logistics support. For example, "Host Nation Support" was provided by the United Kingdom and Australia and later France and the Low Countries in World War II, by South Korea and South Vietnam during wars fought in those countries, and by Germany, other NATO countries, Japan, and other Asian allies during the Cold War, the Gulf Wars, Bosnia, and Kosovo. In fact, there have been only a few conflicts in which the United States has fought alone.

The United States has frequently provided major logistics support to its allies, e.g., "Lend Lease" to Great Britain and the Soviet Union during World War II, airlift to all in the recent past. To confirm the need for a principle in dealing with coalition logistics, the United States' own joint logistics doctrine and its acceptance of NATO doctrine affirm the U.S. commitment to the concept of mutual logistics support.[3]

This principle proposes *how* to implement the concept, how to turn it from lonely negotiated wording to practical reality—in the face of enormous resource, cultural, language, and other differences between coalition partners. Working out practical agreements that will benefit all the coalition partners can seem like climbing Mt. Everest. Implementing the principle of *comparative advantage* will not by itself bring about agreement, but it offers the prospect of greatly easing the climb to the summit. We borrow the term and concept of "comparative advantage" from the literature and practice in international economics, where the meaning is that even though one country is absolutely more productive in producing a set of goods than its prospective trading partner countries, it will be better for it to concentrate its resources on producing the goods where its relative (comparative) advantage is greatest and to buy the other products from its trading partners.

As applied to logistics support arrangements, the principle suggests that the negotiators lay out support requirements that *can* be filled by other than national means. This process will tend to exclude support of complex weapons systems but not fuel, for example. Usually the requirements most amenable to

---

[3] *Logistics Support for Multinational Operations*, Joint Publication 4-08.

other-nation support have had to do with base operations, provision of some food, fuel, and other products, and services of the civil economies of coalition partners. The United States can then make agreements and contracts for the appropriate supplies and services in return for furnishing the support that only it could provide, e.g., airlift services or certain precision munitions.

It is also important to capitalize on this principle and its potential application in both the battle spaces and intermediate staging and support bases at the beginning of campaign planning. Frequently U.S. logistics planners have ignored coalition resources and sought the autarkic, or "we'll do it ourselves," route in early discussions. The almost inevitable result is a troop list of logistics support organizations (if they even exist) that will choke up the force projection pipeline. This "we'll do it ourselves" attitude until recently has driven the logistics resource (people and equipment) requirements and the force structures of the services. Only grudgingly have host nation support agreements been acknowledged—and usually with an argument that "we can't be sure the host nation will keep its commitment." In subsequent chapters, we will discuss some of the options and approaches to making *comparative advantage in coalition logistics* support a dependable influence on force projection and sustainment.

Simplicity

Logistics processes are inherently complex, with many actors and transactions, constantly changing requirements of customers, frequent unanticipated interruptions in plans, and, of course, ever-present human error. So, why establish *simplicity* as a principle? The answer is "because the processes are complex enough that logisticians and DoD leadership should do all they can to simplify them, and certainly should not, out of misplaced bureaucratic zeal, add more complexity." While this idea is only "common sense," the practices have often defied common sense. Affirming that *simplicity* should be one of the five supporting principles we apply in managing defense logistics is a necessary step in the effort to strip needless bureaucratic practices from the logistics processes.

We will apply the principle of *simplicity* in our discussion of each of the components of defense logistics, but it is useful here to outline the functions that have historically been most vulnerable to unnecessary "complexifying." First, command and control (C2), or "management": since this function embodies the exercise of power and influence by some participants over others, it acts like a magnet to tinkerers of command lines, regulations, and "historic" practices. Cultural differences between services and defense agencies and functional joint commands stimulate "I'd rather do it myself" approaches; personal and organizational ambition and ego also play a role. Frequently the result is some negotiated accommodation that no one fully accepts but all think they can live with. As frequently, it also results in lack of accountability, vaguely defined metrics for judging success of outcomes, and the opportunity to point to some "other" agency, law, or regulation as the reason for inadequate performance.

The second target for simplification is management of funds—authority to obligate and expend. Nowhere is unnecessary complexity more evident than in defense funding. Much of this complexity is a consequence of the "many colors of money," referring to the different categories of appropriated and working capital funds. It stems from Congress's historic "balkanization" of committees in appropriations, where the power of the purse confers political influence. These committees jealously protect their prerogatives over their appropriations categories, e.g., research and development, operations and maintenance, and the like. Complexity is added by the "authorization" process, by Office of Management and Budget's "allocation," and the budgeting and obligation controls of each layer of the Defense Department down to the activity that executes the force projection or sustainment tasks. There is constant juggling of budgets even after appropriations are enacted, because some budgeted expenses will exceed their estimates but must be incurred— at the expense of activities determined to have lower priority. The Navy's recent experience with the apparent sad maintenance state of the carrier *John F. Kennedy*, which was in the press from late 2001 until well into 2002, is an example of the consequences of the "robbing Peter to pay Paul" problem. And, as we shall see, the early 1990s modification of working capital fund management included a number of really unnecessary complexifying elements that dramatically increased the quantity of transactions in a system incapable of managing them—although they were touted to make defense "more like a business."

The third function that has attracted a host of complex rules has been sourcing—the procurement of supplies, equipment, and services. Reams have been written on the layering of regulation, procedure, and practices designed to make absolutely certain that no one could spend the public's money illegally or unwisely. Fortunately, the movement to acquisition reform in the

1990s has begun to reverse that process, but it will take the culture some time to move from rule-based acquisition to an ethical-but-business-judgment-based process.

Of course, because the logistics processes are inherently complex, some people in government will always want to protect themselves from criticism about something going wrong. They will invent rules that add complexity, especially after some mishap has occurred. The rules, of course, will be justified on the basis of making certain that mishap never again occurs. The volume of regulations governing most logistics processes has grown as the years passed. Only a focus on the principle of *simplicity* and a succession of stiff "backbones" can reverse this trend, so that logistics processes can yield their customer support results effectively and efficiently.

In the following chapters we will examine how the principle of *simplicity* can be used to measure the effectiveness of force projection and sustainment processes in achieving *timely delivery of forces and support to customers* and to produce a *minimum logistics footprint in battle spaces* in doing so. We will also examine how the application of the *simplicity* principle to logistics management (C2), funding, and acquisition of products and services can produce major improvements in those processes and, therefore, in the logistics support of combat and support organizations.

THE DILEMMA OF EFFICIENCY

Our conceptual framework bypasses the almost sacred quest for efficiency in logistics processes. The reason for focusing on effectiveness so heavily is that logistics is an *enabling* function in preparing for and prosecuting a campaign. Logistics is not an end in itself. Yet it is an enabling function that can mean campaign success or failure, life or death, for service members engaged in the campaign, as well as political objectives achieved or not, with huge consequences for our nation. Thus allocating resources to logistics is a major *risk management* endeavor, and combatant commanders through our history have wisely chosen to attempt to guarantee the availability of ample resources—especially logistics and manpower—to accomplish their missions. The risk of failure or major loss of people has justified the purchase of large "insurance policies." For example, one of those insurance policies was to move an exceptionally large amount of munitions (using several hundred ships) to Saudi Arabia during Operation Desert Shield, resulting in hundreds of acres of storage of several thousand tons of munitions. The amount, which would have supported probably seventy to eighty days of a ground war at intensities twice as great as we had estimated for a war in Europe in the 1980s, represented most of the Army's and Air Force's war reserve munitions stocks. That decision has been ridiculed by many pundits, official and unofficial. But there was irrefutable logic behind the decision. At the time we moved the munitions, the fall of 1991, no one knew how effective the Iraqi forces would be, nor what their ability was to survive the air campaign that preceded the ground attack. We knew only that they had large numbers of combat vehicles, were battle experienced, and might put up a tough fight. The time to prepare is before the fight. The stockage of that huge amount of munitions gave confidence to the war fighters that we would not run out of that critical resource. All they had to do was fly over the storage areas to see the magnitude of our preparation for battle.

What we were doing was simply *repositioning* those war reserves. At the end of the war we returned them to the United States and re-stowed them, having inspected and disposed of the unserviceable items—an effort we could not afford previously. Since the Iraqis had lost any means of mounting a major threat to stored munitions, we were not creating a target by establishing the large storage facility. The transportation was paid for by Saudi Arabia and other coalition partners. The reports of all those ships constantly arriving in Saudi ports must have reached Saddam Hussein and caused some trepidation. And, importantly, in Saudi Arabia we were closer to the other likely theater of conflict—Korea—than in the United States. So there was no real downside to the munitions stock-positioning decision.

Efficiency seekers decried the "waste." Yet they are not responsible for the campaign outcome nor the lives of the U.S. and coalition members who had to fight. That's why the most important dimensions of logistics process results revolve around "effectiveness." Yet we must not ignore the opportunities to become efficient and to stamp out the omnipresent chances for wasteful use of resources to which organizations are susceptible. Each of the logistics objectives and each of the supporting principles has an efficiency dimension, as we shall see in later discussion. For example, predictable, reliable *timely delivery of support* should reduce the need for large inventories of supplies as it has in commercial practice. A smaller *logistics footprint* will mean fewer resources devoted to logistics force structure, people, equipment, and supplies—a potentially large efficiency dividend. Improving *account-*

ability for process performance should, as in industry, focus managers' minds on reducing wasteful practices, improving efficiency as well as process effectiveness. The better the *continuously shared knowledge* principle works, the less likely will be bad judgments and the need to redo, reship, re-repair, and so on. We have already mentioned the potential for efficiencies from contractor support outside the battle spaces, and employing the principle of *comparative advantage* in coalition logistics support means a lower resource demand on the United States than would be possible without it. Implementing the *simplicity* principle should reduce the non-value-added bureaucratic practices that have grown up around organizations and that have become anachronistic with the passage of time. Thus this treatment of defense logistics comes at the efficiency issue by way of effectively supporting campaigns, but with eyes open for the opportunities to avoid waste at the same time.

CHAPTER 2

FORCE PROJECTION PROCESSES

This chapter describes the deployment processes that constitute force projection. Deployment processes can be broken down into a logical sequence of elements required to move forces into battle spaces or ISBs:

> pre-deployment processes
> preparation for movement—following an alert order
> movement to seaports and aerial ports of embarkation; loading aboard ships or aircraft; naval forces embark marines, aircraft, stores, and equipment at naval bases and seaports
> transit aboard these ships or aircraft to ports of debarkation in the area of operation and the en route processes to support transit
> reception, staging, and onward movement to operational sites

Each of these elements includes resource tradeoffs and issues of planning and management to which we can apply the principles developed in chapter 1 when they are appropriate to the particular process. Our objective in this chapter is to understand the issues and to gain insights as to how to approach their resolution *for particular deployment operations.* Meaningful generalities may be scarce; each scenario has its own unique character, which trained staffs and commanders can discern through practice; they can then apply practice-sharpened judgment.

PRE-DEPLOYMENT

Prior to alert for deployment, forces stationed at various CONUS and overseas bases engage in their normal peacetime training cycles to prepare for combat or support operations. An important part of their readiness to perform their unit missions is, of course, to be prepared for deployment—to have accomplished the tasks that are required to have people, the systems that they use, and the organizations themselves ready for entering into the post-alert deployment processes. These tasks involve some of the least glamorous activities that units can undertake, not nearly as riveting as combat training exercises, but failure to accomplish them leaves a unit vulnerable to being ill-prepared when a deployment is ordered. It should be noted that these processes apply to *redeployment* from operational missions either to other operations or to home stations.

First, people readiness. Quite obviously units of all services would like to deploy with a full complement of their people. However, seldom are all *eligible* to deploy, and filler personnel will be required. Some are ineligible because they have insufficient time remaining in the service, some have medical or dental disqualifications, some have assignment restrictions, and some, especially in the reserve components, may not be qualified in their occupational specialties. Thus the people-readiness tasks for deployable units are to keep their people qualified to deploy, to always know which individuals cannot deploy, to update the parent organization continually on the requirement for filler personnel, and to maintain procedures for rapidly integrating new people into the unit.

Equipment readiness for deployment is more than the normal maintenance of operable equipment that is second nature to every military organization. Deployment readiness for equipment requires further steps. Examples are to keep a constant watch over systems nearing periodic depot or other long-term maintenance so that replacement systems can be obtained; to have necessary tie-down kits for rail, truck, or air shipment—and the trained crews to use them; to have load plans for unit equipment on board unit transport or mission vehicles and to have that equipment ready. Equipment readiness also requires assuring post-deployment readiness by having technical publications, test equipment, spare parts, and maintenance equipment on hand and well maintained, and importantly, to have trained maintenance technicians ready to deploy with the systems.

A major element of the unit's readiness for deployment is the preparation and maintenance of unit movement data—the description of all of the unit's equipment and supplies that are to be deployed, complete with weight, cube, dimensions, and other necessary information. Those data are used by the transportation organizations that will load and transport the unit. The data are used to compute the number and type of lift vehicles and to "prestow" or prepare detailed aircraft and vessel load plans. Thus inaccurate data—a not infrequent failing—can result in delays in the deployment schedule that can have serious repercussions for the campaign plan.

Many anecdotes are told of incidents where the units' reported movement data and the actual equipment dimensions did not agree. One that comes to mind is a Sea Emergency Deployment Readiness Exercise (SEDRE) at the port of Savannah. The division's ready task force deployed by road to the port and was met by the Strategic Deployment and Distribution Command (SDDC) terminal unit, which had laid out the holding areas and completed the pre-stow plans for the vessel, using the task force's unit movement data.[1] When the assistant division commander arrived to review the loading progress he found some loading in progress—several hours behind schedule. He also saw a group of trucks lined up outside the loading area. The embarrassed task force commander explained that they were his vehicles, which had been modified so that their dimensions no longer matched the dimensions of the movement data originally provided in the command's system. That failure caused a delay to allow the terminal unit to revise its stowage plans and even remove some vehicles from their stowed locations. It was a lesson that the division commander shared with all his subordinate commanders and staffs and that reinforced the value of deployment readiness exercises.

Here's another example. For the deployment to Somalia in 1993, one of the Army's divisions deployed by sea. On arriving at the port of embarkation, the Strategic Deployment and Distribution Command (SDDC) terminal organization that had planned the stowage of the unit's vehicles and other gear discovered that the division's units had brought to the port far more vehicles and other gear than their own unit movement data indicated. In fact, to load the units as they were on arrival at port would have required complete re-stowage and 20 percent more ships. Needless to say, the division commander, embarrassed by this failure of discipline, ordered the units to configure to their own movement data so that the deployment could proceed and attempt to meet the JTF arrival schedule.

A high state of training for both mission tasks and deployment tasks is essential for organizational pre-deployment readiness. Periodic exercises, such as the Third Infantry Division's "DEPLOYEX," to demonstrate familiarity

---

[1] The SDDC was formerly Military Traffic Management Command (MTMC); the name changed in 2003.

with procedures and an ability to execute deployment tasks to standard, are the major training vehicles. They help diagnose shortfalls both in procedures and in execution pointing toward tasks to improve performance. As in most training exercises, not to embarrass themselves provides a powerful incentive for a unit's people—a factor that helps maintain readiness if exercised frequently enough. The Marine Corps' frequently exercised embarkation processes have long set a high standard. The Army's deployment proficiency improved considerably before Operation Iraqi Freedom, largely as a result of the creation of the mobility warrant officer program, which included training, in part, in Marine embarkation processes.

PREPARATION FOR MOVEMENT

The alert order initiates the implementation of the deployment phases of the campaign plan. The alert order typically designates a deployment date, a sea or aerial port for land forces, and a theater destination, at least in general terms. The deployment part of the campaign plan will include the Time Phased Force Deployment Data (TPFDD) with information about the transportation requirements of each force element included.

The TPFDD is based on the campaign plan's required sequencing of forces into battle spaces and ISBs that are necessary to support the campaign strategy. The TPFDD is the most important element of knowledge about the deployment because it drives the work of the services whose forces are included and who operate the installations on which the forces are stationed. Furthermore, the TPFDD determines the operation of the deployment support organizations, such as U.S. TRANSCOM and its components, the Army's SDDC, the Navy's Military Sealift Command (MSC) and the Air Force's Air Mobility Command (AMC), all of whom participate in TPFDD development. Those experienced in deployment operations understand that the one certainty about the TPFDD plan is that it will change. It will change continually—for perfectly logical reasons.

Force sequencing must respond to the changing theater environment, e.g., threat and host nation and coalition partners' responses. The combatant commander, JTF or CJTF (combined joint task force), for coalition operations must continually adjust the operational scheme to the unfolding missions and enemy situation. Typically, the sequencing of forces will be the principal agent of change so that the appropriate forces will be in the battle spaces when needed. In addition, enemy action can cause port closures, or aircraft or ships can break down, forcing adjustment in the schedules of others and the forces they transport.

To kick off the deployment operation, the TPFDD requires the accurate unit data describing the equipment and people to be deployed as discussed above so that the transportation, staging, and supporting organizations can plan for their support to the deploying units. Therefore, one of the first tasks of the deploying units is to verify the accuracy of the unit movement data, updating for any changes to the unit's equipment or people, e.g., for unit modifications that change equipment dimensions. These unit movement data represent one of the fundamental applications of our principle of *continuously shared knowledge*. They are at the core of the database describing what is to be transported.

At the same time, because lift resources are scarce and not every part of every unit's equipment and personnel may be needed at the same time, tailoring the unit's deployment configuration is a common occurrence. If both the deploying units and deployment organizations have continuously shared knowledge, then adjustments by units can be communicated rapidly to the airlift and sealift planners well enough in advance of deployment dates so as to make the most effective use of lift to support the operational scheme. The knowledge objective in force projection operations, as in combat operations, is to maintain the "common operating picture"—a picture that, of necessity (but frustratingly so), will constantly change.

A second unit task, overlooked by over a dozen Army and Marine units in deploying to Operation Enduring Freedom, is to take the steps to ensure that the unit has an "address" to which its supplies, ordered before and after deployment, can be delivered. The problem arises mainly with task-organized units made up of elements of other organizations. When those units deploy, they frequently change their source of direct supply support, and supplies ordered at home station have to be forwarded to them in the theater of operations. If they have not thought to obtain a unique DoD Activity Address Code (DODAAC), the supply system will not know where they are and to which direct support organization to forward the items. Obtaining the DODAAC is a relatively simple but lengthy process, and as it presently functions, it frequently cannot be accomplished prior to the deployment order since that order creates for the first time the particular task organization for which DODAAC must be provided. (I will say more about the DODAAC in chapters 3 and 6.)

At the same time that deploying units and force providing commands are preparing for deployment, U.S. TRANSCOM and its components are readying aircraft and vessels to provide the airlift and sealift. Air Mobility Command matches the TPFDD movement requirements with military and civilian aircraft assignments. Having determined during the TPFDD preparation phase whether the deployment will require activation of any part of the Civil Reserve Air Fleet (CRAF), it notifies the air carriers of the activation date. (Operation Iraqi Freedom required the activation of CRAF Stage I, approximately forty passenger aircraft, that deployed unit personnel to the theater ISB, Kuwait.) Simultaneously the Navy and Marine Corps prepare amphibious ready groups (ARGs) to embark Marine units in addition to those already deployed with expeditionary strike groups. Those organizations not embarking with ARGs are integrated into U.S. TRANSCOM's air and sea deployment plans.

Sealift planning is carried out by U.S. TRANSCOM, MSC, SDDC, the Maritime Administration (MARAD), industry, and labor organizations using the Voluntary Intermodal Sealift Agreement (VISA) processes. A major component of sealift planning is the joint planning advisory group (JPAG) jointly chaired by the deputy commander, U.S. TRANSCOM, and the MARAD administrator and including representatives of all U.S. flag carriers, the labor organizations that crew the vessels, MSC, and SDDC. Whether in meetings, video conferences, or teleconferences, the JPAG members schedule vessels to meet the TPFDD requirements and the follow-on sustainment shipping requirements. This planning results in a determination of the need to activate VISA's mandatory allocation of U.S. flag vessels to the deployment operation. (Note: For Operation Iraqi Freedom, the carriers were able to provide sufficient vessels so as to make mandatory VISA activation unnecessary.)

Home Installation Support

The installations at which forces are based play a critical role in the preparation of forces for deployment. They are, as the Army has termed them, "power projection platforms." That term applies equally well to the other services' bases. They provide the necessary facility and personnel support to assist the units that must deploy. Typically each power projection platform in all the services has (or should have) contingency plans for deployment support, which they exercise periodically with the deployable units so as to train their people (and the units), fine-tune procedures, and adapt facilities. That support (called "preparation for overseas movement") includes

- facilitating the assignment of filler personnel to the deploying unit
- processing vehicles for rail, truck, or air shipment either to ports of departure or to the theater itself
- assisting the units with the myriad final details of personnel processing, such as final medical checks, immunizations, final checks of emergency notification instructions for families, and wills
- arranging movement of people and equipment to airports and seaports of embarkation
- arranging for support for families of deployed personnel
- taking custody of equipment and facilities not deployed and reassigning non-deploying personnel to other units.

The successful deployment of units depends heavily on meeting sometimes demanding time schedules. Thus the exercise of deployment support plans can show the gaps in information flow, the bottlenecks, e.g., rail loading-ramp access, procedures for coordinating highway movement with state and local authorities, and the many other opportunities for demanding schedules to go awry and jeopardize a carefully orchestrated plan.

One of the most important tasks in this phase is the organizational tailoring that takes place on receipt of an alert order. The Air Force's Aerospace Expeditionary Force (AEF) concept has been especially proficient at tailoring both the mission units and support organizations. While the ten AEFs originally were tailored for normal rotation to such missions as the overflights of Iraq, subsequent operations such as Enduring Freedom and Iraqi Freedom required additional tailoring. The tailoring of forces that cannot self-deploy requires adjustment of unit movement data to establish the baseline for continuously shared knowledge. Frequently exercising such force tailoring and movement data planning builds a culture in the units that such actions are a normal part of going to war—rather than a bureaucratic nuisance that takes valuable time from combat training.

Assistance with the preparations for deployment is a responsibility of SDDC's deployment support brigades, whose teams deploy to the home bases to help both the base command and the deploying units with their preparation and to help coordinate movements to ports of embarkation. They are trained to be "experts" on movement data, railcar loading, convoy procedures, and coordination with civil authorities and with the ports of debarkation organizations. Air Force and Navy base organizations provide similar support for their deploying units.

Finally, one cannot stress too much the importance of the role of active, involved power projection platform bases in launching force projection. Solid procedures, continued training of unit personnel responsible for deployment, disciplined review of the processes described above, and periodic exercises to practice them are all pieces of preparation for deployment.

PORTS OF EMBARKATION: THE GUNS THAT SHOOT FORCES TO WAR

Forces deploy through airports and seaports of embarkation (APOEs and SPOEs). Naval forces sail from the piers at Norfolk, San Diego, or other home ports; marines from Camp LeJeune and Cherry Point road march and fly to Wilmington, North Carolina, to embark their amphibious ready group shipping. The Eighty-second Airborne Division moves about three miles to Pope Air Force Base to board AMC C-17s. The Air Force AEFs being deployed depart from home bases with their self-deploying mission aircraft and AMC lift for the support elements. The two brigades of the Third Infantry Division at Fort Stewart, Georgia, might move their equipment by commercial truck, convoy, and rail to the seaports of Savannah, Georgia, and Charleston, South Carolina, to board MSC's "large, medium-speed, roll-on/roll-off" ships (LMSRs) along with a few mechanics and drivers. Most of the personnel would later move by commercial bus to a military or commercial departure airfield for lift to an ISB, where they would marry up with their weapons systems and equipment.

One can well appreciate the enormous complexity and pace of activity at both APOEs and SPOEs. The process of efficiently moving through these potential bottlenecks is much the same whether the deploying force is five hundred or fifteen thousand strong—just more opportunities for complications with the larger units. Thus the deploying force and the deployment support organizations—Air Force Aerial Port Squadron for APOE and SDDC terminal battalions at SPOE—are compelled to be "joined-at-the-hip" if the out-loading is to proceed smoothly.

Since APOEs and SPOEs have limited holding areas for equipment, the movement from home bases has to be orchestrated through backward planning processes with the aircraft and vessel schedules and loading plans. The object is to feed unit equipment and personnel into the APOE/SPOE so they spend minimum time awaiting loading. One can well understand the value at both ends of the process—the base and the APOE/SPOE—of continuously shared knowledge of the status of the movement and early knowledge of the nearly inevitable glitches in plans, such as broken aircraft, stuck hatches, and the like, that can force changes to the best-laid plans. As we noted earlier, a smooth loading process demands that the unit movement data used by the aerial port or SDDC terminal battalion to do the precise load planning for aircraft and vessels accurately represent each item of equipment that will be loaded.

Of course the same need to replan can arise with last-minute changes to campaign plans, tactical tailoring, and deployment plans. Accommodating these changes and quickly replanning this intricate sequence can be facilitated by advances in information technology. Leaders not intimately involved with deployment planning have to realize that resourcing the acquisition of the necessary decision support systems is as important as resourcing more lift aircraft. Failure to rapidly adjust to inevitable changes can jeopardize operations in the theater. In the next chapter, we will examine this problem, which has bedeviled force projection operations for years and has yet to be solved.

The loading operation proceeds along one of two general lines: combat loading or administrative loading. The choice, generally, is determined by the intended destination. If the deploying unit is moving into a battle space where it may need to engage in combat on arrival, then it must load in a sequence to allow it to exit the aircraft or vessel ready to fight. Typically, marines use the combat loading process to embark the amphibious ready group. Army forces—airborne or air landed—headed for an uncertain reception at arrival drop zones or airfields in the battle space also use the combat loading processes. The loading sequence is geared for rapid unloading of coherent combat power but sacrifices efficient use of available space and weight capability of the airlift and sealift. The unit's personnel accompany the weapons systems or, in the case of airborne assault, jump with them or close by so as to recover, de-rig and move to assembly areas. In both cases the tactical employment plan in the battle space drives the discharge and loading processes. Elements of AEFs may use combat loading to facilitate early employment in the battle space.

Where the destination is an ISB, administrative loading that makes efficient use of the space/weight capabilities of the airlift or sealift is the choice. Unit integrity sometimes is sacrificed to gain efficiency advantages since unit personnel will marry up with their equipment in the ISB port area. The one compromise to the efficiency objective is to spread a unit's equipment, especially combat equipment, over several lift assets so that the loss or delay of an aircraft or ship will cause minimum damage to unit combat (or support) capabilities. This spreading of combat and support assets across a number of aircraft or ships also is practical in combat loading and can allow simultaneous discharge of unit assets from amphibious craft.

Another factor to be considered in loading, as we will discuss later, is enabling en route rehearsals. Command and control headquarters of deploying Army forces, while divided among several aircraft to minimize risk of loss of the whole C2 capability, might be located within the same serial so that data and voice communications over their own radios (via satellite) are possible. Such arrangements are an integral part of the coordination between the deploying organizations and their lift support. Typically, the marines aboard the large amphibious force ships have built-in infrastructure to facilitate en route training and rehearsals.

The (Air) EDRE and SEDRE exercises not only reveal normal procedural and training disconnects but highlight infrastructure shortcomings that can create bottlenecks in the deployment flow. While these bottlenecks—inadequate aircraft parking space, communications, maintenance, and storage space—have created friction in earlier deployments, they could have severe consequences in the rapid deployments required in 21st-century dissuasion or intervention operations. Physical infrastructure improvements that may not be all that expensive can leverage major flow rate improvement through the APOEs, especially.

Pre-Positioned Equipment and Supplies

While the deployment of forces is basic, another set of assets contributes to effective force projection: pre-positioned equipment and supplies. The Army, Navy, Air Force, and Marines all own this capability.[2] The principle of *continuously shared knowledge* deserves careful attention in facilitating the deployment of both sea-based and land-based pre-positioned equipment

---

[2] The great majority of the ground combat systems of both major combat elements in Operation Iraqi Freedom, the First Marine Division and the Army's Third Infantry Division, came from pre-positioned equipment sets. Much of the initial bulk POL stocks and munitions for Army, Marine, and Air Force elements also came from the pre-positioned supplies.

and stocks so that deploying units can marry up with their equipment and supplies at the right time. Both kinds of pre-positioning need to go through the preparation and movement phases outlined above. Vessel crews need to be filled out and the vessels provisioned; land-based pre-positioned sets require some processing and, perhaps, selective tailoring for the specific operation. Deployment readiness exercises benefit these pre-positioned ships and the land-based equipment-holding organizations just as they help hone proficiency of units at home stations. Such exercises, in which Army and Marine units are flown to a country in a combatant command's area of operations, not only provide valuable training but also demonstrate convincing evidence of the nation's force projection capabilities—a reminder to friends and potential foe alike.

EN ROUTE

The major en route logistics activities are designed to facilitate the continuous flow of forces into the theater of operations. Those activities center on

> ▸ air and vessel refueling
> ▸ en route bases for aircraft maintenance, crew, and passenger rest and tanker bed-down
> ▸ contingency plans and resources for emergency repair of aircraft and vessels
> ▸ communications infrastructure aboard aircraft and vessels along with land- and space-based assets necessary to enable en route training and rehearsals.

The United States' ability to air-refuel airlifters and tactical aircraft of all services in strategic deployment contributes a much envied advantage and a vital part of the U.S. force projection capability. This capability, managed by U.S. TRANSCOM from a tanker control center at Scott Air Force Base, Illinois, presents one more intricate ballet involving aircraft, crews, fuel sources, maintenance, international overflight and landing rights, and coordination with deploying forces. Like the other logistics processes we have discussed, aerial refueling depends upon continuously shared knowledge and the ability to rapidly replan to meet the inevitable changes to plans caused by operations, political events, weather, and equipment failure. Aerial refueling is an immense behind-the-scenes operation whose complexity and worldwide scope is unrivaled.

The smooth deployment flow of both Air Force airlift and self-deploying aircraft depends upon the advanced planning (and exercise) of the process prior to alert. A critical element is gaining approval from nations for overflight rights and en route basing. Such agreements, negotiated by the State Department, are frequently the "long-poles-in-the-tent" and require long lead times, anticipating possible need rather than reacting to imminent need. After receipt of alert orders, aerial refueling arrangements between the deploying and airlift organizations and the tanker control center are coordinated so as to gain the most advantage from the available tanker resources. In most operations, tankers, crews, and support personnel must be deployed early to en route bases and coordination made with the Defense Energy Support Center to have fuel available to load at those bases. In this logistics process, both tanker crews and pilots of all refuelable aircraft have the mandate to train continuously to acquire and maintain midair refueling proficiency. There is probably no more dangerous air maneuver short of air combat.

Reception and Staging for Onward Movement to Battle Spaces

The next component of force projection puts forces into position in the area of operations—either in battle spaces or in ISB to stage for further deployment to battle spaces or to support operations in the battle spaces. For units deploying into battle spaces, "reception" could be the tactical employment of the units as in a forcible entry operation. Other units may be deployed directly into battle spaces as "follow-on" reinforcing combat forces or may be deployed for a peace enforcement or humanitarian operation, in which cases the process of reception would combine both tactical considerations and the logistics process outlined below for deployment to ISB. Those forces deploying to ISB to marry up with pre-positioned equipment and stage for future deployment into battle spaces will prepare for the last force projection component, intra-theater movement to and reception in the battle spaces. We will cover the intra-theater movement in the next section.

Once expeditionary strike groups with their carrier battle groups and ARGs arrive in their designated areas of operation, the logistics of force deployment transitions to the logistics of sustainment of the operational scheme directed by the combatant commander. These entities become sea-based ISBs themselves, from which air and naval operations are conducted in accordance with the operational plans. The Marine air-ground task force (MAGTF) is launched ashore and supported in part from the ARGs and from those elements that are moved ashore.

We would expect that most AEF elements would deploy to ISB, although some elements, such as the combat air controllers and parts of the airlift control element and aerial port organizations, might well move into the battle space. Reception for the ISB-located AEF elements is an often practiced routine since it's principally a fly-in and setup operation, with most of the equipment and supplies accompanying the AEF. Some of the bulky equipment, facility modules, and, certainly, bombs and other munitions could arrive at the seaport of debarkation aboard the Air Force–dedicated pre-positioning ships and would require overland transport to the air bases.

The ISB concept is a useful way of thinking about separating the functions and support that are absolutely required in the battle spaces from those that can be performed outside the battle spaces, where the force protection requirement is significantly less. Typically, Army organizations meeting pre-positioned equipment will do so in the ISB. They could then deploy with intra-theater lift or self-deploy on overland routes to battle spaces, as in Operation Desert Shield and Iraqi Freedom, if the ISB is on the same land mass as the battle spaces, e.g., the Saudi Arabia ISB during Operations Desert Shield and Desert Storm and the Kuwait ISB for Iraqi Freedom. Intra-theater airlift and sealift are necessary when the ISBs are not on the same land mass, e.g., Korea battle space and the Japan ISBs.

The ISB's characteristics facilitate the accomplishment of the combatant commander's mission. A primary attribute of an ISB is that it should permit a minimum logistic "footprint" in the battle spaces where force protection is a major challenge—and could soak up combat resources. It should be located so that it is close enough to battle spaces, e.g., two to three hours by air, to permit reaction to emergency resupply or reinforcement requirements. In its staging role, it facilitates acceptance of administratively loaded sealift and airlift, the marriage of equipment with units, their reconfiguration into combat-loaded airlift or sealift—or road convoy as in Operations Desert Shield, Desert Storm, and Iraqi Freedom—and onward movement to battle spaces.

The ISB reception and staging processes require the operation of arrival airfields and seaports, means to assemble people and equipment at those arrival facilities, and means to move them to assembly areas or to AEF air bases, where crews join their equipment and prepare for onward movement or ISB-based operations. The assembly areas are locations that permit the Army and Marine units to organize for tactical employment and to train and rehearse prior to entering battle spaces.

Joint Logistics Over-the-Shore Operations

If there are inadequate port facilities or those in the battle spaces are too well defended, the combatant command must turn to employing an over-the-shore—usually termed a joint logistics over-the-shore (JLOTS)—operation to land seaborne forces. JLOTS are particularly difficult and dangerous operations and are used only if there is insufficient port infrastructure to accommodate the deploying forces. The normal process is to discharge the vessels offshore, where the water depths are adequate and there is some sheltering from wind and ocean swells. Both the Army and the Navy possess lighterage of various sizes and configurations, from Navy floating causeways and tug boats to landing craft and Marine air-cushioned assault craft, even a bulk fuel-discharge facility. Cargo and personnel are off- loaded from the sealift to the lighterage and transported to the beaches or shallow-draft ports. Both services have lighterage stored in or near combatant command areas of operation to hasten the deployment of the lighterage. Some lighterage, of course, accompanies the ARGs. If forcible entry into the battle space is required, the MAGTF executes a combined amphibious and air assault to establish a secure beachhead and facilitate the JLOTS operation. For sea access to ISBs, JLOTS operations replace or supplement the fixed port discharge operations, as occurred in Kuwait during Operation Iraqi Freedom.

Staging for Intra-Theater Deployment

While in the staging or assembly areas, units require external support to upload combat supplies and perform maintenance and repair tasks beyond their own capabilities. They require the normal sustaining services and supplies—food, water, health care, and the like. Normally the service component commanders designate organizations to operate the reception and staging processes, although many reception tasks, including the operation of sea and aerial ports in the ISB, could be performed by a joint organization as part of an overall joint theater logistics management arrangement. (Note: we will return to this joint management issue when we discuss the "support base" role of ISBs.)

INTRA-THEATER MOVEMENT TO BATTLE SPACES

This last phase of the force projection process applies mostly to Army and Marine units who deploy into the battle spaces from ISBs. These are organizations that marry up with pre-positioned equipment in the ISB and then embark on theater airlift or sealift for movement into battle spaces. Some AEF organizations may use theater lift to deploy to operate remote bases as well as to position airlift control and aerial port functions in the battle spaces.

Deployments of MAGTF elements from ARGs or the projection of special operations forces and Army airborne forces into the battle spaces are generally operational but follow deployment processes we have been examining. However, their initial deployments may be direct from CONUS or forward bases and they may not go through ISBs. Yet Army and Marine reinforcing units may operationally deploy from ISBs if their commitment to action is imminent. In any event the processes are similar; the lift resources are the same. Only the command and control arrangements may differ considerably.

Units staging in ISBs for subsequent deployment follow a sequence of preparation and movement to departure airports and seaports in much the same way as we have seen for the strategic deployment processes. Since the probability of meeting enemy resistance is not insignificant, even for "administrative" moves, combat loading of aircraft and vessels probably is the better course of action. Sacrificing some efficiency to reduce force protection risks is the prudent action.

In any case, this deployment process calls for "peaking up" equipment (including test-firing weapons), checking the personal equipment of people, preparing detailed loading plans, checking information flows, and rehearsing actions-on-arrival (in case of enemy action), among other preparation activities. It demands the same thoughtful planning and follow-through as the strategic deployment process described earlier. As noted above, both the theater service component command and the theater combatant command/ joint task force staff and logistics management organization (if employed) will oversee and support the out-loading and movement.

CHAPTER 3

CREATING 21ST-CENTURY FORCE PROJECTION PROCESSES

The framework of the objectives and supporting principles developed earlier in chapter 1 provides a vehicle for assessing the deployment processes through which forces move from home station to the area of operations. To recap—

OBJECTIVES:

➤ timely delivery of support to customers

➤ minimized footprint of logistics activities in battle spaces and ISB.

SUPPORTING PRINCIPLES:

➤ accountability for process performance

➤ continuously shared knowledge of asset status, campaign requirements, "customer" status, and process barriers

➤ maximized commercial contracting of logistics activities in CONUS, forward bases, and ISBs[1]

➤ allocation of logistics tasks to coalition partners based on a principle of comparative advantage

➤ simplicity in planning and operations

This chapter begins with an assessment of how well the deployment processes described in chapter 2 measure up to the supporting principles. It then shows how applying these principles can improve the processes and enable DoD to achieve better results in timely delivery of forces and support with a smaller battle space footprint.

SUPPORTING PRINCIPLES

Accountability for Process Performance

The TPFDD plans of the future may be more like the plans for Operation Just Cause in Panama in 1989 or even the invasion of France in 1944—

---

[1] The forward bases referred to are the foreign bases where forces are normally stationed, e.g., in Japan, Europe, Korea.

simultaneous direct deployments of combat forces into several objective areas from CONUS or forward stationed force locations. Achieving strategic surprise and rapid, violent force applications are key to gaining the initiative against an enemy. Such an operation requires synchronized force deployments of all components, integrated to overcome the enemy's probable access denial efforts and to achieve the desired effects on the enemy. Another part of the TPFDD plan, no doubt, also will resemble the deployments to Operations Desert Shield and Iraqi Freedom, a deliberate buildup of forces in the ISBs, linkup with pre-positioned equipment sets, and establishment of the support bases for sustainment of the forces. The complexity of such TPFDD plans and the necessity for continuously shared knowledge during the planning and execution of the plans is obvious. Managing such a set of processes can be done successfully only if there is a clear line of responsibility, decision and resourcing authority, and *accountability* for the outcomes.

Deployment as Cross-Organization Processes

Over the last couple decades of management evolution the concept of "process ownership" has arisen. Although the language used is different, the concept, as we noted in chapter 1, is the familiar "unity of command" principle of war. The principle requires that someone with authority must be in charge of the operation—or "process." That person must have the resources and be *accountable* for achieving the results for which the process is designed—a simple concept, but terribly difficult to achieve within any bureaucracy, public or private. Competing organizations will each insist on their authorities if they have resources or feel they can acquire resources and influence. Unless directives are clear, process ownership can be vague and accountability unclear, with ample opportunities for participants to blame others if mistakes occur.

Readers with little experience working in bureaucracies will view this discussion with incredulity. They have seen organization charts that seem to imply clear chains of authority and responsibility. Yet the deployment processes *cut across* organizations. Many organizations have roles to play. An example: The Army in 2002 centralized the management of its installations into one agency reporting directly to its headquarters with staff oversight by an assistant chief of staff and an assistant secretary of the Army. Formerly, the major Army commands "owned" the installations that housed their activities. Yet at this writing there is debate about which organization should carry out the force deployment preparation process in support of organizations deploying from those installations. That such an important function could have been overlooked in the organizing directive of the new agency simply underlines the difficulty of fixing responsibility and accountability in large organizations. The major command "owns" the forces to be deployed but no longer "owns" the installations that have the manpower and skills to assist units preparing to deploy. The installations apparently claim that the efficiencies realized in the restructuring took away the resources for that traditional mission. The trick is to determine who among the participants in the processes should be the responsible agent for achieving the required result—in each of its various stages—as well as for the deployment as a whole. Clearly the Army will decide eventually what role the home station will play and who will be in charge. As noted earlier, integration of organization functions into viable deployment processes must extend across services and joint commands.

The issue is how to create unity of command or process ownership with accountability in executing force projection. Certainly, a common process road map is a beginning. Joint Forces Command (JFCOM) has the responsibility to develop the doctrine, the procedures and resourcing methods that constitute the foundation of this joint deployment process.[2] Appointing the JFCOM as the joint process owner in 2000 was a major step that signaled that DoD leadership understood the need for better accountability. The delay until 2003 to begin work in earnest cast doubt on the leadership's commitment. It could be that the furious activity generated after September 11, 2001, on the counterterrorism campaign, the Afghanistan campaign, and Operation Iraqi Freedom simply drained the resources that might have been applied. At any rate there is a great body of lessons to be absorbed as the doctrine is written. That doctrine will be approved by the Joint Chiefs of Staff and the Secretary of Defense and therefore become the common set of procedures for the services and the joint participants in the deployment process. That provisional doctrine is under continual review in order to improve procedures, get rid of bottlenecks, and clarify responsibilities. The discussion that follows offers proposals to improve the force projection process, proposals that should be incorporated into the JFCOM's standard processes

---

[2] "Joint Deployment Process Owner," DoD Directive 5158.5, Nov. 12, 2001.

and doctrine. We will turn first to the deployment or "launching" of forces from their home stations.

Process Ownership for Launching Forces

Each of the services has a key role in deploying its own forces, supporting the transfer of those forces from the JFCOM in CONUS or forward-stationed major command to the supported combatant command. TRANSCOM airlift and sealift resources will deploy the forces (except for self-deploying organizations) as directed by the supported combatant command's JCS-approved TPFDD. Because of the many service and joint organizations involved just in "launching" the forces, there are many opportunities for misunderstandings and mistakes in the absence of some central direction.

Command and control arrangements for deploying organizations are spelled out in the campaign operation order approved by the secretary of defense. Deploying organizations are transferred to the combatant command and will be supported by their service component commanders. But typically the responsibility to oversee preparation for movement and loading remains with the force providing commands, e.g., JFCOM's or other supporting command's service components. All in all this is a reasonably clean, simple command and control transition. Unity of command—and accountability for the transport part of the process—is achieved since the deploying aircraft and sealift remain under their respective TRANSCOM component commands.

Even before the operation order for the campaign is issued, the Chairman, Joint Chiefs of Staff, must give direction to begin planning for the deployment. The logical next step is to form a senior integrated process team, perhaps as a subset of the joint planning and execution community (JPEC).[3] That team should include senior members of the services, Joint Staff,[4] the combatant command and its land, sea, air, and special operations components and their department headquarters, TRANSCOM, JFCOM (the force projection "process owner"), and other stakeholders in the deployment. The team members should be authorized to make decisions for the organizations they represent. Perhaps the team should operate from the National Military

---

[3] Joint Publication 5.0.
[4] The term "Joint Staff" refers to the Organization of the Joint Chiefs of Staff.

Command Center under the direction of the Vice Chairman, JCS or another officer acting for him. This team's mission should be to resolve the inevitable conflicts of schedule and resources that come up in the final planning and execution of what are always complex operations.

If consensus solutions, agreed to by the supported combatant commander, cannot be obtained, the issue can go to the Chairman, JCS, or Secretary of Defense. This team should work with the supported combatant command to complete the TPFDD and with TRANSCOM and its component commands to lay out the allocation and scheduling of the requisite airlift and sealift assets (and their supporting airports and seaports of embarkation and debarkation (APOE/SPOE and APOD/SPOD) to transport the deploying organizations. The AEF self-deploying elements, ARGs, and carrier battle groups (CVBGs), while part of the TPFDD, would not require lift but would be integrated into the en route support plans and theater arrival schedule.

Force providing commands would then appoint deployment process owners for their deploying forces. Forces Command is responsible for Army units deploying from CONUS with the Installation Management Agency and SDDC's deployment support brigades in direct support. It must implement a coordinated plan to facilitate out-loading of deploying organizations so as to meet the TRANSCOM timelines for delivery to the combatant command areas of operation. Army component commands in Europe and the Pacific would manage the deployment of their units that are tasked to the TPFDD. The AEFs' and Marines' non-self-deploying elements must follow a similar process, because they, like the Army, depend on U.S. TRANSCOM's airlift and sealift to move them to the area of operations. In this part of the process the senior integrated process team, JFCOM's process ownership doctrine, and the organization change proposed below could contribute to a more integrated process.

Closing the Gap in the Transportation Network

TRANSCOM is the single command responsible for strategic lift of deploying forces and the management of contracted commercial transportation for both deployment and distribution. Yet it does not manage an important component of the transportation process for either deployment or distribution—the interface between the deploying or distribution organizations and the lift resource owners. The services and the defense agencies (primarily Defense Logistics Agency [DLA]) retain the installation/activity transportation managers who order transportation resources. The absence of this vital part of the transportation network from TRANSCOM's direct (or indirect through one of its service components) control can create obstacles to effective deployments through misunderstandings, lack of communication, and lack of adequate technical knowledge of the processes and effective reaction to the inevitable changes.

One way of resolving the issue is for TRANSCOM to manage the *ordering of transportation*, at least by the largest shippers, the DLA distribution depots and larger installations. TRANSCOM, through one or more of its service components, probably the SDDC, would assume that part of the installation transportation management function requiring off-base service, e.g., deployments, freight shipments, and passenger transportation. The people in the installation/activity transportation offices need not change, and the activities needing transportation/deployment support would continue to place their requirements with the same office. But TRANSCOM, through integrating those offices into its knowledge network and managing personnel assignments and training, could make more effective use of the limited lift resources. A former TRANSCOM commander in the mid 1990s attempted to make this change, but it ran into such service opposition that it was shelved. Had this concept of "defense transportation agents" been implemented, a more closely knit network would be available now. SDDC's deployment support organizations would be more closely integrated with installation "agents" because they, along with AMC's airlift support assets, would operate under a common process within the same unified command.

Such a change also would help resolve a perennial accountability problem in dealing with the commercial air and sea carriers on whom DoD depends for augmentation lift. TRANSCOM, through AMC, has made agreements with civil air carriers for Civil Reserve Air Fleet (CRAF) commitments at different stages of need in times of deployment. It has made similar agreements through MSC for vessel commitments under the VISA process with U.S. flag vessel operators. In both cases these firms expect peacetime business in return for their commitment. While TRANSCOM is accountable to industry and DoD for these agreements, it is difficult for the command to assure that the services' and DLA's transportation offices will use those carriers when their (pre-conflict) interest is to obtain what they believe is the lowest cost transportation. A related example of the need to close this management "gap" is some transportation offices' practice of continuing to use carriers and services that they are accustomed to and not to take advantage of the negotiated services that TRANSCOM's components offer. One example of this practice is the preference of some transportation officers for truck delivery and their failure to take advantage of land intermodal services, which offer reliable service with major cost savings for those shipments that don't require quite as fast service as truck-only carriers provide.

Through integration into TRANSCOM components, better training of the agents, and better knowledge of the services' and defense agencies' shipping requirements, TRANSCOM and its components could achieve low-cost transportation and also assure the commercial air and sea carriers of a fair slice of defense business in return for their CRAF and VISA commitments.

Process Ownership/Accountability for Force Reception

One of the more difficult logistics challenges perennially has been gaining agreement among services, combatant commanders, and the Joint Staff on joint doctrine and procedures to define the responsibility—and accountability—to the theater combatant commander for conducting reception, staging, and onward movement in ISBs. It is especially challenging where common logistics support is to be provided—air and seaport operations, onward transport to battle spaces, local transport between service facilities, real estate management for the activities, contracts for local goods and services, and the like. Depending on the situation, the service components may well have to compete for those limited resources.

Management of Intermediate Staging Bases

Clearly, some ISBs may serve only one service with just a small representation of other services. A Marine or Navy ISB or forward base certainly does not require a joint activity to oversee common support. Normal interservice support agreements can handle any support required by other service elements. The theater combatant command director of logistics (J4) can oversee the allocation of DoD common resources such as fuel and food to the service component commands with little danger of misallocation.

However, as Operation Iraqi Freedom demonstrated, joint use of an ISB may become common practice. The Marines made use of the same staging areas and support infrastructure in Kuwait as the Army. Also, the Navy's plans for the littoral combat ship may require an ISB in the theater for staging its different mission modules for rapid change-out. Only when Marine and/or Navy units are ashore in the same general ISB area with Army and Air Force units would the competition issue arise.

The staging function of the ISB is the set of processes that marries unit personnel, who arrive at an ISB aboard CRAF aircraft, with their equipment, which arrives by airlift or sealift or was pre-positioned. The staging complex contains (1) the arrival airfields –APODs—where units aboard C-5s, C-17s, and CRAF passenger aircraft complete their strategic legs, (2) the seaports— SPODs—where strategic sealift and afloat pre-positioning vessels discharge their equipment, and (3) the assembly areas where the units marry people and equipment and prepare for onward movement to battle spaces aboard C-130 and theater-managed C-17s or surface lift. AEF combat aircraft may also use ISB complexes for their operating bases. The service components may position supplies and repair facilities as well as staging activities in an ISB complex. In addition, other federal agencies, coalition partners, and nongovernmental organizations may be present. The possibilities for competition for limited local facilities, labor, real estate, road space, and aerial and water port capacity are not trivial in this scenario.

Such interservice component command competition is nowhere else a more critical problem than in intra-theater transport. Both theater-owned airlift and sealift must be managed so that the combatant commander's priorities are executed—priorities that will change with little notice. The requirement is for active joint management. In Vietnam, after a lot of trial and error, a joint transportation movement control agency was formed to direct routine lift missions but also respond to emergency requirements, which had to be initiated through command channels and approved by the theater combatant command Director of Operations (J3).[5] All the theater airlift and sealift resources were operated by the owning service but directed through the theater movements control agency. Such a process is necessary to implement intra-theater movement to and from battle spaces and ISBs by common user lift. A similar process was instituted—finally—in early 2004 for Operation Iraqi Freedom, for which CENTCOM formed the CENTCOM Deployment and Distribution Operations Center to centrally manage those processes. It is clear that there must be accountability to ensure that the combatant commander's priorities for support are followed and that the limited resources are not wasted nor the availability of local resources

---

[5] Commander U.S. Military Assistance Command Vietnam (COMUSMACV).

subjected to a "bidding war" between service components. While setting priorities is the task of the combatant commander, he hasn't the means to manage the variety of activities within the ISBs. Instead, the practice of assigning "executive agency" to one of the service components has grown up. (There might be one service component designated to be the executive agent for the theater, or one for a single ISB or group of ISBs and another service component commander for others.) The executive agency concept is accompanied by ad hoc organizations such as a "joint movements control" activity to adjudicate competing demands for intra-theater lift and other transportation services and a real estate management activity to allocate host-nation-allocated facilities.

Yet the executive agency approach to gaining consensus and unity of effort between the service components, supporting commands (TRANSCOM and DLA), and the theater command has the drawback of relying on organizing complex processes in the middle of the initiation of a campaign. That should be the time when the focus should be on final planning and executing the deployment to ISBs and battle spaces and making the inevitable changes as political and threat conditions change. Having to put together a new organization (a heavily augmented base organization such as an Army theater support command or Marine force service support group with joint participation), train the people, and work out procedures is a recipe for potential chaos. Discussions of lessons learned from past deployments have cited this issue repeatedly and suggested the need for a more organized joint process. Still the services (with each new generation of leaders) have resisted the idea of organizing a joint activity and writing joint doctrine and procedures to guide training—before the contingency occurs. One result of this failure to agree on a joint solution is graphically described in the Third Infantry Division's after-action report on Operation Iraqi Freedom:

> *During this initial deployment and operations process, the division encountered numerous challenges and obstacles. Issues such as theater responsibility, training/experience, automation, and sufficient equipment severely affected the RSOI/APS timeline and ultimately the initial stages of forward operations.*[6]

---

[6] Third Infantry Division (Mechanized) After-Action Report, *Operation Iraqi Freedom*, Introduction to ch. 7, p. 45. From *Daily Briefing*, "Related Links," GovExec.com, Nov. 11, 2003.

Joint Theater Logistics Management for Reception and Staging

With the advent of the new national security environment's calling for more frequent deployments, perhaps on short notice, support processes and procedures must always be in place. Furthermore, the people who must manage the processes must know their assignments, have trained with the various other participants in implementing those processes, and have the tools, e.g., knowledge systems, when the campaign is launched. It is too late to start organizing, finding people from all the services, and training them once the short-notice campaign is directed. There is clearly a need for a joint management capability (as the Defense Science Board reported in its Summer Study in 1998).[7] This Joint Theater Logistics Management (JTLM) organization, as we shall call it, reporting to the combatant commander under the staff cognizance of the J4, would be in a stronger position to exercise the appropriate direction of ISB management and allocation of common supplies and services than one of the service component commands. Its task, simply put, would be to implement the combatant commander's priorities for reception, staging, and onward movement as well as operation of the ISB in its sustainment role—since both processes run in parallel and require the same resources.

The JTLM would have a small cadre of planners along with a support contractor to assist in contingency planning for the variety of scenarios likely to be faced by the theater command.[8] It would manage the establishment of requirements for the J4 with the primary provider of common supplies (DLA) and transportation (TRANSCOM), so that the providers' plans are synchronized with the theater plan, and the many processes described earlier are ensconced in plans and procedures—and periodically exercised.

The core of its staff should come from DLA and TRANSCOM or its components for three reasons. First, it would help to cement the relationships between provider and customer that need to withstand the pressures of rapid deployment response. Secondly, those personnel would be familiar with the procedures for managing the common supplies' supply chain

---

[7] *The Defense Science Board 1998 Summer Study Task Force on DoD Logistics Transformation*, vol. 1, Final Report, Dec. 1998 (Washington, DC: Office of the Under Secretary of Defense for Acquisition & Technology, 1998), p. vi.

[8] The contractor selected to provide support services in the ISB. An example is the Army's "Logistics Contractor Augmentation Program" used in Bosnia, Kosovo, Afghanistan, Kuwait, and Iraq.

processes and the transportation processes. The services no longer operate those processes in CONUS and no longer have the institutional expertise. Third, making DLA and TRANSCOM responsible for providing the core staffs for the theater JTLMs would assure a standard set of processes for all combatant commands, rather than home-grown varieties that new people would have to learn on joining. They provide a basis for common training. Consistent, well-understood procedures facilitate the execution of the complex deployment and sustainment processes.

Upon implementation (or, better, warning of an impending deployment directive) the JTLM would assist the J4 in making necessary changes to the campaign plan and its deployment and support annexes and coordinating with the service and special operations components to assure that their revised common support requirements are incorporated into the theater plans. DLA and TRANSCOM would send their augmentation teams to fill out the JTLM staff and prepare for tracking the deployment of forces and materiel and the reception of arriving units and materiel, to include opening airport and seaport facilities, storage sites, and other necessary facilities and implementing host nation agreements. The JTLM would operate the APOD and SPOD and establish distribution centers to accept deploying DLA and service-managed theater reserve stocks. In chapters 5 and 10 I will propose that the JTLM would also operate common supplies inventory management and storage and distribution activities, and manage common transportation resources and base operations services, thus providing the combatant commander a continuum of ISB management from force reception through sustainment and redeployment. The augmentation by TRANSCOM would represent for theater reception and deployment management a capability matching that which TRANSCOM and its components employ for deployment to the theater. There would be common processes, a common language, a network of common procedures and relationships to manage theater terminals (APOD and SPOD), airlift and sealift, that reside in one command, to be provided to the combatant command as a package.

In the cases of humanitarian and peacekeeping operations, the JTLM might deploy organizations and separate teams into the objective areas as well as to ISBs. With adequate force protection, JTLM organizations could establish the same kinds of reception support for arriving forces as in the ISBs. They could conduct JLOTS operations in support of the joint forces either in the ISBs or to gain access to the battle spaces. In the areas where active combat is the task, the service components—that is, Army, Marine, and Air Force elements—and Special Operations Command elements probably would enter through and manage sea and air access points. The JTLM would manage only the ISB activities and provide lift and distribution as well as commit units to the service-managed access points.[9]

Service component commanders would be relieved of the reception and support tasks assumed by the JTLM. Organizations not projected directly into the battle spaces could concentrate on moving their own units through the JTLM's port and cargo holding facilities to service-run operating bases and staging or assembly areas, marrying up deploying personnel with their pre-positioned equipment. They would use the JTLM-provided local transport and other common support. The JTLM also could be assigned a medical element to operate the theater medical evacuation, ISB patient care, and medical supply operations.

Creating the JTLM would materially simplify what has long been a confusing situation in organizing theater common support—support that in the CONUS and many forward bases is provided already by DLA and TRANSCOM, who perform most of those functions in peacetime. Expanding DLA's and TRANSCOM's missions to encompass standing up the JTLM cadres for the theater combatant commands and including augmentation in the deployment flow seems like a practical solution to a dilemma, in spite of what appears to be reflexive fear of another joint activity. The JTLM would provide accountability to the combatant commander for the theater-centered logistics processes in force projection—a valuable contribution to what always becomes a semi-chaotic process of adapting contingency plans to an actual campaign as the events unfold.

Continuously Shared Knowledge

This description of the deployment processes makes it clear that projecting even the relatively few forces that took part in Operation Enduring Freedom in Afghanistan is a very complex process, many of whose elements are in a state of constant and sometimes unpredictable change. Operation Iraqi Freedom deployment was unsurprisingly even more difficult. Therefore, it seems axiomatic that *continuously shared knowledge* is essential to keeping the

---

[9] By placing such units under service operational control.

force projection process synchronized to the campaign plan, which itself will change based on threat, political developments, actions of coalition partners, weather, and a host of other influences. The combatant commander and service and special operations component commanders and their operations and logistics staffs need up-to-date information on the progress of the TPFDD. The operations staffs may have to divert airlifted forces based on a changing operational situation while they are airborne. Battle spaces can change; arrival airfields or drop zones may change. Weather may hold up a key part of an Air Force AEF and require the substitution of another force element. The possibilities for change to a TPFDD are practically endless.

Experience in the latest deployments to Afghanistan and in Operation Iraqi Freedom suggest that progress has been made in attaining force projection knowledge, especially in the use of radio frequency identification (RFID) systems to automate data entry for manifesting, but information gaps continue to plague all the participants in the force projection processes. The sheer magnitude and complexity of the processes offer untold opportunities for difficulty. What follows is not to criticize, but to offer proposals for a major focus on providing what is basically commercially available technology to close the knowledge gaps.

A Force Projection Decision Support System

The principle of *continuously shared knowledge* requires data on deploying forces, their assigned lift assets, and the status of departure airports and seaports, as well as battle space access points and ISB arrival facilities. This information must be evaluated to determine if it matches the "expected" status in the latest update of the TPFDD plan. Staffs can then make an assessment of any deviation (ahead of/behind schedule) and its impact on the TPFDD and campaign execution. This evaluation process, traditionally a combination of computer-generated data and "white board" collaborative assessment, takes place in operations centers at combatant command, service component command, TRANSCOM, and the services' and Joint Chiefs of Staff's headquarters. A decision support system would be of great value if it would bring in all the relevant information on the status of TPFDD progress, use "intelligent agent" technology to continuously compare the status of deployments with the planned schedule, highlight deviations based on parameters it is given, suggest options for changes to the TPFDD (based on programmed "rules") that could restore the schedule, and then make that knowledge available to all the operations centers named above. Such a system would also be used to make necessary changes to the TPFDD based upon changes to the campaign plan by war-gaming various options likely to yield a "best" force posture to meet the objectives of the proposed changes to the campaign plan. This capacity for rapidly assessing "what-ifs" has been a dream of joint planners—to produce a "TPFDD-in-a-day" or better. The concept was demonstrated in 2001 in a joint project led by the Defense Advanced Research Projects Agency (DARPA) and known as the Advanced Logistics Project (ALP).

Such a decision support system would build upon the Joint Operational Planning and Execution System (JOPES) structure, using the TPFDD database. It would contain the set of organizations to be deployed, with each organization given a unique identifying "unit line number" (ULN) as in JOPES. ULNs would be allocated to each *grouping* of people, equipment, and accompanying supplies—to include unique teams and detachments—that deploy as an entity. For example, an Army airborne infantry battalion deploying for parachute drop into the battle space might have a single ULN. An AF fighter squadron, part of an AEF, would self-deploy its aircraft using one ULN, but deploy its extra aircrews, maintenance personnel, and support equipment aboard CRAF airlifters using separate ULNs.

Each ULN represents a set of movement requirements. As important, the TPFDD database for each ULN would include also the names and social security numbers of the people and identifiers for each item of equipment and container of supplies. The container identifier should be linked to the list of contents. Such visibility would be important in the event the deploying organization might need to divert or replace a member of the organization, a piece of equipment, or a container. The personnel identifying numbers would be included in personal data cards embedded with radio frequency (RF) receiver-transmitter tags and carried by the deploying personnel to allow *automated data capture* of deploying individuals. RF tags with identifying numbers would be placed on equipment and containers, enabling automated data capture through tag reading, using remote interrogators at the various nodes in the deployment process.

Automated data capture using automated identification technology (AIT), which avoids the frequent mistakes of human data entry, is critical to the continuously shared knowledge process and the value of the decision support system. AIT, combining hardware, software, and communications, allows more accurate data capture of all supplies, equipment, and people to which it applies. The technology has gone through rapid evolution from the original bar code to new, sophisticated RFID "smart tags" (active and passive) and interrogators. RFID allows the interrogator's remote identification of tagged objects and transmission of the data to a database where it can be aggregated by ULN, parent unit, aircraft, vessel, location, or any of a number of meaningful data sets.

The Army began experimenting with the technology in the late 1980s, placing the then bulky tags on components of tracked vehicles undergoing depot overhaul to track them through the "back shop" process back to the reassembly line. Originally too expensive for all but the most critical items, the technology has blossomed in the commercial sector—to allow retailers to put inexpensive passive RFID labels on some apparel items. One major manufacturer of pilferable items is combining the smart tag on each of the items with a "smart shelf" reader to report unusual quantities leaving the shelf. Millions are in use now; that number is expected to grow to billions by 2005.[10]

DoD made its most extensive use of RFID active tags during Operation Iraqi Freedom, although the lack of operable interrogators prevented data capture for the battle space nodes in the supply chain. However, the active tags on containers and deploying equipment enabled far better data capture and knowledge than ever before experienced. The RFID tags on the three thousand munitions containers aboard the principal land force ammunition vessel allowed selective discharge of less than 10 percent of the containers— all that were required—thus keeping the munitions footprint small in the Kuwait ISB, avoiding the huge real estate demand normally required to maintain explosive safety distances.

The RF tags and interrogators allow fast location of people, equipment, and containers in staging areas and port holding areas. The technology allows rapid manifesting and verification for air or sea embarkation and convoy operations. Accurate RF data capture does away with paper processes and allows rapid verification of an "as-loaded" aircraft or ship against the planned load. (Personal data cards and RF tags on equipment and containers have been in increasing use since the Bosnia operation and were used extensively for manifesting in Operation Iraqi Freedom.) These data capture

---

[10] *Economist*, Feb. 8–14, 2003, p. 57.

devices will—and should—become ubiquitous throughout deployment operations in the future.

In the proposed decision support system, deploying aircraft and vessel cargo and people become "sets of identifier data" and can be tracked for the duration of their transit, using the "intelligent agents" demonstrated in the DARPA ALP project. These agents periodically query the nodes of the process—home station, embarkation and debarkation airports and seaports—as well as the transport aircraft and vessels, to show the status of the deploying organizations (the ULNs). The decision support system compares those agent status reports against the TPFDD schedule to determine if the deploying organizations are on, ahead of, or behind schedule. The system also would "roll up" organization ULNs into sets representing the major force elements such as AEFs, Army and Marine brigades, or naval elements. Thus it can continuously show the proportion of each major force element at the various process nodes, including, for example, the parachute assault into a battle space. The system can then present options to the JFCOM and TRANSCOM deployment process managers and combatant commanders if there is a serious deviation from the scheduled time line.

The important advantages of the ALP technology are

> ➤ its continuous monitoring of the status of deploying organizations and their transport
> ➤ its ability to compare that status with the planned time lines and to present options for the deployment managers and the combatant command for holding or diverting the transport
> ➤ its rapid accurate capture of data on people and equipment being deployed
> ➤ the shared availability of the status update (and all the data concerning each ULN) to *all* the participants from the home station to the combatant command.

The combination of those achievable advantages produces continuously shared knowledge. Without the ALP capability, the deployment process limps along, repeatedly victimized by its inability to react quickly to the inevitable problems that arise. The lack of timely knowledge forces suboptimal decisions because those having to make decisions would have inadequate knowledge of the status of affected participants or of the likely consequences of decisions.

The issue of feasibility of the technology should have been laid to rest by the DARPA ALP demonstrations. Certainly the commercial sector has much experience with using distributed databases, e.g., the credit card companies and banks that handle millions of transactions from around the world, processed through multiple nodes in seconds, updating the variety of databases with charges and fees. Even a large deployment would not equal the magnitude of the credit card process.

Resourcing the fielding of the ALP technology should be a high-priority requirement for short-notice deployments into uncertain environments. Such deployments usually are accompanied by the frequent exercise of the planning/replanning processes. But the budgeting process, biased toward the services, doesn't give much leverage to allow the resourcing of this essentially *joint* decision support system. Senior logisticians who see the value of this method of achieving continuously shared knowledge are left with trying to persuade one of the services to take the lead to flesh out and field the prototype and persuade the combatant commanders and TRANSCOM to place such a system high in their priority lists for funding. The value that the decision support system could bring to force projection should be so clear that the Secretary of Defense should direct funding of its acquisition and designate it as a joint project, with direct oversight by the Joint Staff and the Office of the Secretary of Defense (OSD).

However, before embarking on the development of this decision support system, the DoD must remove a couple of barriers to knowledge that can kill the effectiveness of the decision support system and that have frustrated strategic lift planners for decades. The quality of information about lift requirements has been generally poor. At least one service has been unwilling to provide basic low-level (so-called Level Six) data for movement planning. Secondly, the data provided by some organizations and used in calculating airlift and sealift requirements frequently do not match the characteristics of the organization (equipment number, dimensions, weight, and personnel number) that shows up to load the aircraft or vessel. Both barriers to valid knowledge can cause waste of scarce lift resources, delays in the TPFDD execution, and problems with synchronization of the complex force projection process. Both barriers exhibit a lack of disciplined commitment to the deployment process. They should be dealt with both by JFCOM as the deployment process owner and by the leadership of the organizations that are deployable.

The principle of *continuously shared knowledge* is central to achieving timely delivery of forces. Without that capability, commanders' willingness to deploy no more equipment and supplies than absolutely necessary will be jeopardized, frustrating efforts to achieve a minimum footprint. While the information processes have improved since the Gulf War, the gaps that remain led to complaints that the on-the-ground commanders during the Afghanistan operations were too frequently unaware of what the C-17s were delivering. Major deploying unit status was reasonably well known, but some of the severely tailored support units had more chaotic deployment experiences. In Operation Iraqi Freedom, even with extensive use of RF tags, visibility seemed to end at the Kuwait ports. Many Army and Marine organizations lost visibility of even their accompanying supplies and had little visibility of follow-on and requisitioned supplies (an issue to which we will return in chapter 7's discussion of the application of continuously shared knowledge to sustainment). As in Operation Desert Shield and subsequent deployments, the mistakes and problems had few serious consequences, mainly because there was time to fix them. Trusting that in the future there always will be time to fix preventable mistakes is a high-risk course of action, an unnecessary risk when a modest investment in an ALP-like decision support system can provide continuously shared knowledge.

The DODAAC Problem

A principal reason for the loss of visibility is the continued existence of a major "self-inflicted wound" even after repeated "lessons learned" reports from operations as far back as Vietnam. The culprit is the method of assigning DoD Activity Address Codes (DODAACs). Normally each battalion, squadron, or ship, as well as separate smaller units that independently report their own logistics status, hold their own equipment on property records, and are authorized to use the supply request system, is assigned a separate DODAAC. Each service has a central registry of the location of each DODAAC associated with the supply support activity that directly supports its supply requests and to which requisitions for its needed supplies are sent. The information is provided to DLA by each service registrar. That location designator is placed in the "ship to" space on a material release order that fills a requisition from the unit owning the DODAAC. The deploying units and their support activities must notify the central registry of their new location when they deploy.

The "wound" occurs when units do not report the location change, so that the item is shipped to the home station of the unit even though it has deployed. Another common problem occurs when parts of battalions, squadrons, or separate companies deploy to different locations, sometimes not in the same theater, and are supported by different direct support organizations' supply support activities. The problem becomes further complicated with the introduction of the reserve component organizations. While the DODAAC can be subdivided by adding suffixes, unless the notification is carefully done or a new DODAAC is assigned to the unit, the misshipment of items it requests is practically assured. These DODAAC "wounds" are one of the major causes of the failure of units and their direct support organizations to receive needed repair parts. Their response to this flawed system is to take with them as many parts as they can manage, which defeats the purpose of minimizing the amount of accompanying supplies in order to provide for as much combat power as possible. They would bring the traditional "iron mountain" if they could because of their distrust of the resupply system. We will return to this issue in chapter 7 because of its serious consequences for effective sustainment of weapons and support systems.

Clearly the DODAAC issue is one that cries out for early resolution. Modularization of battalions, squadrons, and other units is a fact of life in 21st-century campaigns. All the services are task-forcing: the Air Force's AEFs are composed of parts of squadrons depending on their missions. Army combat and support battalions habitually are split, with their line companies placed under task force headquarters, sometimes with different direct support organizations than their home station alignment. Similarly for naval construction battalions and Marine air ground task forces. DoD can no longer afford the anachronism of the present DODAAC arrangement if it expects to achieve the level of continuously shared knowledge critical to 21st-century campaign success.

Contracting Logistics Support

Applying the third supporting principle, *maximized commercial contracting of logistics activities outside the battle spaces*, requires that logisticians examine each of the deployment processes we have outlined to decide whether the process is more effectively and efficiently performed by contractors, by organic DoD organizations, or by an appropriate mix, e.g., the maintenance of afloat pre-positioned equipment sets.

For force projection/deployment processes there are several applicable criteria for choosing the option. The first-order criterion should be to gain acceptance of the idea that "effective" generally trumps "efficient/lower cost" in choosing support organizations. But the proper analysis should look also at the tradeoffs to make sure that "effective" doesn't buy more than is needed at a much higher price than the "effective" that meets the requirement with acceptable risk, but at a lower cost.

Criteria for Deciding: Contractor vs. Organic

The following five criteria should be useful in deciding on use of contractors:

> ➤ availability of experienced (in the process) commercial firms
> ➤ availability of trained, experienced DoD organizations that can be made accountable for process execution
> ➤ exposure to battle spaces, possible combat (for ISB processes)
> ➤ availability of appropriate equipment
> ➤ availability of appropriate contractual vehicle (e.g., contingency task order contract)

Contracted Support for Deployment Preparation and Launching

Next, let us apply these criteria to the processes we earlier described. In the home station preparation phase, there may be an experienced commercial firm performing base support operations. Where there is no contractor, the base support DoD organization performs the necessary tasks to assist deploying units to prepare for deployment. It would make sense to augment either the organic or contractor base support organization with contingency contracts to meet the demands of preparing and deploying forces from the base. Augmenting the maintenance capability of deploying units is an example. An on-call deployment support capability coming either from reserve component organizations, such as the SDDC Deployment Support Brigades, or from a contingency contract augmentation—or both—can be a useful enabler for a smooth deployment.

Movement to off-base departure airports or seaports should follow long-established practices of convoying organic wheeled vehicles (for short distances) supplemented by contracted special-purpose truck or rail for heavy equipment. Army and Marine units, Navy construction battalions, and some Air Force AEF units habitually integrate this specialized lift into their deployment plans. Support for contracting for the lift normally is the responsibility of the home installation and should be a frequently checked piece of the base's force projection support plan. To avoid unpleasant surprises, contractors with such lift should be surveyed to assure the needed equipment is likely to be available, and contingency contracts for calling on this capability should be refreshed periodically—just like the contingency contracts for base support augmentation discussed earlier. In both cases, inviting the contractors to participate in dry runs of plan implementation builds a spirit of teamwork that most American contractors, who are both customer focused and patriotic, will welcome. That teamwork is reinforced if these contractors gain revenue from support of field exercises that include even limited exercise of force projection processes.

Industry has long played a most important role in the strategic movement of forces by sea. Contracting relationships for lifting Army forces and parts of the forces of other services are managed for TRANSCOM by MSC for charters as well as United States–owned vessel operation. Loading is accomplished by contract stevedores under the overall direction of an SDDC element that maintains contracts with stevedoring and terminal management companies as well as provisions for temporary storage of deploying equipment and support of accompanying personnel. At the more active ports— Savannah, Georgia; Jacksonville, Florida; Wilmington, North Carolina (for Marines); Beaumont, Texas; Seattle-Portland—a sea deployment means only a temporary increase in operational tempo. Similar arrangements have been made at a total of sixteen "strategic ports" to permit simultaneous embarkation of a number of vessels, should the TPFDD require it.

Where the deployment procedures are used with regularity, such as at the Port of Wilmington, the team of military, civil servants, and contractors is able to maintain continuity and a smooth flow. For the other ports, occasional exercises are needed to keep skills and relationships up to date. Such exercises had become routine for SDDC and its reserve component terminal brigades. During Operation Iraqi Freedom they and their civil servant and contractor team members demonstrated their proficiency.

For all the contracted stevedoring and port operations, the *continuously shared knowledge* principle demands accurate data capture of deploying units' equipment and their location prior to loading and in their stowage locations aboard the vessels. Such data capture must be a contract requirement. RFID tags on equipment and containers enable better data capture, especially if used with interrogators in the assembly locations and ship spaces. The RFID system permits continuous tracking of the equipment before, during, and after loading.

The commercial aviation industry also has a long relationship in supporting deployments, so the above discussion applies similarly to deploying personnel and cargo moving through commercial air terminals. Most of the cargo accompanying deploying personnel using commercial airlift contracted by AMC will be personal baggage and some light equipment such as computers, radios, and light weapons. However, it is quite possible to use third-party logistics providers to airlift initial stocks of parts such as AEF war reserve kits and critical Army reparables stocks into ISBs to take the load off AMC strategic lift. The same requirement for data capture that applies to seaports of embarkation should apply to the departure airfield processes managed by the air deployment support organizations.

Contracted Support for Theater Reception

The reception staging and onward movement processes at ISBs can also benefit from appropriate contract augmentation. Certainly stevedoring and other terminal services should be contracted as soon as possible to relieve the stress on military units so they can be used in places where contracting is not feasible, e.g., at battle space air and sea access points. Earlier in this chapter we noted that the services make use of contingency contracts. These contracts typically are single-award, multiyear omnibus contracts covering the gamut of possible terminal and base operations services needed at ISBs. As experiences from the Gulf War through Iraqi Freedom have proven, these Logistics Contractor Augmentation Program (LOGCAP)—the Army's term for this arrangement—contracts can be rolled out rapidly and operated with people experienced in acquiring and managing the needed services in the ISB's host country.[11] Many of the companies that win these contracts have similar experience supporting oil exploration efforts in these often out-of-the-way locations. They have the contacts, can negotiate standby contracts, and possess knowledge that the services would be hard pressed to replicate.

---

[11] AFCAP and NAVCAP are terms for similar Air Force and Navy contracts.

The services' deployment support organizations work with these contractors during planning phases (in which the contractors need to be intimately involved) and oversee their operations during the execution of plans. Early planning involvement is critical; only the contractors who must deliver the services will be able to ask most of the relevant questions to get clarity about what the service component command needs, and in what priorities. Failure to accommodate this planning association in the critical phase of the Bosnia operation led to the high-cost, risk-prone public relations nightmare of Russian heavy lift aircraft carrying gravel into Bosnia to build base camps on terrible sites. To make effective use of this robust capability, the service component command operational and logistics planners must consider the LOGCAP contractors to be part of the deployment team. They are too important to the success of effective force reception and staging to be ignored during the deployment planning phase. The Army, for example, pays its LOGCAP contractor to maintain a planning team ready to move to the deploying Army component command on short notice to participate in the planning. The process worked well in preparing for Operation Iraqi Freedom for all but the terminal services, which were not covered in the LOGCAP contract. The result and recommendation, as one of the primary ocean carriers noted in discussing opportunities for improvement, was:

> *Port terminal operations were unprepared for the surge in volumes. Although marshalling areas were hastily added, they were not gridded so that yard locations could be assigned to containers coming off vessels. At consignee reception areas, there were and continue to be long delays in receiving containers. These bottlenecks both at the port terminals and at the destinations have resulted in inefficient use of the limited trucking assets in theater. In most cases, a trucker cannot get more than one turn per day, even though the actual distances between the ports and the destinations are relatively short.*[12]

SDDC should discuss concepts for outsourcing the terminal management activities with the VISA carriers who have the capacity and expertise to provide modern terminal and yard management systems, using up-to-date software and computerized systems and processes. These concepts could be

---

[12] Eric L. Mensing, APL Limited, *Operation Iraqi Freedom, The Ocean Carrier Perspective*, presentation at NDTA Forum, Kansas City, September 16, 2003. Chart #10 Notes.

developed in the VISA executive working group (EWG); if they are promising, SDDC should develop its own contracting vehicle or add this requirement to the LOGCAP contract.

This stage of the force projection process also requires the military organizations managing the LOGCAP contracts and the contractors' personnel to be especially concerned with the data capture and information production. Accurate status on the progress of force reception feeds into the continuously shared knowledge process and will be critical to operational planning and timing of those military operations. Timely tracking of units' progress through reception and staging will assure current, accurate knowledge of combat assets available for operational commitment.

Why the verb "maximizing" as applied to the use of contractors in the reception and staging process? One alternative is to rely upon host nation support. However, that course of action subjects the reception and staging operations to political and other uncertainties, makes difficult the necessary advanced planning, and, therefore, adds more risk and uncertainty to the campaign plan. The other alternative is to employ active and/or reserve component units, which certainly can be prepared to perform these support tasks. Yet history suggests that active force structure is an expensive and scarce resource more "profitably" employed to perform the uniquely military tasks of "killing enemies and breaking things." That leaves reserve component units, on whom this burden rested prior to the Gulf War. Then the services came face to face with the realities of political hesitation on reserve call-up, which would have delayed the ability to receive already deploying forces. Thus by using LOGCAP contracts, not only do the JTLM and the service component commands secure a politically dependable set of resources to operate the reception end of the force projection process, but, as expensive as it is, the LOGCAP contracting venture is likely to be less costly than perpetually maintaining equivalent reserve component force structure that may not be available when needed. The only cost to sustain the LOGCAP capability is the cost of the small planning cell. The remainder of the workforce is hired for the particular operation.

The Bosnia operation was the Army's first major employment of LOGCAP. Use of that contract in reception and staging obviated the deployment of most Army combat service support forces beyond those stationed in the European Command. The LOGCAP contractor provided support at the ISB (Tazar, Hungary) but also went into Bosnia to build and operate the base camps in this peacekeeping operation.

Force Projection in a Multinational Environment—and the Principle of Comparative Advantage

The fourth principle treats the case of force projection into a theater in which the United States has coalition partners—such campaigns have been among the most important over the post–Cold War period, the Gulf War and Operation Iraqi Freedom being the prominent examples. The Bosnia and Kosovo campaigns in the Balkans also stand out.

Here we apply the principle of *comparative advantage* to the allocation of force projection tasks among the coalition partners. U.S. forces, of course, are nearly completely self-reliant, and the question arises, "Why should the combatant commander even bother with the incorporation of allies in these processes?" Comparative advantage means that there is an advantage to the overall operation (and even to the United States) in having each of the allies perform tasks that they can execute, even though performance of those tasks may not be absolutely better than what the United States could do.

Applying the Principle of Comparative Advantage

An example: All understand that the United States has the only viable strategic airlift capability and will probably have to assist in deploying allied forces to the theater (the United States' absolute advantage). Yet even though the U.S. forces could handle the intra-theater transport of supplies from the ISB to battle space destinations, other allies also can perform that task, freeing up U.S. forces and lift resources that otherwise would be employed. We say, then, that the allies might have a "comparative advantage" in intra-theater lift (principally land and water). Similar assessments can be made for reception and staging processes in the ISBs or possibly in the battle space.

There are many examples in recent campaign operations, e.g., Desert Shield/Desert Storm and Bosnia, where allied logistics capabilities were employed to benefit U.S. forces. Desert Shield arrangements were negotiated on the fly as nations joined the coalition and brought to the campaign their own capabilities. Thus Egyptian transport units hauled U.S. tanks to forward assembly areas using Saudi Arabian fuel. A less known but major contribution to U.S. force projection was made by the German government, which, through the German national railroad, gave the highest priority to the rail movement of deploying VII Corps units from their garrisons in Southern Germany to North German ports during Operation Desert Shield. In the Bosnia campaign, which had a year of advanced planning by NATO's

European command (Armed Forces Central Europe), a U.S. general (Maj. Gen. Bill Farmen, a former U.S. European Command J4) was designated the "Commander, Support"—"CSupport," as it became known. He led a multinational logistics planning staff to hammer out "role specialties" for the nations. Not only NATO members were involved, but also several (former Warsaw Pact) members of the "Partnership for Peace" were engaged. Agreements were reached to operate various common logistics processes in the force projection phase as well as in the sustainment phase.[13]

Preparing for Coalition Logistics

Exercising the principle of *comparative advantage* should be a critical part of each of the geographic combatant commander's planning and exercise program. For the force projection part of plans, engaging allies in planning exercises to develop coalition support plans aids in assuring them that the United States will keep its commitments to come to the aid of those allies when they are threatened. Commander PACOM and Commander U.S. Forces Korea's annual exercises with Republic of Korea forces as well as with the Japanese Self-Defense Force are important political-military components of the forward presence portion of our national military strategy. Likewise, the continuing process of adjusting those plans compels new U.S. staff officers and allied staff officers and commanders to negotiate with each other and develop the assurances that were the contingency to arise, the coalition partners would meet the mutual support challenges.

The Joint Chiefs of Staff should reinstitute the "LOGEX" series of joint and combined command post exercises once conducted by the U.S. Army but terminated after Desert Storm. Those exercises attracted European countries, both those in NATO's military structure and nations such as France, Sweden, Switzerland, and Austria, when the scenario locale was Europe. They had participation from Korea, Japan, and other Pacific allies when a Pacific area locale was exercised. They were ideal for demonstrating the opportunities for role specialization and other support concepts related to the *comparative advantage* principle. Participating in such planning exercises, even where the target battle space for force projection is fictitious, requires allied planners to go through the process of developing plans that utilize the *com-*

---

[13] William N. Farmen, "Wanted, A NATO Logistics Headquarters," *Joint Forces Quarterly*, no. 18 (Spring 1998): 62–66.

parative advantage principle. In that way each generation of the military planners of allied nations gets to experience the combined logistics planning process employed for the Bosnia campaign—and would be ready should a conflict occur that would require military operations.

Projection of Humanitarian Support

Post–Cold War campaigns have demanded that the United States and coalition partners, including the nongovernmental organizations (NGOs), deploy humanitarian support in the land battle spaces. Such support usually takes the form of food and medicine shipments to assist civilian populations, along with the assistance of members of NGOs and civil agencies of coalition partners to manage distribution and provide medical and rebuilding support. Combatant command logistic planners integrate the shipments and people into the flow of supplies and personnel into the battle space when conditions permit. The *comparative advantage* principle has worked well in this endeavor, with the U.S. forces providing transportation and some force protection to the distribution teams from the aid agencies and NGOs.

Humanitarian support "force projection" requirements pose no particular difficulties except that they are different and need to be jointly planned with the aid agencies and the NGOs, with space set aside at ISBs to handle the strategic leg of transporting the supplies and a mechanism developed to integrate their lift requirements into the intra-theater movement program. The experiences gained during the 1990s operations suggest that working with these non-military organizations will require deft negotiating skill and great patience. The best case for the combatant command would be a total commercial lift process, with no competition for staging or port handling. The reality has been, and probably will continue to be, major involvement by the combatant command. Planning and process development should assume that substantial support will be required of the combatant command logisticians (a suitable task for the joint theater logistics management organization discussed earlier). Yet with all the frustrations logisticians will experience, the aid agencies and NGOs do bring resources to accomplish tasks critical to the successful outcome of the campaign—resources that the U.S. does not have to provide.

Achieving Simplicity in Force Projection

Our final principle to apply in assessing the force projection process is *simplicity*. Our preliminary discussion in chapter 1 noted three areas in which simplicity should be sought and complexity vigorously opposed. These areas were command and control, which relate to the principle of *accountability* reviewed earlier, resource management (funds), and sourcing of goods and services. Let us turn first to command and control of the force projection processes.

Command and Control

Our discussion earlier in the chapter of the principle of *accountability* concluded that command and control of the processes of deploying the forces from CONUS generally follow the unity of command principle and meet the *accountability* principle. And the processes are reasonably simple, with a couple of exceptions. One, already covered, is the responsibility of Army installations for deployment support. The second is the perhaps understandably slow progress in the development of "joint process ownership" for force deployment at Joint Forces Command. Resolving those issues should go a long way toward achieving the desired simplicity of deployment management.

The command and control situation for force reception and staging in the theater ISBs, on the other hand, is in need of simplifying, by removing the confusion of multiple organizations, each thinking it is "in charge." Setting priorities for the allocation of scarce resources in the theater is the task of the combatant commander, but he hasn't the means to manage the variety of activities within the joint organizational structure. Instead, as we discussed in the section on the principle of *accountability* earlier, the practice has grown up of assigning "executive agency" to one or more of the service component commands. In the past few years, the Joint Chiefs of Staff realized the need to gain unity of command for the purpose of conducting joint operations and created joint (or combined) forces land, air, and maritime component commanders for each combatant command and derivative joint task forces.

For some reason, the logistics tasks involved in force reception and staging did not appear to warrant a similar designation, perhaps under the assumption that logistics is a service responsibility. That is certainly only a partially correct assumption. It ignores the large slice of logistics concerned with providing those common supplies and services outside the battle spaces that are of central importance to force reception and staging for onward movement to battle spaces.

On the surface, executive agency appears practical. However, the consequence, as discussed in the section on the principle of *accountability*, is that service component commanders are assigned tasks and workloads that the services have not programmed for in the DoD force planning and budgeting systems. The Army has been the usual "beneficiary" of such executive agent assignments, but efforts to recognize the likely workload resulting from those assignments in the DoD resource allocation process have traditionally been met with little sympathy. The service tasked with executive agency, most often the Army, is expected to take the uncertain resource demand of executive agency out of its force structure and budget, requiring the diversion of resources from other service training and support activities.

Within the Army, such missions have been used to justify a larger slice of the force structure for individual support functions than support of only Army forces requires. Truck and watercraft transport and water production and distribution units are examples that stand out. Resourcing those units would require several hundred million dollars and several thousand personnel. There are strong bureaucratic incentives within both the active and the reserve components to advocate for these units under the rationale of the combatant commands' need for "other service support." More force structure means more units, more leadership positions, and a more important role within the service.

Defenders of the executive agency policy would point to Operation Iraqi Freedom to note that the force structure justified on this basis was available to meet legitimate requirements. They would cite Army support of the Marine force in Operation Iraqi Freedom, which reportedly required some sixteen thousand soldiers. Yet much of the Army support was required because of the campaign's unusual operational concept, employing Marines on an extended battle space line of communications. One could argue with perhaps more validity that the Marine force took the place of an Army corps force that normally would have such a mission, and the sixteen thousand soldiers supporting the Marines would have been required to support the Army force had it been used. The "executive agent" issue would not enter the picture. Further, the preponderance of executive agent–type responsibilities have been ISB functions, not tactical logistics functions. Service organizations generally provide their own tactical logistics support, although an integrated land force (Army and Marine Corps) operational logistics structure is certainly feasible.

The practice of executive agency also has led to creating ad hoc organizations of various kinds, organizing or tasking headquarters at the beginning of conflicts to perform missions for which they have not trained, and creating procedures and theater policies on the fly, as in the first Gulf War. In other words it has been a recipe for minor chaos, which but for the sheer hard work and inventiveness of the people thrust into the leadership roles might have had terrible consequences. And apparently the major reason for not organizing for combat ahead of time has been the services' unwillingness to agree to a joint organization to conduct the planning and operation of the common supply and services functions for the combatant commands. Unity of command as a principle of war has been validated over and over again. But when it has faced bureaucratic territorial imperatives, it has been often sacrificed on the altar of territorial preservation, however dysfunctional that action has become.

Simplicity of command and control should facilitate the assembly of forces and people for operations from all parts of the services, using common doctrine and procedures. It has come to work that way for the special operations, land, air, and naval components of the combatant commands. The creation of JTLMs, as proposed earlier, would establish the similar framework for common logistics support, simplifying the management of that support for force projection operations so as to allow the service component commanders to focus on what is properly the services' responsibility: tactical logistics support and sustainment of their weapons and support systems during the deployment, reception, staging, and onward movement operations.

Simplifying Resourcing

Because of the previous executive agent roles, separating the funding for common support from service-unique support has been a source of confusion, taking time and critical management energy to clean up what is clearly a "self-inflicted wound."[14] This is the second area of potential simplification.

---

[14] Common support would include those services that are used by the forces of all the services but cannot easily be charged to any, e.g., terminal services, real estate leasing, local transportation, and distribution center operations.

With a higher expectation in the Congress that DoD become a more proficient financial manager of the public purse, DoD should be anxious to rationalize funding allocations. A JTLM organization can become the combatant commander's agent for maintaining the linkage between funding and projects—even those required for support of the deployments from CONUS or forward bases. Previous difficulties with funds diversion can be ameliorated by the assignment of direct funding authorization from the DoD comptroller to the combatant commander for the campaign, an authorization that would be used by the JTLM's activities, thus avoiding a service's need to divert funds for common support. The JTLM could also manage the funding transfers for host nation and other allied support.

Simplifying the Sourcing of ISB Support Requirements

The third domain that can benefit from applying the principle of *simplicity* is the sourcing of the goods and services needed to support theater reception, staging, and onward movement. The JTLM mechanism can also deal directly with the force structure required to fulfill the combatant command's common theater support requirements for reception and staging. Through its linkage with DLA and TRANSCOM, it can act as the theater agent for sourcing the many goods and services provided by those commands. It can act as the single contracting authority for all reception and staging requirements not met by military and civil service resources. For example, the JTLM or its subordinate activities can procure all the local supplies, such as perishable food, bottled water, and construction materials, as well as labor services and local transportation. Service components would provide their requirements for such supplies and services but would not have to compete with each other for the sourcing. I proposed above that it be allocated the operational funds by the combatant command for supplies and contract services it would source, an action that would facilitate this simplified sourcing arrangement for reception and staging operations. The JTLM would have the sole ability to place requirements on the local economies of ISB hosts so as not to create destructive price competition (and gouging), with the attendant political problems that have arisen in the past from such competition for scarce resources. The JTLM could also be the U.S. component of a coalition organization to manage common support, joining with allies to minimize competition for support resources among the national forces.

Since the JTLM is part of the combatant command force structure, units of all services can be placed under its operational control for the execution of its ISB responsibilities. Such an arrangement would help to assure that only those functions that could not be contracted to ensure timely delivery of support would be provided by DoD organizations.

The issue is by no means trivial. But it is perhaps more easily solved than heretofore through the use of LOGCAP-type contracts to perform many, if not most, of the tasks previously handled by logistics units. The JTLM can then be the reasonably unbiased (no stake in the outcome other than good force planning) arbiter of force requirements. In this day of force structure and military-in-theater limits, the combatant command undoubtedly will opt for LOGCAP, host nation, and/or coalition national support, if it can, rather than having to employ U.S. logistics units in the ISBs. While there will always be a requirement for some military organizations for sensitive missions, the requirement can be minimized through JTLM-managed contracts. Military logistics units still would be required in the land battle spaces and for technical support functions where contractor support is not feasible. And the bureaucratic competition to have more force structure justified as "other service support" would certainly be lessened.

ACHIEVING THE LOGISTICS OBJECTIVES

How will the proposed improvements to the force projection processes enable 21st-century forces to be delivered to the combatant commands when needed to meet the campaign operational objectives and require a minimum footprint in the battle spaces for their logistics support? The first task is achieving timely delivery of forces and support to the theater.

Timely Delivery of Forces and Support to the Combatant Command

Clearly the demands of the force projection component of the campaign plan dictate a complex, time-sensitive game plan designed to deliver forces to battle spaces and ISBs on the schedule required by the campaign operations plan. The objective of timely delivery of forces and their support—in the proper sequence—is critical to tactical and operational success. Our descriptions of the deployment processes have illuminated the complex time-phased marriage of deploying forces, home station facilities, and support staff, departure airports and seaports, lift assets, en route support, and reception and staging resources. Because of the intricacy of the simultaneous operations by all the supporting logistics groups who operate the processes, there must be a commitment to manage to the objective.

Investing for Timely Delivery of Forces and Support

DoD can drive major improvements in assuring timely and more rapid delivery of forces through a combination of the process improvements proposed earlier and five major investment commitments: continuously shared knowledge, force and equipment design changes, deployment infrastructure, new mobility platforms, and pre-positioned unit equipment sets and supplies (the latter two to be discussed in chapter 4). Application of the supporting principles also yields several process improvement recommendations that require modest investments but will contribute greatly to timely delivery of forces.

Improving accountability through creating, at the highest staff level of DoD, a senior integrated process team will reduce the chances of miscommunication and resulting delays in force projection planning and operations. Assigning TRANSCOM or its SDDC component the installation transportation requirements generation process and staff will enable a disciplined knowledge network for originating the deployment movement requirements and overseeing the movement of organizations from home stations into the deployment flow. Establishing combatant command joint theater logistics managers will allow speedier reception, reducing the delays that have plagued arriving forces as recently as Operation Iraqi Freedom.

Enlarging the area of contracted support for the deployment process will allow smoother operation of all parts of the process, especially at home station and in the reception and staging functions in the ISBs. The critical first weeks of a deployment could be supported by contractor organizations who have planned for these operations under the oversight of military leaders.

Of the five major investment commitments, continuously shared knowledge probably has the greatest short-term impact on achieving the timely delivery objective. The technology to enable the fielding of an ALP-like decision support capability has been demonstrated; the investment required is nowhere near the magnitude of that needed to acquire additional lift capability. The DARPA-led work supports the conclusion that, in conjunction with the demonstrated data capture capabilities of RFID tags, it can reduce the effects of the inevitable breakdowns in complex deployments. DoD's investment in this capability and the training and exercise program to institutionalize it will equip force projection process participants with the tools to manage TPFDD execution and to quickly respond to necessary changes in order to assure timely delivery of forces.

Procedures that enable more responsive DODAAC and unit identification changes to the information processes in order to accommodate rapid task force changes must precede the investment in continuously shared knowledge. Without new procedures there will be no guarantee that the distribution process will deliver materiel to the proper units in a timely way—no matter how good the knowledge. Similarly, as discussed earlier, deploying organizations must provide valid data about equipment and personnel to the deployment support organizations in the deployment planning process to avoid deployment delays and misuse of lift assets.

Force Design Changes for Improved Deployability

The second investment commitment requires resources, but also an investment in changing service culture. Units are configured generally to reflect their intended mission in the battle spaces and to incorporate the appropriate technology for those missions. However, Navy, Marine, and Army airborne units have always been configured with their deployment means clearly in the forefront, along with their battle space missions. And more recently both the Air Force and the Army have redesigned forces for speed of deployment, usually at some sacrifice of endurance capabilities and self-sufficiency. Configuring units for rapid deployment thus results in focused changes to organizations, equipment to be deployed, and accompanying supplies.

The Army embarked on a major effort to configure a set of brigades that are more easily deployed directly into battle spaces than heavy (tank and mechanized infantry vehicles) brigades, yet are more capable of maneuver operations than light infantry brigades. Protected maneuver and support units in vehicles that can fit on C-130 intra-theater aircraft are the centerpieces of this new "Stryker" brigade combat team.[15] The brigade's units have

---

[15] "Stryker" is the name of the multi-mission basic 8-wheeled vehicle that is the principal carrier of weapons and soldiers.

been tailored to minimize the number of C-130 or C-17 sorties required to deliver them into the battle space, and its logistics support has been tailored, as with the Air Force AEF, to bring minimum sustaining supplies. An even more ambitious effort is under way to create the Army's Future Combat Systems with a similar restriction on vehicle size so as to facilitate C-130— or a future tactical airlifter with the same general internal dimensions as the C-130—access to unimproved airfields. Developing the Stryker brigade has also required a major financial investment, and the Future Combat Systems will require an even greater investment in order to yield the desired effects-based operational capability. Both new combat and support configurations are designed to drastically reduce the accompanying support structure.

The Air Force made major adjustments in structuring its Aerospace Expeditionary Forces. Rather than deploy whole squadrons and groups, it selected only the mix of aircraft and support necessary for the range of anticipated missions and left itself the flexibility to tailor the mix prior to and during particular missions. From the standpoint of providing support to aircraft, it has made a significant conceptual change by shrinking the range (number of items) and depth of stockage of accompanying spares kits, relying on communication and fast transportation to mitigate the risk of availability-affecting shortages. In addition, the Air Force positioned the back shops that perform component repair in regional centers rather than move their large footprints to the area of operations.

Likewise the Marine Corps has applied "appetite suppressant" to its expeditionary logistics force structure, agreeing with the Army and Air Force that component repair doesn't have to accompany combat forces to effectively provide ready spares to units. Efficient repair sites, good communications, and inventory management, along with fast, precise transportation of carcasses and repaired components, will allow the forces to maintain ready systems.

Another force design option for increasing the air deployability of the force stirs controversy. Land forces can leave behind portions of their indirect fire support if they can depend upon air power to provide the continuous precise support that their own missile and artillery systems produce. Just as the special operations forces were able to provide targeting to bombers and land- and sea-based attack aircraft to support their missions during operations in Afghanistan, so could other land force elements, with guaranteed air support, do likewise. The rapid achievement of air superiority over the battle spaces allows for more on-call air tasking as aircraft can loiter close to engagement areas—an advantage demonstrated many times during Operation Iraqi Freedom.

The concern of Army land forces has always been the responsiveness of on-call air support within those engagement areas. If this support proves itself, the Army may be able to hold back medium- and longer-range attack missile systems, e.g., Multiple Launch Rocket Systems (MLRS) and Army Tactical Missile System (ATACMS), and the Army and Marines may delay deploying some of their tube artillery units—at least in the initial phases of the campaign. These units can sea-deploy to ISBs so as to be ready for air deployment into battle spaces when needed.

As effects-based operations—the joint campaign planning that endeavors to apply the best mix of combat power to missions—continues to mature, we can expect combatant commanders to insist on the allocation of scarce airlift resources to the services' units that can best provide the needed effects for the campaign objectives. Thus air-delivered target effects will likely be favored if they are responsive to on-call missions because delivery systems such as Air Force bombers and carrier-based strike aircraft require no lift. That benefit suggests the value of having processes that assure responsiveness to land force needs since they will operate frequently in a close air support role as well as a battlefield interdiction role. This requires a cultural adaptation of both land and air forces, but the payoffs in reduced lift requirements for early phases of the campaign are considerable.

Improved Deployability through Focused System/Equipment Design

Force design changes are making better use of airlift resources to deliver combat power rapidly. Equipment design supports the force design changes. For example, the new Army force designs—the Stryker system and the projected Future Combat System—enable operational maneuver from strategic distances, providing the combatant commander the capability to insert a force into the battle space with the speed much closer to that of an airborne force and the staying power approaching that of a mechanized force. The new designs in those examples are critical to the success of the force design. The Army needs to reduce the size and weight of the weapons and support systems of the air-deploying organizations in order to get more delivered combat power and accompanying support from the available lift resources. The new design objectives are not only to fit more weapons and support systems into each airlift sortie but also to increase their endurance once in the battle space so they do not require as many fuel or maintenance assets to accompany them into the battle space as did predecessor systems.

The Marine Corps similarly is searching for vehicles that will fit the V-22 (vertical/short takeoff and landing) aircraft that will be the centerpiece of its operational maneuver from the sea capability. Therefore, we can see that the need for rapid air deployment has become a dominant component of the nation's military strategy. The two land force services have taken equipment design steps to increase their ability to project lethal force into battle spaces in efforts to exploit in the land battle spaces the force projection advantages of air and naval forces.

Air and naval forces' equipment design changes complement the land forces' changes. For example, precision munition design changes, most notably adding the Global Positioning System (GPS) fuze assembly to conventional bombs, have produced an unequalled precision strike capability for air operations. Improved air targeting pods for fighter bombers have increased their lethality. The Navy's littoral combat ship represents an important design change to allow more effective combat in the littoral regions of battle spaces. Both kinds of changes support the objective of enabling timely delivery of forces in the era of effects-based operations.

The third investment in timely delivery of forces is to continue the development of the deployment infrastructure—the physical facilities that enable a rapid flow of equipment and people from their bases through the APODs and SPODs. Great progress was made in modernizing and adding to the "force projection platforms"—the home bases—of CONUS-based Army organizations during the post–Gulf War period. But the embarkation pace of Army divisions committed to Operation Iraqi Freedom ran into structure inadequacies at the strategic SPODs and at APODs. There was insufficient terminal space to assemble the many vehicles, to unload them from rail cars, and to arrange them for vessel loading. Investments must be made with the port authorities at the designated SPODs to provide for the smooth flow from rail to vessel, else any advantage in rapid deployment bought by investing in higher speed vessels in the future will be wasted. Rail access must also be structured to enable this flow.

In addition, the heavy-duty rail cars needed for combat vehicles are slowly being retired, making it necessary for DoD to buy or lease sufficient cars to support whatever force level of heavy and Stryker brigades must be deployed in the first phases of future operations. Provision must be made to store these cars and keep them in a well-maintained condition. Similarly, cargo containers will be required to be immediately available for loading at home bases if the aggressive deployment schedules required by the nation's defense strategy are to be met.

Of the three investment commitments we have covered, force and equipment design changes require the greatest investment and take the longest time. Force design changes that can be accomplished without major equipment changes, such as relying on more air munitions for fire support of land forces, and the relatively small investment needed for the continuously shared knowledge capability can do much to improve the timely delivery of forces necessary to the effects-based operations of future campaigns. The next chapter will cover the remaining options for improving timely delivery of forces: more and better lift platforms and changes to equipment and supplies pre-positioning.

Timely Delivery through Process Management

We should not leave the assessment of how well the force projection processes contribute to achieving the timely delivery of forces and support without treating the crucial ingredient: process management. Even with the improvements proposed earlier that come from adhering more closely to the five principles, these complex processes still are operated and managed by humans, subject to all the frailties of any other human endeavor. Continuously shared knowledge serves to lubricate the processes to facilitate timely delivery, but the capabilities and commitment of the logisticians who perform and manage the many embedded tasks must overcome the inevitable "glitches" that develop in planning and implementation. Of course continuously shared knowledge is not yet a fact of life, so the logistics managers at all stages of the deployment process need to follow that time-proven rule given by one former commander of the Army's SDDC: "Check, check, check!" My own experience—gained, sometimes painfully, as a lieutenant training for deploying on airborne operations, and reinforced for the next thirty-three years—is that there is no substitute for "check, check, check!"

President Ronald Reagan made famous the saying "Trust—but verify." Just like athletic teams that practice to become proficient in executing different plays, logistics organizations that plan and manage deployment and reception and staging operations must practice the operations until they can perform them blindfolded. Then they may have confidence they can execute them to achieve "timely delivery of support to customers." More importantly, their customers, the deploying combat and support forces, will have confidence that the logistics organizations taking them through these involved deployment processes know how to make them work. As with most other logistics activities, "the devil is in the details." The deployment details must be right; for example, checking dimensions and weights of equipment for airlift and sealift to permit accurate loading and stowage and ensuring that cargo identification systems—whether sophisticated radio frequency tags or painted-on unit designators—are correctly applied are only a few of the myriad details in the deployment process that if not done properly, can change "timely delivery" to "late delivery," with its consequences for the success of the campaign plan. The Army's recent addition of mobility warrant officers, trained specifically for deployment management, to brigade, division, and corps staffs is one healthy step forward to assure high standards of planning and execution. But all deployable units must internalize the fact that deployment is a critical component of the campaign and deserves the training time and focus that its complexity demands.

Minimizing the Logistics Footprint in Battle Spaces

Minimizing the logistics footprint in the battle spaces is our second objective of effective force projection processes. It facilitates the agility of the combat force and minimizes the requirement for force protection in the battle spaces. To the extent feasible, the actions supporting this objective can also reduce the impact of having a major U.S. presence, with the political and cultural stresses it brings to traditional societies, in ISBs.

"Footprint" planning should, therefore, occupy an important position among the factors in planning the actions in theater access points (drop zones, landing zones, airfields, beaches, and ports). In airborne and air land operations into battle spaces, ground forces seek to seize their objectives with rapid, decisive operations. Those operations require great tactical agility, which, in turn, requires minimal but highly mobile logistics support.

Logistics units accompanying the combat force must be equipped and trained to meet the tactical force's agility requirements so as not to become a force protection burden. In the pre-deployment phase of the campaign, logisticians need to plan according to the principle "Bring no more than prudent risk assessment says you must have!" No more should logistics planning be guided by rules of thumb such as "thirty days of supply on the ground." That practice ties up much more strategic lift than necessary, creates lucrative targets for the enemy, undermines combat force and logistic unit agility, and creates a huge force protection problem for the service component and joint task force commander. With a renewed emphasis on rapid force projection and decisive operations as the 21st century dawned, footprint reduction has assumed a prominent place in the services' force designs and deployment planning.

Disciplining the amount of accompanying supplies will work only if the resupply process is responsive to the ever-changing requirements that combat may demand. Thus the principle of *continuously shared knowledge* becomes essential to keeping the stocks in the battle spaces within the parameters required for maintaining the agility of the logistic units. We shall cover this area in more detail in chapters 5 through 8.

The force design changes involving substitution of air support for land force missile and artillery also contribute to footprint minimization: only a minor part of the air munitions requirement (Marine and Army aviation) must be transported into the battle spaces, rather than the entire munition supply for the land force missiles and artillery. The fewer munitions consumers there are in the battle spaces, the lower the footprint.

The system and equipment design changes necessary to improving the timely delivery of forces will also contribute to reducing the consumption requirements and their footprint effects. Technology improvements in engines that are part of the Army's newly designed Stryker vehicle system vastly improve endurance through reduced fuel consumption per mile and reduced maintenance requirements. Improving the endurance of land and air vehicles reduces the requirement for fuel, the commodity with the largest consumption. With lower energy consumption, less fuel must be transported to weapons systems, and they can endure longer missions "per tank of gas." In addition, reducing the demand for field electric power—also part of the new force designs—reduces the requirement for generators to power command posts and other power-eating facilities in the battle space.

One of the most dramatic footprint reducers made its major debut first in the Bosnia/Kosovo and then the Afghanistan campaigns. Precision munitions played a minor role in campaigns as far back as Vietnam, and more recently in Desert Storm. In the Afghanistan operation, technology and resources finally delivered on this long-held promise. Because it takes only one or two precision bombs, missiles, or artillery rounds to kill a target rather than six or eight times that number of "dumb" munitions, precision munitions acquisition enabled a major shrinkage in the movement, storage, and maintenance of munitions, allowing a major reduction of dedicated personnel and the accompanying equipment, their support, airlift and sealift, and facility space. Munitions "productivity," in terms of target kills per unit of footprint, has skyrocketed—a major facilitator of rapid force projection. The impact of substituting precision munitions in the battle spaces is only now beginning to have an impact on the munitions supply; but as the new generation of GPS-equipped bombs, missiles, and artillery munitions become available to Army and Marine forces, the footprint reductions will be more dramatic. At the present time the GPS-equipped munitions are reducing both the strategic lift requirements for Air Force and Navy bombs and missiles and the battle space resupply for the Navy aircraft carriers.

Minimizing the U.S. Logistics Footprint in the ISBs

Our five supporting principles all can play a role in minimizing the logistics footprint of U.S. forces in the ISBs so as to reduce the chances of political difficulties with the host countries. Through improving *accountability* for ISB operations by creating the joint theater logistics management organization, DoD can ensure that there is one face to the host nation for infrastructure, labor, and other kinds of support, and a U.S. force no larger than necessary will be present. Implementation of the principle of *continuously shared knowledge* will contribute to a smoothly orchestrated reception, staging, and onward movement process, lessening the possibilities of port and staging area congestion and the buildup of hard-to-identify containers and equipment at the ports and airfields. It will enable the positioning of only enough theater reserves of supplies to assure uninterrupted resupply to organizations in the battle spaces. It will allow direct delivery from CONUS to battle spaces when appropriate and will facilitate a streamlined flow of supplies through theater distribution centers to airports and seaports for shipment to units in the battle spaces. Following the principle of *maximum contracting* of ISB support activities will lessen the U.S. force requirement and the potential for misunderstandings so common between United States and host nation cultures. It will provide jobs to local nationals, with a beneficial impact on the local economy, and make U.S. presence much more palatable than if U.S. forces members performed the work. Taking advantage of the principle of *comparative advantage* for support-sharing with coalition partners will also diminish the U.S. presence in the host nations, as with, for example, the commitment of Egyptian heavy equipment transport units to move U.S. armored vehicles from ports to assembly areas during the first Gulf War. Lastly, with the employment of the *simplicity* principle, the simplified organizational structure in the ISB, utilizing the simplified direct funding arrangement and centrally directed sourcing of needed supplies for reception and staging, will also contribute to smoother operations and smaller staffs than under the present arrangements, in which each service component (with the possible exception of the Navy) feels compelled to bring a complete logistics staff to look after its interests.

Need for Logistics Leadership to Minimize the Logistics Footprint

Even with all the technology-facilitated materiel changes, the incentive to enlarge the footprint will be ever present, and it will require smart but ruthless logistics leadership to keep the beast at bay. Logisticians—perhaps genetically—seem to be risk-averse people. "More is always better; do not run out of . . ." are the nursery rhymes of logisticians—including the author. Thus, their incentive is to bring more "stuff." Combat commanders who have experienced supply shortages are no different. But the lift resources and the footprint that allow force agility are both limited; it takes continual review of processes to squeeze out "nice-to-have" and modulate "desired" supply levels so that the combat and support organizations have enough—but not too much. The risks of stock-outs, demand "spikes," and other phenomena need examination and explanation to component and task force commanders so that both they and their logistician planners and operators agree on the levels of supplies and such, and on the risks involved. Once again the rule is "plan well but check, check, check!"

CHAPTER 4

FORCE PROJECTION PLATFORMS

This chapter examines the platforms used to deploy forces and their accompanying supplies—those in present service and potential additions to the set. Chapter 3 set these parameters for strategic lift:

> *Achieving strategic surprise and rapid, violent force applications are key to gaining the initiative against an enemy. Such an operation requires synchronized force deployments of all components, integrated to overcome the enemy's probable access denial efforts and to achieve the desired effects on the enemy. Another part of the TPFDD, no doubt, also will resemble the deployments to Operations Desert Shield and Iraqi Freedom, a deliberate buildup of forces in the ISBs, linkup with pre-positioned equipment sets, and establishment of the support bases for sustainment of the forces.*

The examination covers the following areas:

> - strategic systems—those that transport forces from home stations to battle spaces and intermediate staging and support bases for either forcible entry or routine lift
> - sea-based and land-based theater pre-positioned equipment (treated as another strategic force projection system since that program relieves the pure lift assets of some of their requirements)
> - intra-theater airlift and sealift that is present and potentially available during the early 21st century
> - contributions of the platforms and pre-positioning policies to enabling timely delivery of forces and a minimum logistics footprint to support combatant command campaign plans, focusing especially on platforms that could counter the access denial strategies likely to face combatant commanders aiming to project forces into enemy-held territory

STRATEGIC AIRLIFTERS

The Organic Fleet

The United States' ability to project forces *rapidly* to trouble spots around the world is the envy of armed forces throughout the world. At the beginning of the 21st century, the core of this capability is the strategic airlift force composed of the older C-5s and the new C-17 aircraft belonging to TRANSCOM's Air Force component, Air Mobility Command. These aircraft are the principal air deployment platforms for Army and Air Force units. When required, they also deploy Marine and Navy organizations and equipment. The C-130 aircraft, whose early versions began operations in the 1950s, are used principally for intra-theater airlift, but can also contribute to strategic deployment. Until the C-141 airlifter (now being retired) came along in the 1960s, C-130s were the workhorses of strategic lift. The organic fleet consists of over 100 (building to at least 180) C-17s, 110 C-5s, and a few C-141s, plus 54 KC-10s, which can perform both aerial tanker and airlift missions.[1] C-17s are continually being added and C-141s retired.

The airlifters have been designed to carry personnel, mobile equipment, and palletized cargo and to offload cargo quickly with their organic ramps either after landing or by parachute. C-17s and C-130s can land at austere airfields, provided their loads are adapted to runway length and hardness. The older C-5 takes a longer, wider runway and wider offload areas than the C-17. All three aircraft are air-refuelable, thus extending their mission radii to whatever is required.

The limitations of the still very capable C-5 were taken into account in the design of the C-17, which provides the combatant commander a short field landing capability and ramp agility. This agility factor is important since ramp areas may hold three C-17s, yet only one C-5 at a time. The C-17, unlike the C-5, has the ability to back up, a valuable capability when operating into austere fields with small ramp areas. That capability alone increases the maximum number of aircraft on the ground (MOG) that airfields can handle. In addition, the C-17 is also the airlifter of choice for long-range forcible-entry airborne operations. The C-17 is probably the most used strate-

---

[1] General Accounting Office, "Civil Reserve Air Fleet Can Respond as Planned, but Incentives May Need Revamping," GAO Report 03-278, Dec. 2002, p. 3.

gic airborne assault platform, frequently traveling halfway around the world for airborne insertion exercises, e.g., from Pope AFB to Uzbekistan. During Operation Iraqi Freedom, C-17s air-dropped part of the 173rd Airborne Brigade into Northern Iraq after a flight from Italy, the aircraft's first combat airborne assault of a major unit.

Civil Reserve Air Fleet

Augmenting the Air Force's organic fleet of airlifters is the Civil Reserve Air Fleet, consisting of 927 personnel and cargo aircraft.[2] These aircraft, governed by agreements between DoD and the owning airlines, become available for employment under AMC's operational control in three different stages of emergency need. The table below shows the distribution of aircraft by stage:

Stage I: Cargo – 31	Passenger – 47	Aeromedical – 0	Total – 78
Stage II: Cargo – 95	Passenger – 171	Aeromedical – 25	Total – 291
Stage III: Cargo – 271	Passenger – 610	Aeromedical – 46	Total – 927

Stage I and Stage II aircraft are to be made available with crews within twenty-four hours of activation; Stage III aircraft are to be available within forty-eight hours; Stage III requires either multiple-theater wars or a national mobilization before activation.

These commercial airlifters can provide a significant boost to the CONUS to ISB leg. There is reluctance to activate them except in emergencies because withdrawing them from commercial service can hurt the owning airlines, whose customers would migrate to non-CRAF carriers. In fact, CRAF has been activated only twice in its history. CRAF Stages I and II were activated for Operations Desert Shield and Desert Storm.[3] CRAF Stage I was activated for Iraqi Freedom; forty-seven passenger aircraft delivered 93 percent of the troops to the theater. Normally AMC contracts for passenger lift from the charter carriers, as well as the scheduled airlines, and tries to use contracted lift to minimize the need for activating CRAF aircraft. (The

---

[2] Ibid., p. 4.
[3] Ibid., p. 4.

Iraqi war deployment of 2002–03 occurred at a time of low utilization, leaving the airlines with an estimated nine hundred excess aircraft. Thus the activation's effect on industry was to produce airline revenue they would not otherwise have had.)

For augmentation of cargo lift, AMC has sought to expand its peacetime usage of the package carriers (FedEx, UPS, etc.) and cargo carriers rather than call for their CRAF commitments. In most cases it is far better to have the air carriers voluntarily provide the passenger or cargo service rather than call up the aircraft and crews under the CRAF arrangements. Normally the cargo versions of the 747 are used. Yet many of the all-cargo carriers with smaller aircraft, e.g., DC-10s, have complained they were not getting a fair share of AMC's charter work and have considered leaving the CRAF program. TRANSCOM should oversee the allocation of traffic to maintain a balanced peacetime use of the CRAF carriers so that they will still be available to meet the emergency requirements. In addition, the Government Accountability Office (GAO) made the case for use of the less expensive MD-11 and DC-10 aircraft since "over 40 percent of these recent missions flown by B-747s did not utilize all the available pallet positions and carried less than 55.7 tons."[4]

The size requirement of the organic airlift force and CRAF objective is assessed periodically through major simulations and usually expressed as "$\underline{x}$ million ton miles per day" (in 2002, the latest mobility requirements study [MRS][5] by DoD, the requirement was 54.5 million ton miles).[6] The airlift requirement is sized for different contingency operations, such as a major theater conflict, as well as for peacetime requirements, to include channel routes and the occasional major airlift operations required when the President travels overseas. The capability of the organic airlift force is expanded for short periods of time through more intensive use, by augmenting the number of air crews and maintenance crews from the reserve components so that the aircraft achieve high utilization rates (e.g., 18–20 hours/day). Now that C-5 aircraft are replacing C-141s in reserve component squadrons, they are habitually integrated into the airlift mission schedule. The airlift wings can also defer scheduled maintenance for short periods to generate more sorties.

---

[4] Ibid., p. 10.
[5] Study name changed in 2004 to Mobility *Capabilities* Study.
[6] GAO 03-278, p. 6.

Airlift Control

Strategic airlift missions are centrally controlled by AMC's Tanker and Airlift Control Center (TACC), which tasks and monitors individual aircraft. Even though the airlift aircraft are assigned to airlift wings, they are centrally tasked and controlled because of the need to have a single plan that includes en route base support, permissions for overflight of foreign countries, crew changes, and other necessary mission details. The strategic airlift wings are responsible for generating the aircraft and crews to meet mission requirements, including the vital tasks of maintenance and training.

Aerial Refueling: The Tanker Fleet

The strategic refueling fleet operated by AMC is composed of 523 KC-135s—a modified B-707, the first of Boeing's passenger aircraft—and 59 KC-10s, a newer modified DC-10. The KC-135s are over forty years old; all but 131 have been re-engined. Those which have not been re-engined need an investment of about $5 billion to bring them up to date—essentially a remanufacturing process.[7] As with the airlifters themselves, the decision to modernize—or just to continue safe use—is an economic one of weighing the relative costs of buying new, leasing, or upgrading to the needed capability.

Operation Iraqi Freedom gave new impetus to the need to upgrade the tanker fleet. It severely stressed tanker resources to the point that most observers concluded that the fleet could not have supported another, even modest, deployment. That critical situation undoubtedly helped bring the decision process to lease new aircraft.[8] In the Defense Authorization Act of 2004, the Air Force received congressional authority to lease 20 Boeing 767 aircraft and procure 80 more after their conversion to tanker configuration. (Subsequently, the unethical behavior of one of the principal Air Force acquisition officials caused the program to be suspended). While simple arithmetic would suggest that the 100 more capable 767s yield the equivalent fuel carrying capability of 130 KC-135s, those familiar with tanker

---

[7] Neil Curtin (director, Defense Capabilities and Management, GAO), "Considerations in Reviewing the Air Force Proposal to Lease Aerial Refueling Aircraft," testimony before the House Armed Services Committee, July 23, 2003, Report GAO 03-1048T, pp. 1, 2.
[8] Ibid., p. 1

operations point out that the sheer number of missions—increasing as commitments have increased—and geographical spread suggest that even though the modern aircraft has more capacity, it still can perform only one mission at a time. A promised tanker requirements analysis to develop fleet size, as well as total capacity, can make use of the same kinds of simulations that have been in use to do the periodic MCSs conducted by the Joint Staff and the OSD. In all probability such an analysis will indicate the requirement for further increases in the size of the fleet. Clearly it is urgent that the analysis be conducted and resources be committed to the program.

Airlift's Contribution to Timely Delivery of Forces

As the requirement for timely delivery of forces grows with additional national security commitments, the need for additional capability grows. Part of the strategic airlift requirements analysis must turn to expanding the number of airlift options in addition to just buying more C-17s, as capable as that aircraft has proven. The analysis also considers strategic sealift and prepositioning, but in the end there is a need to get some forces to troubled parts of the world more quickly than even the fastest sealift. Other airlift options warrant examination. There are at least three interesting candidates.

The first is to sell the air cargo industry on buying a commercial version of the C-17, with DoD picking up some costs for having those aircraft available, perhaps in CRAF Stage I. Generally industry is reluctant to buy military-design airlifters because their added weight to absorb landings on marginal airfields makes them more expensive to operate. It is not clear how to make that option economically attractive, especially in view of the current excess capacity in cargo airlift due to the downturn in demand and because of the large number of excess wide-body passenger aircraft available for conversion to cargo configuration.

The second option is another commercial alternative, a high-capacity hybrid aircraft with perhaps half its lift coming from a lighter-than-air dirigible feature. Designs thought to potentially interest the large package carriers such as FedEx and UPS would carry 1–2 million pounds of cargo on large decks on 4,000–5,000 mile legs at speeds of 100–150 knots. The commercial concept is to allow the expansion of air cargo into the high end of the commercial sea container market by allowing profitable operations at a price per pound midway between normal air cargo and expedited sea container services. Several small prototypes of this hybrid aircraft are possible in the next few years. However, both the aircraft and the cargo carrier industries will be reluctant to invest the large capital requirements until the concepts, technology, and costs are better understood and show an investment return surpassing that of converting excess wide-body passenger aircraft. DARPA has a program to examine the feasibility and technical risks of a hybrid air-foil and lighter-than-air aircraft. Such an aircraft would offer advantages in being able to deliver units the size of an Apache helicopter squadron directly to a large cleared area in the battle space.

The third option is another high-capacity aircraft concept advanced by Boeing's Phantom Works and known as the "Pelican." The design would use the tremendous advances in engine technology to employ eight engines in four turbo propeller pods to power the aircraft. It would take advantage of the "wing-in-ground effect" aerodynamic technology that would allow it to carry some 750 tons for 10,000 miles over water or 6,500 miles over land.[9] The Pelican design or the hybrid airlifter would be a particularly useful addition to the airlifter fleet in deploying follow-on Army brigades, Marine and Air Force elements, and sustainment forces to ISBs. C-17s would deploy the initial entry forces into the battle spaces and then could switch to intra-theater missions from ISBs to and between battle spaces rather than having to recycle for more strategic deployments. The opportunities for more rapid deployment of significant forces can be modeled in the (MCS) simulations to assess the cost-benefit estimates and the value of the R&D and acquisition investment.

Yet another addition to the strategic airlift fleet—powered air delivery systems—would further increase its utility in supporting force projection. This adaptation of unmanned air vehicles would launch from airlifters at stand-off ranges and altitudes to minimize the airlifters' exposure to the enemy's air defenses and would deliver supplies and equipment directly to land force elements. This alternative air delivery system would be employed when resupply by normal airlift means is not feasible because of the threat, weather, or topography. The incorporation of these air delivery systems into the airlift platform fleet would enable direct CONUS-to-battle space sustainment, useful for special operations and for other operations where there is no accessible ISB.

---

[9] William Cole, "The Pelican, A Big Bird for the Long Haul," *Boeing Frontiers*, Sept. 2002, http://www.boeing.com/news/frontiers/archive/2002/september/i_pw.html.

SEALIFT—THE MAIN STRATEGIC TRANSPORTER

Sealift generally carries well over 90 percent of strategic deployment requirements. That has been the case in most conflicts up through the first Gulf War and for Operation Iraqi Freedom. Whether it will continue to hold true in the 21st century in the face of more frequent smaller deployments of the type seen since the end of the Cold War depends on force size and composition and on conflict location. Both Operation Just Cause in Panama and Operation Enduring Freedom in Afghanistan relied mainly upon strategic airlift to deploy forces in order to achieve strategic surprise and a rapid commitment of combat power. Nevertheless, as Operation Iraqi Freedom proved, larger operations cannot be conducted without sea deployment, and sealift will be critical to sustainment in nearly all campaigns—as it has been in the past.

Organic Fleet[10]

The organic government-owned or chartered sealift fleet has three major components to fulfill the 10 million square feet capacity requirement specified in the Mobililty Requirements Study 2005:

1. MSC's Sealift Program vessels. This component has eight fast (33-knot maximum) and eleven large (greater than 300,000 sq. ft., over 900 feet in length) medium-speed roll-on/roll-off ships, five 238,000-barrel tankers, and several special purpose vessels. These vessels are kept in reduced operational status with cadre crews and can be activated in four days.
2. MSC's afloat pre-positioning force: These vessels are available for sealift once they have discharged their equipment and supplies.
    ➤ Thirteen maritime pre-positioning force vessels organized into three squadrons berthed in Diego Garcia in the Indian Ocean, in the Mediterranean, and at Guam, loaded with the equipment and sustainment supplies for a Marine air ground task force. They are operated under twenty-five-year time charters by three ship operating companies.
    ➤ Eight combat pre-positioning force large medium-speed roll-on/roll-off ships, each with over 300,000 square feet of deck space. At this writ-

---

[10] Navy League of the United States, *2003 Almanac of Seapower*, Jan. 2003, pp. 123–128.

ing they are being reloaded with the equipment of a heavy brigade, sustainment supplies, and a "port opening package" of equipment required to discharge vessels. They are to be berthed at Diego Garcia and operated by MSC's civilian mariners.

> Seven logistics pre-positioning ships for the Navy, the Air Force, and DLA.

> Several container, crane, and break-bulk ammunition ships.

3. The Maritime Administration's ready reserve force, composed of thirty-one roll-on/roll-off and forty-six other ships berthed on all three coasts and maintained in reduced operational status with cadre crews. They are staffed to meet four-to-five-day, and up to twenty-day, availability objectives. They continually deploy on exercises to test their readiness and were used on the deployment for Operation Iraqi Freedom.

Voluntary Intermodal Sealift Agreement

Several other vessels can be made available through an arrangement, similar to the CRAF program, between U.S. flag carriers and DoD. The VISA program makes available vessels (mostly container ships) in the active trade. It is a "quid pro quo" for these mostly U.S. subsidiaries of foreign shipping firms, in return for preference in carrying U.S. government cargo in normal trade. But as in the CRAF program, these carriers stand to lose nongovernment customers if their—mostly container—ships are diverted to defense use under the program (unless, of course, the carriers have excess capacity). Such was the case during the deployment for Operation Iraqi Freedom. The industry provided needed vessels under the peacetime contracts, and DoD did not have to activate VISA.[11]

Sealift Control and Crewing

Overall management of sealift is the responsibility of the Navy's MSC—like AMC, a component command of U.S. TRANSCOM. MSC, which also operates the Navy's auxiliary ships and fleet support vessels, uses a combination of methods for obtaining and crewing the sealift vessels. The United

---

[11] Eric L. Mensing (APL Limited), *Operation Iraqi Freedom, The Ocean Carrier Perspective* (presentation at NDTA Forum, Kansas City, Sept. 16, 2003), Chart #5 notes.

States-owned fleet is crewed by civilian mariners with a small Navy detachment for liaison and communications. The vessels have cadre crews that are filled out for exercises and missions. These arrangements minimize the very high marine personnel costs and, providing civilian mariners are available, have proven their ability to meet their availability times to load deploying forces. In activations over the past several years, of 170 vessels activated, only 3 failed to meet their availability objectives.[12] However, as the United States-owned merchant shipping fleet continues to contract and graduates of the federal and state maritime academies find fewer opportunities to go to sea and more opportunities for industry work, crewing these vessels may become more problematic. A further demand, albeit a healthy one for the civilian mariner workforce, is the continuing conversion of the Navy's auxiliary vessels to civilian mariner and contract operation. This conversion means more steady employment and an addition to the base of experience for the merchant marine academy graduates and new seamen, but in the short term it may stress the existing mariner pool.

Sealift and Timely Delivery of Forces

The continuing disadvantage of strategic sealift in force projection operations is the time required to deliver forces—albeit large, lethal, survivable forces—to ISBs and, perhaps, battle spaces. Pre-positioning equipment sets aboard vessels and stationing them near likely conflict areas (as at Diego Garcia) has helped reduce the delay, especially when there is sufficient warning to allow those ships to sail close to debarkation sites.

Yet the strategic operational and tactical advantages of compressing that delay time for projecting robust land forces—say, cutting in half the transit time from CONUS to ISB or battle spaces—argue for development and acquisition of the types of vessels that can meet this need. Clearly the possession of a fleet of twenty to twenty-five high-capacity (150,000 sq. ft.), high-speed (capable of forty knots or better) vessels able to access austere ports would be a formidable capability in the nation's strategic arsenal.[13] Such a fleet would complement the airlift elements by its ability to deliver

---

[12] Navy League of the United States, p. 128.

[13] These vessel characteristics require modest advances in naval architecture and marine engineering, but such a design appears to be feasible within the second decade of the 21st century.

medium and heavy land forces with the lethality, survivability, and sustainment resources to overmatch any likely adversary. It could move seven or eight heavy and medium Army and Marine brigades and support organizations to a joint operational area halfway around the world from CONUS in twelve to fourteen days—less if moving forward-based forces from Europe or the Pacific. The shallow-draft capability would permit access to many ports not accessible by deep-draft LMSRs. The large number of potential sea access points also would complicate the enemy's ability to deny access. Thus a combatant commander, given strategic warning, could have the capabilities of two or three carrier battle groups, a Marine expeditionary brigade aboard its ARGs, airlift-delivered special operations forces, airborne and medium-weight Army brigades, a couple of AEFs, and, for the knock-out blows and ground-taking and holding phases, the high-speed sealift-delivered heavy and medium brigades. What potential state adversary would not be influenced by such an array of forces?

Need for High-Speed Sealift

Strategically, this set of forces, as it deploys, can dissuade or deter. If the adversary persists, the operational options open to the combatant commander would be bountiful. Together these forces acting in integrated joint (and perhaps coalition—combined) maneuver could achieve tactical superiority nearly any place the combatant commander would pick. High-speed sealift would complete this integrated set of forces, albeit at a likely cost of 20–25 billion dollars. Without it there could be delay in bringing the heavy force punch to the fight and a risk to maintaining the initial momentum gained from the airlifted and amphibious forces. Afloat pre-positioning, however, may enable nearly as rapid medium/heavy force projection, as explained in the next section.

The last time this kind of argument for dedicated fast sealift was made was in the mid-1960s as the nation was just entering the major force commitments of the Vietnam War. In the winter of 1967, the Secretary of Defense and the President went to Congress proposing in the FY 1968 budget a fleet of twenty "fast deployment logistics" vessels ("fast" then meant 20–25 knots). The following spring the politics of the time caused the Congress to reject the proposal. The coalition of merchant marine shipowners and operators, the maritime unions, and the shipbuilders all believed that DoD would use these vessels to carry DoD cargo in peacetime, thus reducing considerably its use of the commercial carriers.

But the passage of almost four decades has changed the political environment such that the merchant marine and shipbuilding industry probably would welcome such a program. Some will argue that these should be commercial vessels, and DoD can then enlist them in the VISA program. While that is an attractive idea, the U.S. industry neither has the resources to invest nor is likely to find the rates of return on such a major investment attractive enough. Witness the last decade's effort by a U.S. company to attract capital for a fast vessel (the Fast Ship Atlantic project) to use in transporting containers.

No Commercial Market

Commercial resistance to paying for fast oceangoing ships is perfectly logical. The kinds of cargo carried by commercial vessels generally do not benefit from higher speed ocean transit. Cutting a few days off the transatlantic or transpacific crossing probably would not justify the higher container or auto rates the ship lines would need to charge to recoup their investment. Dependable service is much more valuable. If a U.S. manufacturer can depend upon the steady flow of components from offshore vendors, the manufacturing process can gear itself to a supply chain that includes present transit times. The key is "dependable" service. The cost of an extra three or four days of inventory probably is less than the cumulative costs of higher rates for fast sea transport. Further, DoD's need is for open-deck, vessels able to transport the combat vehicles of medium and heavy brigades to austere ports. There simply is little commercial cargo that requires such vessels.

Promising Technologies

There is no cheap solution to buying the fast sealift capability. Several promising technologies are available, one of the more promising being the upscaling of the increasingly popular twin-hulled catamaran ferries in service in Australia and in the Baltic and North Seas. Developing the technology to produce large, fast ships had not been a Navy priority until (possibly) recently. However, their value in moving medium and heavy forces to a theater in half the present time argues for making such development a DoD priority. Such ships could then replace the aging converted Sealand container ships, and complement the large medium-speed roll-on/roll-off vessels bought during the late 1990s.

The particular design of the high-speed twin-hulled ferry has appeared to mitigate the physical barrier that has long bedeviled the maritime quest for higher speed, namely the huge power increase necessary to attain even modest speed increases for surface vessels. Advances in speed up to one hundred knots have been conceived in paper designs and in some experiments—principally through air-cushion technology. However, bringing such developments forward would require considerably more resources than have been allocated heretofore. The high-speed ferry demonstrations, as well as the U.S.-U.K. joint experimental ship using similar technology, give promise that the concern with naval littoral warfare and the impetus behind the littoral combat ship and the Army-Marine Corps program for the theater support vessel (TSV) may at last place a higher value on high speed.

Other technologies also warrant exploration, such as upscaled air-cushion vessels, semi-swath hull designs, and semisubmersibles that could "fly" through the water like fast attack submarines.

Another alternative receiving some attention is the concept of "joint use" platforms. These vessels could well embark sensor suites in unmanned aerial/undersea vehicles and command and control suites for the joint task force. They also could carry tactical missile systems (for attacking access-denial targets) that could be packaged in mobile launch cells that could be stowed out of the way after launch to allow the embarked land force units to move ashore. The large-deck amphibious ships have some of these capabilities, but the advances in technology suggest that new platforms could contribute more.

At the same time, this R&D program for high-speed strategic sealift might be a needed shot in the arm both to invigorate shipbuilding and to encourage the buildup of the merchant mariner workforce: new technology that could sweep the world of shipping if the industry can make the business case to justify the investment. Adding in new information technology and infrastructure investments that will reduce the in-port dwell time of containers could materially reduce overall supply chain cycle time. That combination might attract products now transported by air, since even premium sea rates could still undercut airfreight rates.

STRATEGIC PRE-POSITIONING—ASHORE AND AFLOAT

Through most of the post–Korean War period, pre-positioning of equipment and supplies has been recognized as a means to project forces into areas of conflict. It complements strategic airlift and sealift by shortening the distance (and reducing the reaction time) to get forces and critical supplies into the area of operations. Pre-positioning, whether ashore or afloat, therefore reduces the demand for common-user airlift and sealift.

One of the earliest uses of pre-positioning was the Army's pre-positioning of most of the equipment of an infantry brigade aboard the "forward floating depot" (FFD) based in Okinawa during the early 1960s. These half dozen or so former World War II Victory ships were a primitive—by today's standards—means to place the equipment set closer to Southeast Asia and thus reduce the need for airlift and sealift to lift the Twenty-fifth Infantry Division (the anticipated user). The concept was to airlift the personnel and some not easily stored equipment to the operational area, where they would marry up with the FFD's equipment on its arrival. The concept received an early and successful test in Vietnam. However, the concept of afloat pre-positioning was shelved after the Vietnam War, because the U.S. strategic interests in the Pacific could be met with positioning units in Korea and Japan.

At about the same time (in the late 1950s), the United States made a decision to set a goal of "Ten Divisions in Ten Days" for the Army in Europe. Since augmenting the four and a third divisions already deployed with sealifted units in that time was clearly impossible, DoD and the Congress agreed to allocate equipment from a variety of sources to create most of the required equipment sets in various sites in Europe, principally the BENELUX countries, Italy, and Germany. Thus was born the POMCUS (pre-positioned equipment configured to unit sets) acronym. Unlike the FFD concept in the Pacific, these sets were land based and required a sizable organization to care for and manage the several thousand pieces of equipment and tons of supplies. But the concept was the same as in the FFD case—fly the troops to airfields near the sites, recover the equipment, and move to tactical assembly areas to prepare for operations.

Pre-Positioning Now

Pre-positioning has extended to the Marine Corps, which has three MAGTFs' equipment afloat on the maritime pre-positioning ships, and to the Air Force, Navy, and DLA, which store supplies aboard the logistics pre-positioning ships mentioned earlier. In all cases, the services and Congress have determined that this is the less costly politically feasible way of meeting some contingency plan deployment requirements. While it requires investment in the equipment sets and ships, owned or chartered, only one set of people is needed—usually the highest cost ingredient in the services' budgets.

Since the Gulf War, the Army has revised its POMCUS approach by placing brigade sets in Korea, Kuwait, Qatar, and Italy, along with the afloat set in Diego Garcia. The Kuwait set has been perpetually exercised since Operation Desert Storm to demonstrate the U.S. commitment to defend Kuwait from Iraqi attacks. It was issued to a brigade of the Third Infantry Division in the fall of 2002 in preparation for the Iraqi campaign. The remaining two sets were issued to the other two brigades subsequently. In addition, the Army removed all but one brigade set of equipment from Europe in constituting the sets in Southwest Asia. The post–Gulf War pre-positioning also includes one major new ingredient mentioned above: the "port opening package" of watercraft and port operations equipment in the afloat set, designed to allow early establishment of seaport operations–to provide intra-theater sealift capability and tug support and, if needed, to discharge the remaining pre-positioning vessels and follow-on sealift.

Maintenance and storage management of pre-positioned equipment has evolved along with the continual adaptation of the pre-positioning concept to meet new requirements. The services' own military and civil service personnel continue to manage and now oversee contractors, who perform the cyclic maintenance and storage operations. Although such contractor support is not trouble free, it has proved less costly than the large service organizations of the Cold War era. As in most contracting operations, awards made for a long term—five years or longer—and based upon "best value" and good past performance in similar tasks rather than lowest cost seem to get far better results. There also is less need to terminate poorly performing contractors if "best value" awards are made and the incentivized performance metrics are vigorously enforced by the services' managers.

Limitations of Pre-Positioning

As with the other force projection means, pre-positioning has its own set of advantages and limitations. We have covered the critical advantages. The limitations—in addition to the investment and maintenance cost—are less obvious. Perhaps the most significant is the political acceptance of the proposed site by the host nation and its willingness to allow the deployment of the equipment when the United States requires it. Basing any U.S. force components in areas between the Mediterranean Sea and Hawaii can be problematic—more so for the ashore option than the afloat option. Force protection is a major concern. The quid pro quos of the plan are worked carefully by the Defense and State departments. The host nation gains a measure of protection by the United States because of the site's existence—perhaps its most attractive feature. And it gets the economic benefits of jobs, supplies, and services purchased and spending by the site operating staff. The disadvantage to the host nation is that too frequently the site becomes a "red flag" to various opposition groups, who will attempt to use the existence of the site as a symbol of "U.S. imperialist designs" and undue influence. They can stage protests that require the host nation to react, if not retaliate—all to be captured by the world press because a U.S. interest is involved.

To minimize such limitations, all the services have turned to afloat pre-positioning. U.S. force presence is not so obvious in a theater if it is contained on ships that are reasonably unobtrusive and can sail away if the political climate heats up. However, the major advantage of the afloat pre-positioning option is that it allows the quiet movement of the sets based on strategic warning of just a "possible" deployment. In this way this force projection asset is part of the dissuasion arsenal, like the carrier battle groups and amphibious ready groups. Deploying the land-based sets cannot easily be accomplished quietly; it involves too much activity. And getting access to the equipment can be problematic if the host nation does not support the particular campaign, as was the case with Turkey in Operation Iraqi Freedom.

Yet another limitation of pre-positioning is the phenomenon of "out of sight, out of mind." The active forces' unit equipment is constantly being upgraded; extending that same upgrade to the pre-positioned sets requires great discipline and resources, or units directed to fall in on the equipment will find themselves operating pre-positioned weapons one or two generations behind those on which they have trained. This is hardly a recipe for confidence building in preparing for a fight, but was a fact of life for the Third Infantry Division units that drew pre-positioned equipment for Operation Iraqi Freedom. Services planners can short-circuit the problem with an adequate exercise and maintenance program where the scheduled con-figuration changes will be applied and vigorously overseen by the combat unit commanders. On the other hand, with sufficient knowledge and time to modify training, the experience of the Third Infantry Division in draw-ing pre-positioned equipment for Operation Iraqi Freedom suggests that older models of important systems do not have to degrade readiness. The tanks and infantry fighting vehicles that the division drew were older mod-els than their systems at home station. However, the equipment was in ex-cellent shape, reportedly better than that at their home station.[14] They were given adequate time for the crews to adapt to the systems before launching the attack into Iraq. The systems performed as desired.

Some observers recommend returning to the time when an equipment set was designated for a particular unit. Certainly the commanders had a great interest in assuring that the configuration remained as close as possi-ble to that on which their troops trained. Yet, with the continual deploy-ments of the post–Cold War era, it is difficult to predict which deployed unit might receive a particular equipment set. If the situations were more predictable, a more permanent relationship would present advantages in al-lowing a more rapid equipment draw and preparation for onward movement to battle spaces.

Transforming Pre-Positioning

Like the other force projection systems, pre-positioning likely will undergo transformation over the next decades of the 21st century. With increasingly complex land systems under constant technology upgrade, the first compo-nent of transformation should have pre-positioning evolve to contain fewer combat assets. The development of lighter air-deployable ground com-bat systems will hasten this transformation; fast sealift and the possible Pelican/hybrid very large airlifters could move the Army's modernized heavy ground systems that now reside in the forward land based pre-positioning sets directly from CONUS to the theater ISBs or directly into battle spaces. (The Marines' heavy systems would continue to be embarked aboard the ARG and maritime pre-positioning vessels, although follow-on MEF elements

---

[14] Army Materiel Command Briefing, "Emerging Lessons Learned, Operation Iraqi Freedom," o/a 15 May 2003, Chart 10 of 14.

could be lifted by the strategic lift platforms as they are today). The result for both services should see the less technology laden support equipment, e.g., transport and engineer vehicles, along with combat supplies such as munitions, fuel, rations, barrier materials, and other consumables, placed in pre-positioned sets. The transformation should yield faster delivery of sustainable combat power since sustainment supplies and systems could be introduced into battle spaces nearly simultaneously with the air-delivered land and air combat systems.

The second component of the transformation should be to establish most sets afloat. While locating pre-positioned sets on land at or near potential ISBs could save marry-up time and possess a cost advantage over the afloat mode, the political uncertainties of many of the potential host countries argue for investing in the vessels necessary to give the combatant commanders the flexibility of stationing and movement to potential trouble spots without having to ask national governments' permission.

The afloat mode could also be configured to host containerized weapons system repair centers for the Army as well as for special operations and Marine forces to support, for example, C4I systems. Two vessels already are designed to be loaded with containerized Marine aircraft intermediate maintenance equipment and parts. Such vessels would provide a climate-controlled, secure work environment for technicians and storage for parts and components. They would employ helicopter/VSTOL (vertical and short takeoff and landing) transport for components, repair parts, and technicians moving to and from battle spaces or theater APODs. Such possibilities require exploration as DoD continues to shape its force projection means to fit the anticipated demands of the national military strategy and the political realities presented by potential ISB hosts.

In the meantime, the advent of a high-speed intra-theater vessel can make heavy and medium brigades available to combatant commanders much faster than heretofore—in times close to what might be achieved by the high-speed strategic vessel described earlier. The concept is to marry the intra-theater vessels, versions of which have seen service in support of Operation Iraqi Freedom, with heavy Army brigade sets pre-positioned afloat. The vessels carrying the brigade equipment could sail to a deep-draft port in the region of the major combat operation, to be met by the brigade's soldiers, and transfer the equipment, now fully manned, to the theater support vessels. These vessels' forty-knot speed would allow them to travel nearly a thousand miles in twenty-four hours, and their shallow draft (twelve–fourteen feet) would enable debarkation in very austere ports. The vessels could each carry a tank-infantry company team or equivalent. Thus a fleet of twenty of these vessels could lift a brigade from its LMSR debarkation at an ISB to battle space access points in one lift in a day or so. They could repeat the operation for several more brigades as long as necessary, probably at a slower pace to allow movement of sustainment cargo.

INTRA-THEATER OPERATIONAL LIFT

Intra-theater—or operational—airlift and sealift complement the strategic force projection means by supporting the deployment to battle spaces from ISB staging areas of land and air component elements that marry-up with their pre-positioned equipment.[15] These platforms also deploy forces between battle spaces—operations likely to be used frequently in 21st-century campaigns—redeploy them to ISBs, and provide a major in-theater supply chain linkage between the ISBs and battle spaces.

The air platform for nearly fifty years has been the C-130 in its evolved configurations (the latest being the C-130J). An extremely versatile aircraft able to air drop over sixty paratroopers or air drop or land over thirty thousand pounds of equipment, it has proven to be a major contributor to both deployment and sustainment from the Vietnam War to the present. Its capability for in-flight refueling allows it to carry maximum loads over extended theater air lines of communication. Its limitations are speed (60 percent of a C-17's), capacity (compared to the C-17), and the required runway length for landing. While it can land with a full load in about five thousand feet, repeated cycles of short field landings, albeit with a 20 to 30 percent load reduction, can cause a high stress-induced failure rate. Also loads must be further decreased if armor plate is added to improve its survivability when operating into some airfields in battle spaces. Thus the search continues for upgrades or other aircraft to better perform missions requiring speed, higher capacity, and/or shorter landing and takeoff capabilities, all badly needed for operational force projection in 21st-century campaigns. The C-130's limitations have become operational liabilities for future combatant commanders.

---

[15] For the purposes of this book, operational lift includes platforms that can comfortably reach 1500nm. There is overlap in platform use for shorter range missions, e.g., Army and Marine helicopters may be used as well as the C-130 and C-17s on airlift missions.

The C-17 was developed primarily as a strategic airlifter able to deliver forces into relatively small airfields in the battle spaces. It also can be allocated to the combatant commanders to support intra-theater missions. It has both the desired increased speed and four times the cargo capacity of the C-130, and yet requires a runway no longer than the C-130 does. In many ways the C-17 is an ideal platform for many intra-theater deployment and sustainment missions.

The V-22 VSTOL aircraft now under development for the Marine Corps, Air Force, and Special Operations Command can achieve the short takeoff and landing requirement but only with limited cargo capacity. It will be able to move Marines, special forces teams, and light vehicles into inland unprepared landing zones, out-ranging the helicopters now part of the Marines' and special forces' organic lift. Its range can be extended through in-flight refueling. When AEFs are equipped with the V-22, they will add to the Army's capability to move forces into more distant unimproved landing zones than is possible with the Army's organic helicopters. The V-22 will become a useful component of the AEF's operational airlift support to land forces, although with the limitations described above.

A preferred solution to the difficult intra-theater airlift requirement—combining speed, range, C-17 capacity, and the VSTOL's unimproved landing zone capability—may be found in the advanced tactical transport concept. This large VSTOL design is a decade or two away, with both technology and resource barriers to its acquisition. Design options that include ducted fans or a compound rotary wing whose blades become fixed for horizontal flight may also be feasible and justify some development resources to explore their potential.

Although we generally don't consider the Army's and Marines' cargo helicopters as operational lift, in many cases they do perform the critical function of projecting forces the "last mile" to put decisive combat power on objectives. For example, those helicopters, capable of in-flight refueling, can move from ISBs into battle spaces, pick up combat units where the fixed-wing airlifters have landed, and rapidly move them to their objectives. Continued development investment will increase their capabilities for operating at progressively longer ranges, e.g., with the compound rotary wing technology mentioned above, as in the type of high, hot conditions that prevail in many areas of the world, such as Central Asia, that are likely to be campaign locales.

Like the V-22 discussed above, cargo helicopters have been and can continue to be used for moving forces from sea bases to inland positions, as in the deployment of the Army's Tenth Mountain Division from an aircraft carrier "sea base" into Haiti in 1994 and in frequent Marine expeditionary unit (MEU) operations.

INTRA-THEATER OPERATIONAL SEALIFT

Low-Speed Fleet

With so many potential areas of operation partially accessible from the sea, attention has finally turned to better intra-theater sealift capabilities. The LST was the workhorse of Vietnam, carrying units and cargo along the coast of Vietnam and up the Mekong River to the base of the Ninth Infantry Division and the Army-Navy riverine force. Its great advantages were its cargo capacity and its shallow draft. Low speed was a disadvantage, especially on the Mekong, since it became an easy target. The Army now contributes two vessel types to the intra-theater mission. The three-hundred-foot-long logistics support vessel (LSV) was first built and deployed in the 1980s; seven have been procured, and the last one is under construction at this writing. The LCU-2000, a large landing craft capable of ocean travel, albeit at only eleven knots, is the latest of the ramped landing craft. The Army's vessels were intended mainly for the JLOTS operations described earlier, although they have been used in the intra-theater role to deploy some forces, as well as to transport supplies in Southwest Asia.

High-Speed Theater Support Vessel

The major opportunity for a robust intra-theater sealift capability has emerged from the development, principally in Australia and Europe, of fast ferries—the three-hundred-foot, forty- to forty-five-knot twin-hulled, shallow-draft (thirteen feet) catamarans. This vessel's intra-theater force projection capability has been demonstrated by the Marines, who chartered a vessel to transport an entire battalion at a time from Okinawa to mainland Japan and to Korea—over 1,100 miles—overnight, with several hundred marines and their organic vehicles. It was also used to move cargo from the Persian Gulf ports to Karachi, Pakistan, as part of the Army-Navy concept demonstration. And it was employed to move units and logistics cargo during Operation Iraqi Freedom. It has demonstrated over this period such great potential that there has been nearly unanimous agreement for its acquisition, leading to a joint Army-Navy-Marine program. The joint program's prospective purchase of about twenty of these vessels will provide an important intra-theater lift capability. On a four-hundred-mile deployment from an ISB, that fleet of theater support vessels could transport in one ten-hour sortie one of the Army's Stryker-equipped brigades, taking the place of 254 C-17 sorties.[16] Its shallow-draft capability would allow multiple sea access points.

Its employment has been played in joint exercises where its utility was demonstrated (conceptually) for intra-theater force projection: from ISB to battle space, between battle spaces, and as a special operations force support base. Its prospects for adoption and for other uses, such as mine countermeasures, fleet command and control, special forces operations, as well as a logistics support vessel, improve as its multipurpose utility is demonstrated. The vessel also could complement the fleet shuttle ships resupplying deployed carrier and amphibious groups. It could take some of the load off the carrier-on-board-delivery aircraft, carrying-time urgent cargoes, such as aircraft components and fresh food, as well as personnel replacements.

In all probability these vessels will be operated by both Army and Navy crews. Because of their mission to operate near enemy littorals, they should have military crews. The Army has the task in joint doctrine to operate some intra-theater sealift and intends to operate the first dozen vessels. Since they have multiple potential uses, there is a case for Military Sealift Command to operate some as "auxiliaries." Experience with the first increment can inform the decision.

IMPROVING TIMELY DELIVERY OF FORCES THROUGH PLATFORM MODERNIZATION

More, Better (Capacity), Faster

Clearly timely delivery of forces can be improved by having more, faster, better (higher capacity) airlift and sealift platforms—both strategic and

---

[16] Association of the U.S. Army, "Force Projection Capability for a Transforming Army: Issue 5: The Theater Support Vessel," May 2002.

intra-theater—and necessary aerial tankers. The upper limit might be the capacity of battle space access points—particularly when the enemy pursues an access-denial strategy—and ISB APODs/SPODs to accommodate them; this is not a trivial point in the parts of the world likely to be the locales for 21st-century campaigns.

The "more, better, faster" platforms limitation, however, is not likely to be reception capacity as much as budget capacity. Given the frequency of simultaneous deployment requirements of one kind or another in different parts of the world, one can argue that a particular campaign's limited access should not limit fleet size. Rather, periodic MCS simulations should continue to be the analytic basis of lift requirements. The objective should be the capability to execute force entry ("forced" or not) operations with great speed and overwhelming combat power, if necessary. Timely delivery of sufficient force argues for continued investment in lift. Therefore part of the MCS must focus on platforms to allow the combatant commander to overcome denial of access to airfields and seaports. Let us now examine ways of overcoming access-denial strategies.

Overcoming Access Denial

Enemy access-denial strategies consist of defending airfields and potential landing zones with ever more plentiful surface-to-air missiles and denying seaport access by mining and land and air defenses. Historically U.S. forces have overcome such strategies by inserting early-entry special operations forces that can target enemy defenses, by employing amphibious assault of Marine forces, soon to be equipped with both a high-speed amphibious assault vehicle and the V-22, both launched by the amphibious ready group vessels off the coast of the land battle space, and by using Army forces' airborne assault to establish airheads and pave the way for reinforcing units. The problem with the historical approach is the sacrifice of strategic surprise. The airlifters cannot be expected to deliver initial entry forces unless there has been a considerable effort expended to suppress the enemy air defenses. And the forces they deliver by parachute are very light and are overmatched by enemy armored vehicles and artillery. The historical amphibious assault likewise must begin from areas that are difficult to hide from enemy intelligence unless the objective areas are reasonably close to the shoreline.

What is needed is the ability to launch the airlift and sealift from strategic distances, e.g., one thousand kilometers or more, achieving strategic surprise by making simultaneous attacks on a number of critical targets and inserting forces capable of achieving the desired effects against enemy forces. Ideally the airlifted land and special operations forces should be able to approach stealthily, avoiding air defenses by landing at unprepared landing sites. Amphibious forces operating from a sea base a hundred miles offshore can launch Marines in V-22s to seize key targets and then launch heavier amphibious vehicles nearer the shore. The combat vehicles of both airlifted and amphibious forces should be able to fight immediately on landing. Follow-on seaborne forces should be able to enter the enemy ports after mine clearing with both the high-speed, shallow-draft, strategic lift and theater support vessels described earlier, and debark the force's combat vehicles quickly. The Army, Marine, and special operations forces should provide the combatant commander the flexibility to base them, at least initially, at sea as the Marines customarily are, and as Army forces were for the Haiti operation. Therefore operational airlifters should be capable of being operated from sealift vessels. The V-22 and helicopters meet that requirement. The challenge is to develop the advanced tactical transport to do the same and to be capable of carrying C-130 type loads of approximately twenty tons, e.g., combat vehicles of the kind the Army is deploying to Iraq, the just-fielded Stryker vehicle. Once the initial objectives are taken, and the enemy air defense threat minimized, the fixed-wing airlifters and other sealift can bring in the reinforcing units and sustainment supplies, and both the vessels and the aircraft can be made available for intra-theater lift and sustainment.

These investments in R&D and acquisitions could yield a step-function increase in DoD's ability to project decisive force to the combatant commander in just *days* instead of weeks. Realizing that potential requires not only those advanced platforms and pre-positioning changes, but also the transformation of deployment processes as described in chapter 3, especially the capability for *continuously shared knowledge*. They go together to produce rapid, potent force projection.

CHAPTER 5

SUSTAINING FORCES IN THE BATTLE SPACES

"Whenever armed forces . . . are used, the idea of combat must be present. . . . The end for which a soldier is recruited, clothed, armed, and trained, the whole object of his sleeping, eating, drinking, and marching is simply that he should fight at the right place and the right time."[1]

Force projection gets the forces to the battle spaces and the intermediate support bases. The second set of logistics tasks kicks into high gear with their arrival in those locations, sustaining the people and the systems they use so that their organizations maintain the combat effectiveness for which they were designed throughout the campaign. Sustainment, executed simultaneously with the deployment and employment of forces, is critical to the success of the rapid decisive operations concepts. Once the combatant commander commits forces in a campaign, employment begins. Those forces will become engaged. Sustainment of those forces must also begin simultaneously and grow to include the follow-on forces so as to maintain operational momentum.

The quote at the beginning of this chapter, from Karl von Clausewitz's famous treatise on warfare, *On War,* states the case for the linkage of sustainment to operations in simple but graphic language. As many other observers of warfare have rightly pointed out, the maintenance of (designed) combat power is the principal task of logistics once the forces have been moved to the area of operations. Combat power rests in the military organizations deployed to the campaign area of operations. Those organizations have been designed, manned, equipped, and trained to contribute their elements of combat power to the overall combat power of the deployed force. Their contributions are woven together for operational employment in the campaign plan. Combatant and service component commanders of

---

[1] Karl von Clausewitz, *On War,* trans. Michael Howard and Peter Paret (Princeton, NJ: Princeton University Press, 1976/1984), p. 95.

the JTF,[2] through their own experiences and training, do the weaving. They depend upon each organization's capabilities to perform in the campaign as designed. It is the logisticians' task—the focus of the logisticians' mission—to see to it that they can! This chapter will provide an overview of force sustainment as a foundation for examining its major components in chapters 6–10.

LOGISTICIANS' SUSTAINMENT MISSION FOCUS

To sustain combat power, organizations must have a continuous flow of consumable supplies, e.g., food, water, ammunition, fuel, and medical supplies. Periodically they need replacement people and equipment. Logisticians are responsible for providing everything except the people, although equipping those replacements and moving them to their organizations are logistics tasks. The life blood of combat power sustainment is in the hands of logisticians. It is a heavy responsibility that requires the utmost in skill and a thorough knowledge of logistics processes to manage the complex tasks, paying attention to the vital details. The responsibility also demands innovation and creativity to overcome the inevitable barriers. It demands dynamic leadership to develop the high-performing organizations necessary to deliver the support that is crucial to campaign strategies.

Supply Chain Concept

This mission focus drives the many sustainment processes and supply chains needed to accomplish it. It is the "demand" function of the conventional supply-demand relationship. But unlike consumer demand as we know it, sustaining the people and systems in the JTF organizations also requires (1) rapidly deploying the *infrastructure* necessary to *facilitate* the *supply and systems support processes* to sometimes remote areas of the globe, and (2) operating these processes in all kinds of *adverse environmental conditions* under the pressures of knowing that both the campaign's mission success and the JTF's members' lives are always at stake.

---

[2] Could be a "combined joint task force." This chapter uses the term "JTF" as a shorthand way to describe the combatant command's campaign organization.

From this mission focus we derive the "demand" for the means by which sustainment processes can be accomplished. The "rapidly deployed infrastructure" that links a highly developed CONUS sustainment infrastructure to the combat forces provides the means to cope with the remote location of the "customer" organizations and the adverse environmental conditions under which the sustainment processes must operate. To visualize these sustainment processes, we can borrow from industry the concept of "supply chains"—the joining of customers who demand goods and services, through the various links and intermediate nodes of the supply chains, to the original producers of the products or services.

An example: the customer who wishes to buy a new automobile customarily goes to a dealer, who then can order from the auto manufacturer the specific model of the car that the customer wants. The manufacturer may have to instruct one of the plants to produce the specified car and then ship it to the dealer (or ship it from already produced inventory). In turn, the plant orders the auto's components from its suppliers so that it can assemble them into the specified automobile, and the suppliers then replenish the materials they have bought from their own vendors, and so on back to the mining or manufacturing of raw materials. Just as there are unique supply chains for each of the goods and services we consume in everyday life, so also are there unique supply chains for the goods and services needed to sustain the people and systems in the JTF's organizations.

Two Categories of Defense Supply Chain

Figure 5-1 illustrates a generic defense supply chain. The ellipses in Figure 5-1 represent supply chain nodes. The primary flow of goods and services goes left to right, ending with the node marked "customer," the combat or support unit/ship/squadron that delivers combat power. There also is a critical right-to-left flow—primarily the return of unserviceable equipment and system components for repair. The flow also connects the nodes from right to left with information on orders, availability status, and people and materiel being evacuated from the customers. The schematic is divided into two regions: "CONUS," which includes for our purposes bases abroad where forces are normally stationed, and "Theater," the geographic combatant command areas, e.g., Central Command and Pacific Command.

FIGURE 5-1   Defense Supply Chain

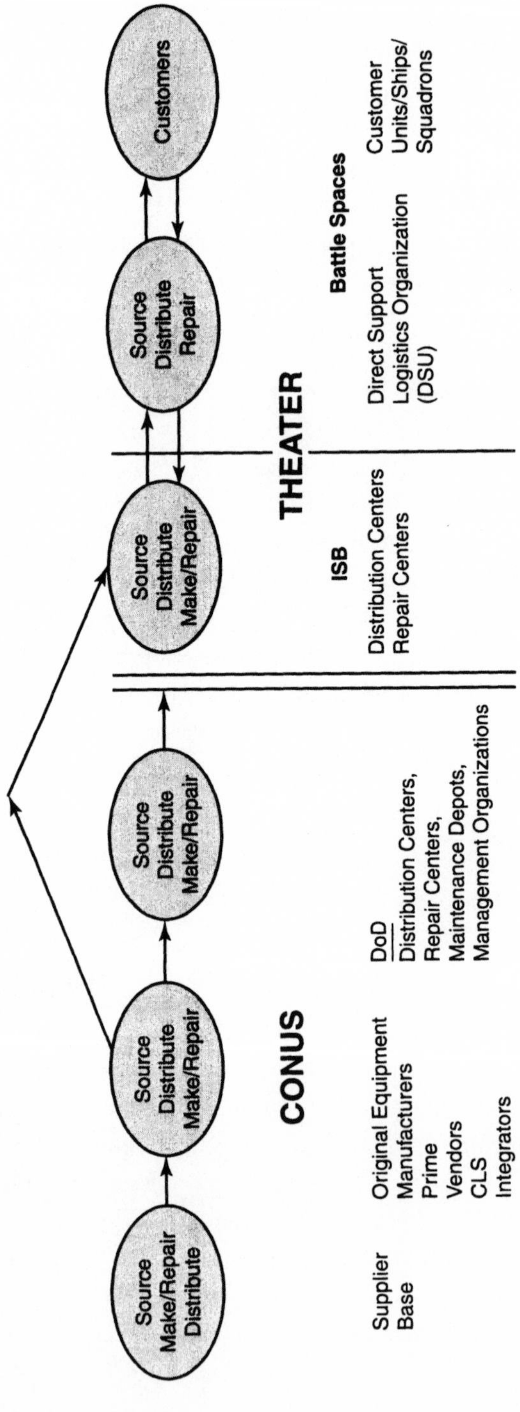

CLS: Contractor Logistics Support

Theater is divided into "battle spaces" (the locale of combat and support customers and their direct support logistics organizations—commonly known as direct support units [DSUs]), and ISBs (the configuration of support activities outside the battle spaces that include distribution and repair center nodes of the supply chain). The CONUS region, from right to left, portrays the node containing the DoD organic components of the supply chain, the distribution centers, maintenance depots, and other repair centers operated by the services, and the management organizations such as inventory management activities; next are the two industry components: the principal suppliers, such as the original equipment manufacturers and the prime vendors (of consumables such as food and medical supplies), and their "supplier base," such as sub-tier vendors and component manufacturers.

Figure 5-1 also depicts, within the node symbols, the major supply chain activities in each node. "Sourcing" refers to that node's acquisition of materiel and services to perform its manufacturing, repair, or distribution functions. Generally, industry's job is to manufacture or remanufacture ("make"), and sometimes to repair and then distribute the products to DoD. The DoD activities in CONUS have to "source" materiel and services to perform mostly repair, but sometimes manufacturing, activities, e.g., gun tubes in arsenals, and to distribute within CONUS or to the theater. The ISB activities also source materiel and services to perform their distribution and repair activities for the DSUs and combat and support units in the battle spaces. The ISB repair centers may also make repair parts, circuit boards, and the like if they have the capability.

We will differentiate between two basic categories of defense supply chains—those dealing generally with the support of the people in the JTF organizations and those focused upon maintaining the mission availability of the weapons systems and support equipment in those organizations. The term "product support," common in the commercial world, will apply to the latter.

These two categories of supply chains incorporate both the goods and the services needed to sustain the organizations' people and systems and maintain their combat power. It is of little use to either war-fighting or support organizations to focus only on the goods, e.g., repair parts for the systems or types of food needed to support people. The consuming organizations require the combination of parts and maintenance and repair services necessary to keep their systems mission ready. Likewise, they need balanced tasty nutrition, safe drinking water, and other life-preserving supplies to keep their people ready. The supply chain concept allows logisticians to focus on the processes necessary to achieve ready systems and ready people in the JTF organizations through the timely delivery of the required support with a minimal logistics footprint in the battle spaces, our two primary logistics objectives.

Within the two categories of supply chains, each commodity or weapons/support system will have its unique supply chain. It is the logisticians' responsibility to understand the components (our ellipses) and to ensure that these supply chain nodes are integrated through information and incentives so as to produce the needed products and services on time and at reasonable cost.

THE SUSTAINMENT INFRASTRUCTURE

In everyday life we take for granted the commercial infrastructure that enables supply chains that serve us to function. The telephone, computers, and point-of-sale systems—*knowledge* systems—in retail stores are important parts of the infrastructure that facilitates inventory management and ordering. The transportation infrastructure, composed of highways, rail, airports, and pipelines, provides the physical structures along which our goods travel. The well-equipped facilities that house the goods and services we use and the security infrastructure that minimizes loss and damage, as well as keeping us free of personal attack, are all central to enabling the supply chains to serve us effectively and efficiently. All these attributes contribute to the smooth functioning of the supply chain processes. The military logisticians' challenge is to create the same level of performance as the commercial infrastructure-only in a rapidly established, remote area of operations on land and sea, where the physical infrastructure is sparse or nonexistent.

We will make use of the generic defense supply chain shown in Figure 5-1 to describe the components of the proposed sustainment infrastructure of the 21st century. That infrastructure is similar in many ways to the present one, yet modified to take advantage of technology and the necessity to meet the 21st-century logistics objectives, timely delivery of support and a minimized battle space footprint. We begin at the right side of Figure 5-1, the nodes representing the principal customers of the sustainment processes that operate outside the battle spaces: the DSUs that deliver that sustainment support to the operating units of the forces of all services.

THE DIRECT SUPPORT LOGISTICS ORGANIZATION: CENTERPIECE OF BATTLE SPACE SUSTAINMENT

Direct logistics support organizations have three primary roles in supporting their combat and support organization customers: distributing the supplies necessary for sustainment, supporting the continued availability of their weapons and support systems, and providing health care. Now let us turn to examine these centerpieces of battle space sustainment, first in their distribution role: replenishing the supplies carried by the combat and support organizations that the DSUs serve.

A first requirement is that the DSUs should be every bit as agile as their supported combat units. In order to move quickly, not present an attractive target to the enemy, and remain in reasonable supporting distance of their combat forces customers, the land force DSUs generally can hold only a minimum inventory of truly critical items—perhaps a couple days' consumption of water, rations, fuel, and munitions and a few repair parts. Within the land forces, the MAGTF DSUs are the combat service support detachments (CSSDs) that are task organized from the MEF to support the particular configuration of combat and support organizations in the MAGTF. Army land forces have support battalions for the brigade task forces and for other groups of command and control and combat support organizations, such as artillery, engineers, signal, or aviation. These support battalions also are task organized, like the Marines' CSSDs, to support the particular configuration of the supported task force.

The AEF DSUs that operate frequently on bare bases—even in ISB locations—must constrain their logistics footprints to minimize force protection and relocation requirements, but once established, normally do not relocate as frequently as the land and naval force DSUs.

The DSUs supporting naval forces, the station ships and logistics elements of the combatant crews, have agility requirements similar to their land forces' counterparts. They must be prepared to relocate as task forces are moved to different engagement areas in support of the campaign plan. They have an advantage over the land forces' DSUs in that naval combat organizations are more self-sufficient, requiring less frequent replenishment. Also they can afford to carry a greater volume of supplies on the station ships without losing mobility; hence they don't require the same frequency of resupply as land-based DSUs. They do need to restrict the amount of cargo handling required in transferring supplies from shuttle ships to station ships to their combatant customers in order to minimize the transfer time, when the vessels are more vulnerable.

Establishing DSU Agility

We have noted that the requirement for rapid decisive operations puts a premium on the operational and tactical agility of both the combat forces and their DSUs, which means that the land force DSUs, especially, can hold only a minimum inventory of critical items if they are not to lose their ability to keep up with their customers. This requirement forces rethinking of sustainment concepts. The concept of *rapid decisive operations* requires minimizing the footprint of logistics activities, including storage and distribution, thus requiring that the resupply of customer organizations be synchronized by the theater and DSU distribution activities so as to meet their sustainment needs at windows convenient to them—usually *between combat engagements.* I propose that a significant contribution to the DSUs' agility and to minimization of the logistics footprint would be land and naval forces' adoption of two complementary logistics concepts: *cross-docking (cross-decking* for naval forces) and *log pacs.*[3]

Cross-Docking

The DSU should act as a cross-dock/cross-deck activity, accepting supplies—log pacs—designated for particular customer organizations, assembled by and delivered from CONUS or theater distribution centers to the DSUs supporting the customer organizations. The DSUs would then add to or subtract from the log pacs to account for the latest customer needs and then deliver them to the combat and support customer organizations when scheduled by the customers—usually during inter-engagement windows. The commercial analogue of this process is the "market basket" concept used by "e-tailers" such as Lands' End or Amazon, which allow the

---

[3] "Log pac" is a term used for years in the Army to denote an assembly of different supplies intended for a particular unit. The DSU delivers the assembly, or log pac, to the task force, usually at the same time, rather than having the individual commodities delivered separately.

consumer to add items to a market basket and order shipment of the whole basket when it is convenient. The log pac is just such a market basket, usually containing rations, water, fuel, ammunition, medical supplies, mail, and specific items the customers have ordered, such as repair parts and components, barrier and construction materials, and replacement clothing and equipment.

Cross-docking enables a leaner, more agile DSU resupply function. In earlier days, DSUs were expected to be the major source of supplies for their customers. "Demand accommodation," the percentage of customer orders that could be met by the range of inventory carried by the DSU, was a principal metric of successful operation. Higher demand accommodation was better. The best performing DSUs not only had a high demand-accommodation record, but also had the stock to fill 85–90 percent of orders for items they normally stocked. It's not hard to imagine the size of the inventories and the sacrificed mobility these DSUs and their supported organizations experienced. Now the emphasis has to be on quickly satisfying the customer's requirements without sacrificing agility—a policy that incentivizes lean inventory and the supply chain's rapid reaction to fill orders. Shifting the DSUs' primary role from carrying inventory to cross-docking orders filled by theater or CONUS distribution centers promotes the minimized logistics footprint objective; the rapid response of the distribution centers promotes timely delivery.

If the theater (or CONUS) distribution center can assemble the periodic log pacs into packages for each of the DSUs' combat organization customers, a DSU can simply transfer those packages from the theater transport (air, land, or sea) to its own delivery vehicles. It can add the items from its own lean reserve stocks that were ordered too late to meet the current theater log pac shipment time. Thus, readying log pacs for delivery to combat organization customers can be a much faster operation than having to fill most of the requirements from the DSU's own stocks and then restock its inventory from subsequent theater log pacs. Since the DSU in the continuously shared knowledge environment will know what is contained in the theater-assembled log pac for each of its customers, it can assemble the supplemental package from its inventory in time to have it ready for loading when the theater log pac arrives. Therefore, the DSUs will require fewer inventory stocking and issuing activities, and thus require fewer people and less equipment—and a smaller footprint—than if they bore the whole log pac assembly burden. We will return to the log pac discussion when we examine the ISB activities, showing how the log pac concept is key to enabling a direct link between the theater distribution centers and the DSUs, minimizing the need for intermediate supply activities.

Modernizing DSUs for Agility

Cross-docking (or *cross-decking* for maritime DSUs) dictates a materials-handling system designed for that purpose. Materiel should be loaded into containers that will easily fit both in airlift and sealift platforms and the DSUs' trucks or helicopters and that can be handled by small, agile forklifts or truck-mounted cranes, quickly and easily emptied by the combat unit personnel into their ship spaces or vehicles, and returned to the DSU.[4] The DSU can "back load" the containers with system component "carcasses" destined for repair centers and return the containers to the theater/CONUS distribution centers. The containers with their RFID tags provide the in-transit visibility of customer orders from distribution center to customer and from DSU back to distribution and repair centers.

Use of these modular containers by all the services could also reduce the amount of dunnage required by the present pallet system. Dunnage reduction offers not only a significant weight and volume savings but, more importantly, greater speed in stowing materiel in both vessels and land force vehicles.

Such containers could be the basic building block for designing the Navy's new combat logistics force station and shuttle ships and for dry-cargo supply stowage on combatants. Equipping the vessels with the compatible materials-handling equipment would allow containerized log pacs to be prepared at forward naval bases and cross-decked from the shuttle ships by helicopter (the "vertical replenishment" process) to the combatants or to station ships. The station ships, like the DSUs ashore, hold the reserves for the combatants, supplementing the log pacs delivered by the shuttle ships or accepting the combatants' containers if operations preclude direct replenish-

---

[4] The palletized load system (PLS) flat racks and container inserts serve this purpose for throughput of munitions, rations, fuel bladders and pods, and other high-volume consumables; the Army DSU could receive them from the theater distribution centers, cross-dock the entire 8 × 20-foot flat racks from the theater transport to its trucks, and deliver to the combat units to rearm and refuel them.

ment. Modernizing both the design of the vessels and the shipboard materials handling by use of these modular containers and automated handling systems could improve the accuracy and speed of replenishment and help the Navy's efforts to reduce crew size on both the combatants and the combat logistics force vessels.

The modular containers should become the basic building blocks for designing land force and AEF DSU storage equipment. For example, interlocking several containers on PLS flat racks could allow rapid download—and upload—of the DSU inventory and allow the trucks to be used in distribution to customer organizations. The land force DSUs' distribution function is one of the more difficult. It requires either truck or helicopter delivery of log pacs, frequently at night over unfamiliar terrain, often only partially secured from enemy action and in narrow time windows. Lean DSUs with expensive transport vehicles should have modern location and communications technology to enable successful delivery missions. The main ingredients are GPS-RFID transponders linked to satellite communications, so that location is always known to transport operators, the parent DSU, and customers awaiting log pacs. The transponders will facilitate recovery of empty containers, a perennial problem for supporters.

Weapons/Support System Sustainment

The DSUs' second role, of maintaining weapons and support system availability, will appear in greater detail in the following three chapters. Two aspects of that function, however, relate to the previous discussion on distribution to forward elements of land, maritime, and air forces. The first is the utilization of log pacs to "pull" to the DSU the replacement components, consumable parts and supplies, test and diagnostic equipment, and, when the combat situation permits, technical assistance. The DSU will maintain an inventory of repair parts and supplies, but, as with other supplies, it should be confined to the fast-moving items that do not take up much of its limited mobile storage capability and hamper its ability to keep up with its supported force.

The second aspect of its distribution-like system support task is the requirement to send "contact teams" to work at remote sites—expeditionary airfields for AEF and Marine air DSUs and at locations near land force engagement areas where equipment has sustained failure or damage.

These contact teams are the "do-ers" of the product support work, exposed to the risks of encountering the enemy in the course of their work. They must rely upon GPS and communications technology to navigate to the remote sites, maintain awareness of the enemy situation, and order parts and technical assistance. They are responsible for restoring broken multi-million-dollar systems to combat ready status. The GPS and communications technology enable them to utilize their technical skills without unnecessary risk and are vital to the capability for continuously shared knowledge, which, in turn, allows a minimum logistics footprint and timely delivery of support.

Unfortunately, the services have seldom so equipped these teams, a result of their focusing technology investment on the combat units and giving the support units "hand-me-downs." (The Navy maintenance technicians are much more fortunate because they work aboard the combatants, which have modern communications.) Even as late as the beginning of the Iraqi Freedom operation in 2003, individuals in support units in the first Army division to enter combat had bought their own commercial GPS receivers. Their units relied upon range-limited FM line-of-sight radios. One group of soldiers from a DSU (the 507th Maintenance Company) became disoriented, got separated from its parent organization, ran into an Iraqi ambush, and were killed or captured. That might not have happened had they been equipped with GPS and adequate communications.[5] (We will return to issue of the absolutely ineffective Army logistics communication infrastructure in chapter 7.)

Sustaining Health

The third major role of DSUs is to be the primary health care agent for their supported organizations. (Chapters 9 and 10 explore this task in greater detail.) Its relationship to the DSUs' distribution and systems sustainment tasks is such that an overview is useful. As with the distribution of log pacs and the contact team work of systems sustainment, the medical trauma and evacuation teams in the land force DSUs operate between the combat organizations and their DSU bases, where patient holding and medical supplies are located. The trauma teams and air and ground ambulances, like the

---

[5] "Texas Base Stunned to See POWs," Washington Post, March 25, 2003, p. A11.

maintenance contact teams and log pac distribution teams, need GPS and communications technology to navigate over unfamiliar terrain, maintain situational awareness of their supported organization to prepare to receive casualties, manage the air or ground evacuation of patients, and order supplies. The trauma teams treat the most critically wounded in order to stabilize them for evacuation to hospitals and are therefore critical nodes in the continuously shared knowledge system for health care.

Continuously Shared Knowledge Infrastructure for Sustainment

With an understanding of the customer end of the supply chain, we turn to the most critical part of infrastructure performance: the same continuously shared knowledge we covered in the force projection discussion. It is the adhesive that binds the supply chain nodes together and enables them to deliver the required support. Knowledge of the consuming organizations' ever-changing sustainment status, their needs, and fulfillment status in as near real time as possible must be shared with

> - order-fulfilling activities (nodes) and their sourcing activities in the supply chain
> - JTF command and control activities that must monitor the organizations' mission readiness
> - the transportation link and terminal and distribution node operators who must plan for the fulfillment demand on the transportation and warehouse operation resources, throughout the supply chain
> - the health care providers from the combat unit through the DSU and patient evacuation system.

The major elements of the continuously shared knowledge infrastructure are the logistics and health care managers, the knowledge systems, and the necessary secure communications links between the sustainment activities. This infrastructure should be functioning during the force projection operations so that forces' sustainment requirements can be anticipated and satisfied promptly. The continuously shared knowledge network components should be able to "unplug" from CONUS and forward station communications means and "plug in" to the theater means as they deploy, maintaining continuity of forces' status, requirements, and fulfillment progress.

Knowledge Communications

Continuously shared knowledge—the data and information as well as decision support systems to convert information to "knowledge"—works best within the sophisticated commercial communications infrastructure of the developed world. There is little such infrastructure in the remote areas of JTF operations. The JTF must bring its own infrastructure, perhaps including supplementary low earth orbiting satellites or manned/unmanned aerial communications vehicles launched for the campaign. The lessons of late 20th- and early 21st-century operations suggest that such extraterrestrial communications are no longer a "nice-to-have" component; they are essential to sustaining widely separated land, sea, and air forces in the remote areas of the globe. Terrestrial communications alone will not be sufficient to allow that continuously shared knowledge. In fact, commercial practice in both the developed and undeveloped areas of the world has come to rely upon satellite communications to transcend the limitations of terrestrial infrastructure.

Operation Iraqi Freedom provided the most recent example of the utter failure of communications support to Army and Marine logistics organizations in the battle space. The reliance on terrestrial, mainly line-of-sight FM or microwave communications resulted in their inability to order repair parts and monitor the status of orders already placed before the entry into Iraq. The consequences for the DSUs and combat and support unit customers was a resort to cannibalizing broken or damaged equipment in order to obtain needed parts when the stocks they carried with them ran out or did not include the needed items. Fortunately, the "push system" for critical consumables such as food, water, fuel, and ammunition worked sufficiently well to supply those needs, albeit not without times when supplies ran extremely low. The four-day pause prior to entering Baghdad allowed those supplies to catch up and also provided some rest from the rapid advance for the soldiers and Marines. And the patient evacuation system, which used both the operational communications and the Iridium satellite phone system, also functioned—because it was not tied to terrestrial communications.

Belatedly, the land force in Iraq is receiving satellite terminals linked to INMARSAT for the DSUs after having been denied the capability before the operation commenced. The INMARSAT linkage is the same system used effectively by the Army Materiel Command logistics assistance representatives during Operation Desert Shield/Desert Storm twelve years before—a current example of "lessons *not* learned." Somehow combatant commanders must learn that without satellite communications to support logistics knowledge in their areas of operation, they will be forced to create large footprints of inventory echeloned along their lines of communication, with many trucks, forklifts, and people necessary to manage the risks of supply shortages affecting combat operations.

Knowledge Software

The JTF's requirement for continuously shared logistics knowledge mandates that the supporting communications infrastructure be designed to facilitate the supply chain management processes described above. Thus orders for supplies and services, order fulfillment, asset status, and conditions (e.g., the inter-engagement resupply windows, delivery points, threat, weather, etc.) can be shared with all parties in the supply chains. Commercial software such as that used by e-tailers such as L.L. Bean or Amazon now allows multiple items on a single customer order, each item in the order forwarded through the information infrastructure to a source of supply, whether a theater or CONUS distribution center, a vendor, or another DSU in an emergency. That order fulfillment software then facilitates assembling each scheduled log pac in the theater distribution facilities (joint and/or service component) into containers or air pallets to meet scheduled resupply deliveries. Similarly, "reverse log pacs" need the same kind of careful planning and incorporation into the continuously shared knowledge process. As noted in our discussion of the generic defense supply chain (Figure 5-1) they may include casualties, component carcasses destined for ISB repair centers, mail, returning technicians, and excess supplies. The continuously shared knowledge system should facilitate that important operation.

Use of Automatic Identification Technology

In past campaigns it has been very difficult for logisticians to have knowledge of "asset status and conditions" and be able to easily assemble supplies into log pacs. By the end of the Gulf War in 1991, over 20,000 sea containers of unidentified supplies were in the storage areas around Damman. Unidentified and misidentified "gray boxes" have been a tradition in logistics experience. They are stark symbols of supply chains' failure to get needed items to the customers and not to waste resources. Simply answering, "What do we have, how much, and where?" has been enormously difficult. Certainly to assure timely delivery and avoid the kind of footprint represented by those 20,000 containers, DoD must place a premium on putting in place the knowledge infrastructure that will answer that question: "What do we have, how much, and where?" Automated identification technology linked to asset databases, retrievable by the components of the supply chain, is the means of providing the source data for that infrastructure.

The following example illustrates the value of AIT in assembling log pacs for land forces and replenishment packages for naval and air forces. Vendors would put passive RFID labels on DoD- and contractor-procured items showing the item description—the stock keeping unit (SKU) number and order identifier. A larger capacity RFID tag goes on each pallet and container, showing the packing list of all items on the pallet and in the container. The list is prepared automatically as the reader "sees" the labeled items being packed. Thus items can be pulled accurately from CONUS or ISB distribution center storage locations to match log pac requirements and assembled into containers, their packing list can be burned into their tags, and they can be moved through the inter- and intra-theater transportation systems to their DSU customers in the ISB and battle spaces—a process very similar to that of FedEx, UPS, and other distribution firms. In-transit visibility is achieved automatically through readers sited at distribution and transportation nodes. With the readers at the nodes and on board the aircraft, vessels, and trucks also communicating their GPS signals, the knowledge database can know where each container or air pallet (with its contents also visible) is located so that DSUs can track critical items and prepare to give those items high priority for cross-docking to combat unit customers.

Decision Making with Knowledge

It is clear from this process description that timely, accurate *continuously shared knowledge*, employed by trained, disciplined logistics units, is key to orchestrating this continuing resupply operation so essential to sustaining the forces' combat power. The opportunities for missteps are bountiful. Only part of the combat organizations' sustainment needs are predictable. Some needs become urgent, and both the DSU and, often, its supporting theater distribution or repair centers and CONUS sources must react quickly. The urgently needed items might have to displace other items scheduled for the next log pac because of the weight or space constraints of the transport vehicles. Or the loss of an aircraft scheduled for a log pac delivery may require reshuffling the items to assure that those most urgently needed can make the next scheduled delivery if no replacement aircraft can be found. Alternatively the enemy situation may force the rescheduling of the log pac or require a different delivery point. All these changes are unpredictable. But if the logisticians do not get the timely information on the changed conditions, the unpredictability may jeopardize the combat force's ability to accomplish its mission. It is also critical that the ongoing changes made by logisticians in the theater distribution center are visible to both the DSU recipients of the log pacs and their combat forces' customers so they can take appropriate actions to prepare to receive the log pacs and replacement personnel. The combat forces and DSUs must agree with changing delivery points-landing or drop zones or ship rendezvous locations—to assure force protection and preservation of freedom of maneuver.

The DSUs' health care mission, as noted above, also depends heavily on continuously shared knowledge. Assured communications tied to GPS and RFID readers for the patients' ID tags and medical supplies and equipment are critical resources for both trauma and evacuation teams (as well as for the medical teams internal to combat organizations). These resources are a small price to pay for the large payoff they bring in restoring health to wounded, injured, and ill people and in maintaining a healthy force.

Implementing the Knowledge Infrastructure

The necessary information infrastructure to produce continuously shared knowledge is available in commercial applications today. But adapting it to the needs of battle spaces requires different approaches. For example, processing in the battle spaces should be limited to genuinely mobile hardware linked to the communication system, with computation and decision support processing accomplished elsewhere. The preference should be for laptops, personal data assistants (PDAs), or even wearable computing devices, depending on the user and the RFID readers. The wearables are particularly useful for those who benefit from hands-free technology, e.g., for the technicians doing diagnosis and repair of systems or the crews managing underway replenishment and cross-dock processing from theater transport vehicles to DSU transport and later to customer units. Transport vehicles and land forces' DSUs must be equipped with GPS receivers in their communication and RFID reader systems in order to make the linkage of location with information content automatic.

The backbone communications systems servicing these devices should be wireless, like the commercial wireless intranets and networks growing across the nation, but equipped with appropriate security means. With such a system, linked by wideband satellite communications to the ISBs and CONUS, databases and decision support systems could be sited either at ISBs or CONUS locations. Even in 1990, deployed Air Force wings in Saudi Arabia had their parts ordering and inventory management processing handled at Langley Air Force Base, thus minimizing their logistics footprint.

Equipping the DSUs with Continuously Shared Knowledge

This discussion underscores the critical role for the principle of *continuously shared knowledge* described earlier in this chapter. It illustrates the need for knowledge not only of the consumers' needs but also of locations for cross-docking, knowledge of the ability of the DSUs to accept the log pacs, knowledge of the threat situation and anticipated inter-engagement windows of time—all of which can rapidly change. Continuously shared knowledge is critical to permitting the *synchronization* of the sustainment activity with combat—and the direct logistics support organizations' ability to absorb the support. Just as an aircraft carrier cannot replenish its aviation fuel tanks from its supporting AOE during aircraft launch and recovery operations, neither can an Army or Marine maneuver battalion refuel its combat vehicles during a fight (although its organic fuel carriers may be able to accept resupply during that period). Thus the combat units, their DSUs, the parent command and control (and mission tasking) headquarters, and the theater distribution and transportation organizations must synchronize their activities. These inter-engagement periods deserve the same kind of planned but anticipatory action as the combat operations, or the inability to deliver needed supplies will make the chances of combat success even more risky. Then combat commanders will attempt to create more "piles" of supplies to ensure they never run out. More piles, requiring a buildup of inventories, more support people, equipment, real estate, and force protection, will only reduce the force's agility by increasing its logistics footprint and becoming attractive targets for enemy action. Preliminary conclusions from initial assessments of the logistics support of land forces during Operation Iraqi Freedom may, unfortunately, support the "more piles" behavior, which may cause even greater harm since it impedes battle space agility and creates lucrative targets for the enemy.

DSU Command and Control

In our discussion of sustaining forces in the battle spaces, we have thus far covered the importance of providing rapidly deployed infrastructure for the continuously shared knowledge system and the ISB and battle space infrastructure of terminals, hospitals, and repair and distribution centers. We have argued that packaging sustainment resources into log pacs using the market basket concept allows direct sustainment inputs to go to DSUs for cross-docking to the customer combat units. We have also noted that the process described seems to work equally well for land and naval forces. In fact, naval forces have long used the market basket concept with their shuttle ships and carrier-on-board delivery (COD) aircraft delivering from forward naval bases to the CVBGs and ARGs—their ISBs afloat. Because Marines are initially supported by ARGs, they are quite used to the concept.

However, the direct delivery of log pacs to DSUs sets up potential problems of communication between the DSUs and the CONUS and theater distribution centers that should be anticipated. Because many of the JTF's land- and sea-based organizations in the battle spaces are themselves continually engaged in combat and often moving, the theater support activities responsible for their sustainment must orchestrate the delivery of sustainment support to the continually changing locations of the DSUs.

The arrangement demands a "trust" relationship between the DSUs, their combat and support organization customers, and the theater distribution center. With hundreds of miles separating them, and the possibility of periodic communication gaps, the theater distribution centers must have help either from the service theater logistics organization or the DSUs to minimize the chances of inadequate support. This book proposes a practical way to avoid the potential problems. The DSUs' own command and control headquarters—both Army brigade task force and its support battalion headquarters and MAGTF CSSDs—should split themselves between the battle space and the ISB (and/or CONUS) distribution centers, assisting the DSUs and the distribution centers (ashore or afloat) where the resources to build the log pacs are found. Those DSU elements represent the DSUs to their service theater support organization that controls the product support repair centers and to the joint logistics management organization that operates the distribution centers and the intra-theater airlift and sealift. Their role is to provide face-to-face contact with the distribution and repair activities to assure timely delivery of support to their parent DSUs.

The DSUs of each of the services have a common mission to act as the intermediary between their supported combat units and the out-of-battle-space support sources, whether they are supporting a CVBG, MAGTF, or AEF element in the battle space or Army combined arms, aviation, missile, or air defense organizations. Lean and ready DSUs, "plugged in" closely with the supporting product support and distribution centers and transport managers, can take much of the sustainment anxiety off the combat commanders' shoulders. The challenge is to keep the combat units well sustained without reducing their agility or requiring major force-protection resources.

Turning now to the air component, Air Force AEF support is less vulnerable than land force support since its theater aircraft generally operate in a more secure base environment. It is no less complex, requiring the same infrastructure to meet its requirement for continuously shared knowledge for robust support of sortie generation with minimum footprint. The AEF poses a simpler challenge for sustainment, if for no other reason than that it moves far less frequently than land forces combat consumers. And it is likely that some AEF sortie generation will take place at ISB locations, where each AEF's support needs might be met with direct delivery from the ISB facilities (fuel facilities, ports for ship-delivered munitions stocks, rations, water, construction supplies, etc.). Its product support needs for component repair may be met by civil aircraft transporting replacement components from its peacetime bases as well as the war reserve kits that it brings to the forward base when it deploys.

Naval air wings operate from their aircraft carriers, which contain all their required support. The carriers provide both operational agility and a self-contained base infrastructure. The Marine air component of the MAGTF is based partly on carriers, partly ashore with the ground component. The land-based Marine air elements' supporting DSUs require the same tactical agility as their land force counterparts and would benefit from the same log pac direct delivery approach.

Direct Log Pac Delivery to the DSUs: A New Support Paradigm

Rapid decisive operations require the logisticians to facilitate the operational and tactical agility of combat forces to allow them to fully exploit superior knowledge of the enemy. We have discussed above the role of the DSU as the principal sustainer of the combat forces in the battle space, enabling them to achieve the operational objectives of the campaign. I have proposed direct delivery of replenishment supplies (and services) in log pacs to the DSUs from CONUS or theater distribution centers, where they would be cross-docked/cross-decked for delivery to the combat and support customers. DSUs would then be capable of the timely delivery of support with a minimal battle space footprint and would maintain the agility required to support rapid decisive operations. The central question is how best to provide the log pacs to the DSUs. What should be their pipeline of support?

The concept of direct delivery of log pacs to DSUs from the distribution centers in CONUS and/or ISBs is antithetical to the traditional support concepts of land force logistics and, to some extent, naval force logistics. Traditionally (and at present) land force supplies flow through their own unique echeloned commodity stovepipes such as ration, or fuel, or ammunition supply points, to be delivered by convoy to mobile land forces. That concept of logistics support was necessary during World War II, Korea, Vietnam, and the first Gulf War because of the lack of adequate logistics communications and the paper-based order fulfillment processes. While it usually provided adequate supplies to the combat organizations, the concept inevitably produced numerous and often huge logistics installations in or near the battle spaces, which hampered combat force agility and required significant force-protection resources to prevent interdiction of the flow of supplies and destruction of the installations.

Agility Demands a New Paradigm

The requirement for agility inherent in the rapid decisive operations concept would fall victim to the echeloned, commodity-centered support arrangement of the 20th century, especially in the land forces' battle spaces, but also in supporting naval operations. Movement of Army brigade and Marine air-ground task forces would be hampered if they had to drag with

them multiple commodity "tails." Instead, the combat organization customers should be able to relocate rapidly, with their own lean direct logistics support organizations, to new engagement areas, while their theater
support organizations redirect their support pipelines to the new engagement
areas. Similar logistics agility is necessary as AEF elements relocate to better
support the air campaign. The maritime forces' sustainment pipelines are
designed for that agility and well practiced in sea-based support. They too
have moved to multiple commodity station ships to provide the single integrated resupply capability to the combatants.

The echeloned land supply points also present a major force-protection
risk in the battle spaces. They require diversion of combat forces to protect
both the installations and the roads linking them and the combat forces.
Both the Vietnam War and Operation Iraqi Freedom provide recent evidence of the kind of combat force commitment required to supplement the
local defensive capabilities of the logistics units. Even in the relatively benign environment of Saudi Arabia during Operation Desert Shield/Desert
Storm, Iraq's crude tactical ballistic missiles caused damage and loss of logistics troops' lives. Similarly, convoys and intermediate supply installations
along the line of communications have provided lucrative "soft" targets to
Iraqi insurgents even after the end of major combat operations in Iraqi Freedom. The lesson for future conflicts, demonstrated in Afghanistan and Iraq,
as this is being written, is to limit the physical presence of support forces so
as to minimize the need for combat forces to protect them and their installations: thus the quite proper emphasis on minimizing the logistics footprint
of deployed forces in the battle spaces.

To achieve the objective of minimized footprint in the battle spaces, the
optimum arrangement for land and naval forces theater sustainment infrastructure is to have **two echelons** of sustainment support, only one of which,
the DSU, is in the battle space. This concept would eliminate to the greatest extent possible the intermediate echelons of logistics support. Distribution centers should be sited outside the battle space, with the mission to
configure combat and support unit replenishment supplies into log pacs that
can be cross-docked/cross-decked (with some additions and deletions) at the
DSUs. This arrangement would be managed so as to meet the timely delivery of support objective; its very nature minimizes the battle space logistics
footprint.

The elimination of the intermediate echelons does pose risks of dependence on air or sea delivery of the log pacs. Aircraft delivering log pacs into expeditionary airfields will be vulnerable to surface-to-air missiles or guns; vessels will be vulnerable to suicide bombers in small boats or similar threats. For example, reportedly the AEF C-130s were not allowed to land on forward airfields during the early stages of Operation Iraqi Freedom, requiring the Army forces to maintain a four-hundred-mile ground line of communication with its ambushes and other attempts to interdict it. Curiously the Marine Corps C-130s did not have the same restrictions in supporting the MEF forward forces, but, of course, they are part of the MEF. And the 173rd Airborne Brigade that parachuted into the Kurdish areas of northern Iraq was resupplied by C-17 and C-130 in those forward airfields—since the threat in that area was far less serious than in the areas to the south. The special operations forces also were continually resupplied by airdrop, so the problem is not insurmountable.

While the interdiction threat should not be minimized, a number of options for air delivery, including those described in chapter 4, can reduce exposure. For example, fixed-wing aircraft can land on safer airfields, and the log pacs can be transferred to cargo helicopters and delivered to protected landing zones, operations practiced frequently during the Vietnam War.

The Army faces the most far-reaching changes in its logistics doctrine and organization if it is to reduce its echelonment footprint. As a general rule, the Army should have no support echelon other than DSUs in the battle spaces; general support organizations, traditionally the operators of fuel, munitions, food, repair parts, and other supply storage activities, belong in the ISBs—if footprint is to be minimized. Land force headquarters and clusters of combat support formations such as aviation, air defense, or missile artillery that operate in the battle space in general support of the land campaign will have their own DSUs and can be log pac customers just like the brigade task forces. Those formations most likely will locate in brigade task force operational areas and utilize some of the task force DSU support structure. Such a change would result in combining the materiel management centers of the division and corps support commands (the parent organizations of the DSUs) with the theater support command in the ISBs in order to provide the oversight of the log pac order and distribution processes. Thus the preferred flow of sustainment would move from the ISB distribution centers via log pacs to the DSUs without passing through intermediate storage activities.

Cautionary Note: Heavy Land Force Logistics Footprint

However, as all logisticians with scars have learned, there always must be flexibility in concept as well as in planning and execution. The exception to the general concept of keeping general support assets out of the battle space is most likely to occur for bulk fuel, artillery munitions, and construction/barrier materials for the land forces. As long as the campaign plan requires heavy (tank-mechanized infantry) task forces supported by self-propelled artillery, VSTOL fighter-bombers, and attack and support helicopters, the fuel requirements likely will exceed the capability to deliver by air to the brigade task force/MAGTF areas. Each heavy brigade task force may require a daily fuel resupply of 200,000 gallons—too much to move by air. Most likely bulk fuel must be moved from battle space sea access points over a land line of communication (LOC) by tactical pipeline and/or trucks, using thirty to forty of the 5,000–7,500 gallon tanker trips per day from the source to the DSU supporting each brigade task force. MAGTF and Army aviation brigades may require more. Also, depending on the capabilities of the enemy forces, the howitzers supporting the brigade task forces and the MAGTFs could go through three to four thousand rounds a day in major combat operations even though they are far more precise and require fewer rounds per target kill than even during the Gulf War. Similarly, bulky construction and barrier materials likely will travel to DSUs over a land LOC, along with fuel and munitions.

While some campaigns may not require heavy forces, the last major war of the 20th century, Desert Storm, and the first of the 21st century, Operation Iraqi Freedom, certainly did. Thus each brigade task force might require daily convoys of one hundred or so large trucks such as the sixteen-ton palletized load system trucks and five-thousand-gallon tractor-trailers to replenish the fuel and munitions supplies the task force consumes. Given the depth of attack into Iraq, it was necessary also to establish POL storage areas along the lines of communication, feeding them from the ports with fuel pipelines. The amount of munitions expenditures will determine the need for munitions stockage on the lines of communication. With low rates, none may be necessary; a high rate would indicate the need to establish intermediate stock points to avoid the risk of depletion in case of intense combat. The advent of more precision munitions may contribute to lowering the consumption rate of land force munitions and enable mostly air resupply to the DSUs.

Intermediate stock points along land LOCs present command and control and major force-protection challenges, a price that must be paid until log pacs can go direct to brigade/MAGTF DSUs from the ISB or CONUS. Such a probable scenario undergirds the continued requirement for a command structure for both the DSUs supporting (non-brigade) combat support formations and the necessary general support units required to operate the land LOC, the intermediate storage areas, and the transport organizations to move the sustainment supplies.

While minimizing the logistics footprint is the goal and intelligent planning and discipline can move toward it, logisticians always must keep in mind that no goal trumps that of assuring timely delivery of the required support in order to sustain combat power. And that will require the maintenance in the land forces structure of a capability to operate a long land LOC like that of Operation Iraqi Freedom.

Two Echelon Sustainment

With the above cautionary note on the need for a contingent land LOC capability in mind, the Joint Chiefs of Staff and the regional combatant commanders should require the Army and Marine Corps to modify doctrine, training, and organizations to establish the two-echelon theater sustainment concept, with DSUs as the focal point of battle space sustainment. That two-echelon doctrine should then be embedded in the regional contingency plans. For some small-scale campaigns, e.g., Panama, Haiti, and others in the western hemisphere, the CONUS infrastructure can serve as the ISB echelon. However, in the more distant theaters, time and distance will reduce responsiveness, and a theater ISB infrastructure must be created, as has been the practice in regions from Southeastern Europe to the Western Pacific. That infrastructure must be capable of performing at the same level as the western commercial infrastructure, but do so in a remote area where the physical infrastructure is sparse. It must be established rapidly, usually simultaneously with the deployment and initial sustainment phases of the operation.

The theater sustainment infrastructure outside the battle spaces, as we first saw in chapter 1, consists of ISBs, ashore and afloat (as shown in

Figure 5-1). There may be several supporting a campaign. They should be geographically separate from the battle spaces to remove them from most direct threats. They should be no more than approximately one thousand miles removed—two to three hours' flight time—and closer if possible. They should be relatively secure from likely missile/guerilla threats so as to minimize force-protection requirements. Saudi Arabia served that purpose in the first Gulf War as a single ISB; in the Afghanistan campaign, there were several ISBs: Kuwait, Uzbekistan, Bahrain, and Romania. In Operation Iraqi Freedom, Kuwait and Bahrain were two principal ISBs, joined later by Turkey and Jordan. DoD had hoped to add Turkey early in the operation, but the political situation did not allow it. The Turkey case illustrates the potential of uncertainty for host nation support agreements at the political level—agreements that can come apart because of the differences in political support among even allies for particular campaigns.

Having made the case for siting as much of the sustainment infrastructure as feasible outside the battle spaces in sea or land ISBs, we next examine the nature of that physical infrastructure.

ISB SUSTAINMENT INFRASTRUCTURE

The ISB nodes of the continuously shared knowledge process described in the discussion of the DSUs represent the first priority for infrastructure in the ISB. Linkages to DSUs, CONUS, and other bases make the ISB nodes a critical gateway for campaign sustainment.

Health care, component repair, and distribution infrastructure represent a second critical set of infrastructure that should be established rapidly in ISBs—afloat and/or ashore. The hospitals must be prepared to accept casualties from the operating forces and prepare them for evacuation to hospitals at forward bases and in CONUS. The repair activities are important parts of the product support supply chain as immediate sources of serviceable components for weapons and support systems and of diagnosis and repair (Help Desk) expertise. The distribution centers are needed to hold theater stocks of supplies to replenish the minimal inventories carried by DSUs in the battle spaces. They also store "project stocks" such as barrier and construction materials and POL pipeline components and may keep spare systems (vehicles, communications equipment) for replacement of combat losses. They conduct cross-dock operations to forward shipments from

CONUS sources to designated direct logistics support organizations in the battle spaces. The land-based ISB facilities to house the hospitals, repair, and distribution activities should be part of prearranged host nation and/or contracted support. The workforces and equipment—both organic and contractor—should deploy early enough in the operation to set up and, like the hospitals, be prepared to provide the required sustainment to battle space forces when demanded.[6]

Transportation Infrastructure for Sustainment

The third critical set of infrastructure elements necessary to facilitate timely delivery of sustainment is the transportation infrastructure—the POL pipelines and storage facilities and the intra-theater airlift and sealift with their terminals in the ISBs and battle spaces, e.g., the expeditionary airfields and ports and the carrier and ARG decks. This infrastructure is essential to force projection and should be in operation or being installed within hours of the entry of forces into the battle spaces in order to assure the timely delivery of critical supplies and the evacuation of casualties by the lift platforms (discussed in chapter 4). Use of terminals in the land-based ISBs, like the repair and distribution infrastructure discussed above, should be part of the host nation and/or contracted arrangements negotiated during the campaign planning. Their workforces and equipment deploy early enough to meet force projection needs and remain for the sustainment operation. The intra-ISB transportation network established for reception, staging, and onward movement of forces is augmented to link health care, repair and distribution centers, and AEF bases with terminals. Battle space expeditionary airfields and airports must likewise be planned so that the proper engineer and operations units and equipment can be inserted with the combat forces so as to meet the demands for sustainment and additional deployments.

Role of the Afloat and Ashore ISB in Sustaining JTF Operations

The ashore and afloat ISBs do not operate under nearly as risky threat conditions as the DSUs in the battle spaces and can therefore focus on the more

---

[6] Negotiating early TPFDD status has always been a challenge for logisticians. Somehow they must convince the war fighters who control the TPFDD that combat power will suffer if they cannot bring this infrastructure into the ISBs in time to meet forces' demands.

time-consuming tasks, such as operating the distribution and repair centers shown in Figure 5-1 to support the brigade task forces and MAGTFs in the land battle spaces and the naval task forces afloat. Those ISBs also provide the same kind of support to the Air Force AEF, usually colocated with or in close proximity to the land ISBs. The distribution center is the focus of ISB logistics support.[7] Equipment, consumable supplies, and repairable components are delivered from CONUS to the ISB airports and seaports by strategic airlift and sealift. Sea containers destined for the AEF's bases at the ISB are delivered directly by the ISB's local truck fleet, while other supplies are delivered to the distribution center's warehouses to maintain its designated stock levels. Air pallets destined for the AEF bases are cross-docked at the center's facilities to the regular delivery trucks for the AEF, and the AEF's needed common supplies such as food and medical items are distributed from the ISB distribution center's inventory on an agreed schedule. AEF forward operating bases separated from the ISB probably will have direct commercial air and surface delivery from CONUS.

A similar scheme supports any Navy or Marine units that may be located at the ISB. In addition to the distribution center and the airports and seaports, the land ISB also can host the services' component repair centers that are deployed to the theater, hospitals to care for casualties, replacement processing centers for the land forces in the battle spaces, staging areas for reinforcing forces (as described in the force projection phase) and for forces rotated out of the battle space for refitting and rest, multinational and humanitarian support activities that depend upon the U.S. military lift, and distribution activities for entry into the battle space.

MINIMIZING THE LOGISTICS FOOTPRINT— ALSO IN ISBs

Although the force-protection requirements would be far less than in battle spaces, a large support force presence in the land-based ISBs still has undesirable political effects.

---

[7] Distribution centers have traditionally been service operated. This book proposes in chapters 7 and 10 that they be operated by a joint logistics management organization that is subordinate to the combatant commander. However, the discussion of distribution centers applies to both cases.

Such a large presence of foreign troops, even support personnel, aggravates latent distrust and plays into the hands of those who oppose U.S. interests. And it may place at risk the very political objectives for which the campaign is waged. The large presence of support troops at Cam Ranh Bay, Long Binh, and other huge logistics installations in Vietnam overwhelmed local populations. Likewise, the similar installations near Damman and Dharan in Saudi Arabia during the first Gulf War became a symbol fastened upon by extremists as evidence of America's objective of cultural and political domination of Arab peoples. Unfortunately, this reaction was echoed at the theater distribution center and port complex in Kuwait during Operation Iraqi Freedom.

Combatant commanders have to take into consideration the footprint effects on nations willing to host ISBs. Facility siting should minimize the visibility of logistics activities. Service component commanders must be particularly sensitive to the necessity to limit the equipment and people to those tasks that cannot be accomplished in CONUS or forward bases. For example, if avionics components' reliability indicates low demand and stockage is adequate, there may be no need for a repair activity in the ISB. Repair parts stocks in the DSUs can be replenished by air delivery from CONUS to the ISBs and cross-docked to the DSUs. On the other hand, in cases where component failure rates are likely to result in frequent stock-outs if only the CONUS source is used, an ISB repair activity would be prudent.

Yet another approach is to copy a commercial practice and leave the theater stocks aboard the sealift vessels until needed. This approach was used to good effect during Operation Iraqi Freedom when a container ship with a couple thousand munitions containers discharged selected containers as required by the theater munitions managers. The ship retained the great majority of containers, which in the end were not required because of the short duration of major operations. Commercial firms habitually use this "inventory-in-motion" concept to avoid landing cargo for which payment is in doubt. Thus the services and JTLM could employ this concept for sensitive cargo requiring major force-protection resources, e.g., munitions or major combat systems, or for high-bulk cargo. Periodically the vessels could off-load only the necessary containers to maintain a small operating inventory physically on the ground. Of course, this concept requires the use of the GPS-RFID transponders and cargo visibility for the theater managers to determine which containers to land.

Best Case—No Land ISB

The preferable strategy would be to avoid using intermediate support bases in host nations. That may be possible for sustaining some parts of a joint task force. Naval and Marine organizations may be able to rely partially upon afloat ISBs—the "sea base" concept—supplemented by direct strategic lift sorties into the MAGTF's expeditionary airfields in the battle space. Direct strategic lift might also be sufficient to sustain special operations forces and Army light infantry and airborne brigade task forces. To the extent that the organic airlift fleet can sustain the required sortie rates, the ISB footprint can be contained.

However, it is unlikely that the combatant commanders can completely do away with ISBs since the AEFs will require main operating bases for fighters and tankers and other support aircraft in the theater. They will require bulk fuel and munitions, which are most likely to be moved by ocean tanker and container ships, respectively, and off-loaded at host nation ports. Where heavy land forces in large numbers are not required in the campaign, the AEF bases could perform double duty to house the necessary ISB structure for land and maritime forces to supplement the support provided by afloat ISBs and direct-to-battle-space strategic lift.

A Vietnam War example illustrates this point. The Ninth Infantry Division was located in the Mekong Delta region of southern Vietnam with the Second Brigade and its direct support artillery battalion afloat, constituting the "riverine" force. It could have been sustained with one to two C-5 sorties per day from Okinawa (a U.S. forward base) if the airfield close to its Dong Tam division base camp could have been improved to accept the C-5. A weekly landing ship tank (LST) carrying munitions, barrier materials, and canned beer and soda, and a fuel barge two to three times a week that delivered cargoes to the Dong Tam Mekong River port would have resupplied the remainder of its requirements. Its ISB for those three commodities was a bulk fuel terminal for the barges and storage areas for the barrier materials and munitions at Vung Tau at the mouth of the Mekong River. Even the munitions and barrier material footprint in Vung Tau might have been removed by adding an additional daily C-5 sortie or two, depending on the expenditure rate. Unquestionably the large logistics footprint in Vietnam created major force-protection problems.

Sea Basing

We have mentioned the afloat ISBs in terms of the support of ARGs to MAGTFs and the station ships of the combat logistics force that resupply much of the carrier battle group and surface action group needs. "Sea basing" has gained wide notoriety in the last decade and has become an objective of the Navy's sea power concept. Sea basing first stirred imaginations in the mid-nineties with the studies on a mobile off-shore base (MOB), a derivative of deep-sea oil drilling platform technology. The MOB would be large enough to allow C-130 operations, could be repositioned between and within theaters, and could uncouple the forces ashore and afloat in the theater from dependency on a land ISB. Two major problems—technical feasibility and affordability—need to be solved before the concept can transition into a capability. The former is the more challenging.

At least two kinds of technical problems face proponents of the concept. The first is the feasibility of constructing such a platform even with the expertise of constructing oil platforms. A five-thousand-foot platform with several decks is a far more challenging project than present oil platforms. Several engineering firms have claimed they can complete the project. So far, DoD has not decided to make the investment to find out. A second technical problem faces the sea basing concept no matter what platforms are employed: bringing supplies to the platforms in the quantities that would make it a useful distribution center for forces ashore larger than the present Marine expeditionary units and supporting air elements in the MAGTF. At this time the ARG large-deck amphibious ships can support the MAGTF for a limited period of time, but restocking them at sea is a challenge.

Supplies and equipment for the initial deployment and some period of sustainment can be loaded aboard an MOB or other vessels at pier side. However, replenishing those stocks at sea would necessitate transferring twenty-foot and forty-foot sea containers from container ships. Transferring containers in other than calm seas with no wind—a rare occurrence—would be extremely hazardous. That hazard is the reason that the Navy does not reload empty missile cells with Tomahawks at sea. Imagine a forty-foot container on the end of a container crane with a ten-knot wind and slightly rolling sea. Trying to position that swinging container on another platform without it colliding with something on the vessel would require a lot of luck. Until that problem can be solved, sea basing will need to stick to the long-practiced transfer of smaller packages by helicopter or "high line."

Potential for a "Mini-MOB" with Large VSTOL

If a solution to the problem of safe transfer of containers could be found, the affordability problem would still confront DoD. The MOB was expected to cost as much as an aircraft carrier: $4–5 billion. However, that cost assumed a C-130 capable flight deck. The MOB size could be reduced to the size of a large medium-speed roll-on/roll-off ship (950–1,000 feet) if the C-130 cargo capacity could be developed in a large VSTOL aircraft like the V-22 or a "Super STOL" capable of operations from a carrier-sized deck. Such a combination would present fewer technical challenges than the five-thousand-foot MOB. While the acquisition program for the combination of the "mini-MOB" and the large VSTOL would certainly run to $60–80 billion and probably take twenty years to develop and put into operation, one must remember that the national leadership was willing to pay $30 billion to Turkey just to gain access to its infrastructure for Operation Iraqi Freedom. Several mini-MOBs and the large VSTOL or STOL aircraft would have obviated such pricey "rent" for a theater ISB.

The political advantages of such an investment certainly warrant technical exploration of its three challenging components: container transfer at sea, the mini-MOB platform, and the large VSTOL. Freedom from reliance on the cooperation of even dependable allies for sustainment of forces in campaigns the nation must wage would itself constitute a powerful deterrent to potential state transgressors. Otherwise the nation will either be forced to pay handsomely to persuade ISB hosts to allow support operations on their soil or, as in the case of Turkey, be forced into more risky campaign support strategies.

The CONUS Sustainment Infrastructure

The third component of the sustainment infrastructure is that located in CONUS or at forward bases. Figure 5-1 shows the principal nodes in the generic supply chain. Note that materiel comes to the theater ISB distribution and repair centers from the DoD distribution centers and other facilities or from contractors, whether original equipment manufacturers (OEMs), "prime vendors" (normally commercial distributors), or weapons system/ equipment integrating contractors and their subcontractors performing contractor logistics support (CLS). Materiel also may come directly to DSUs or customer units, e.g., through the U.S. mail or the distribution centers, marked for the DSU or customer. In this section we will describe in broad terms the nodes in the CONUS (and forward base) sustainment infrastructure, but their roles in the weapons system and people support processes will be described and analyzed in chapters 6–10.

Most consumable and reparable materiel still comes through the DLA-operated CONUS (or overseas) distribution centers, but increasingly CLS contractors and prime vendors are bypassing those centers, preferring direct shipment, usually to container consolidation points (CCPs) near the large DLA distribution centers and onward to the ISBs or DSUs. Materiel originating at DoD maintenance depots, repair centers, or inventory storage activities almost always flows through the CONUS distribution centers DoD logistics management organizations, a term that includes the services' system and commodity commands and DLA product centers, direct the distribution of materiel to the theater in response to orders from the JTF organizations. For example, requisitions (orders) placed by DSUs are sent to the CONUS management organizations if they cannot be satisfied at the ISB. The management organization directs the distribution centers to ship the requisitioned items to the requisitioning DSUs if they are in stock. If not, the management organizations order from the suppliers—usually a lengthy process. The supplier might be an OEM, a prime vendor, one of the firms in the supplier base, or a DoD maintenance depot for a reparable item, where there is no serviceable inventory on hand.

Prime vendors may respond directly to the theater distribution centers or to DSUs, although the relevant management organization is normally copied on orders so that it can exercise its contract oversight responsibilities. CLS integrators who respond to system program managers may fill orders from the inventory positioned anywhere in the world or from system repair centers in the theater or any other place they may be located. Their processes for order fulfillment resemble the commercial product support operations of such firms as Boeing (commercial airplanes) and Caterpillar (construction machinery). These firms fill customer orders from the optimum location, including other customers' supplies, if necessary and agreed to by the customer.

Equipment items are normally shipped by the OEMs directly to particular units (through CCPs, theater distribution centers, and the supporting DSU) designated by the CONUS management organizations, although some may be held in theater stocks in the ISB to replace items destroyed in battle. These major, or principal, items (aircraft, tanks, weapons, etc.) are monitored through a chain of custody to the recipient unit.

Materiel shipments to the theater ISBs travel by military air through the AMC aerial ports, by commercial air, commercial container ship, and by MSC-owned or chartered vessel. The materiel that is shipped via commercial air and sea will go from CCPs through commercial terminals. Munitions generally will be moved through military air and ocean terminals for safety and security reasons. Mailed items are sent through U.S. postal facilities and use the same modes of transportation as other shipments, depending on size, weight, and priority.

As contractor activity has increased, the need has become more acute to maintain asset visibility, both in CONUS storage (distribution center or with vendors) and in transit. The *continuously shared knowledge* principle demands the tracking of items of supply and equipment using source data automation such as active and passive RFID. That visibility gives the organization that ordered the item confidence that the needed item is not lost and allows commodity and system managers to monitor system performance.

Munitions and Bulk Fuel

The munitions and bulk fuel supply chains operate differently in that both are managed by commodity specific organizations—the Joint Munitions Command (JMC) for conventional munitions and DLA's Defense Energy Support Center (DESC) for bulk fuel. They manage the supply chains from their sources to the theater ISB. JMC procures conventional munitions on behalf of the services, oversees munition production at government-owned contractor-operated facilities, manages storage at several ammunition depots in CONUS, and distributes munitions to the various services' activities. Each service, however, manages its own missiles.

Explosives safety is a primary concern, and quality surveillance of storage and shipment is a fundamental factor in the distribution of munitions. For safety reasons, munitions generally are not placed on pre-positioned equipment nor on vehicles loaded on vessels. Only a few ports are used for shipping quantities of munitions and for arming naval vessels. In host nation ports, the same explosives safety factors determine the limits on discharge of vessels and storage ashore. Packaging of artillery and naval gun munitions also requires separating the fuzes, primers, and propellant from the warheads. Efforts continue to desensitize propellants, especially, to enable the lifting of those restrictions.

The conventional munitions industry is small and requires careful husbanding by DoD to maintain its viability. Unfortunately it had been the victim of budget-balancing cuts that seemed all too necessary during the 1990s. But the cuts left the industry weaker and smaller. The consequences of these cuts were seen during Operation Iraqi Freedom. Peacetime restrictions on allocations of training ammunition induced by the budget cuts left both active and reserve component forces less well trained than they should have been, with grave consequences especially for reserve combat service support units. The small production base (reduced to a single plant) for small-caliber ammunition could not respond to the unforeseen needs dictated by the long insurgency following the overthrow of Saddam Hussein's government. Sourcing of small-caliber ammunition required purchases from European manufacturers and investment in greater plant capacity. On the other hand, production of major air-delivered munitions such as the joint direct attack munition was increased in anticipation of the campaign, and no shortages surfaced.

The characteristics of the munitions supply chain require particular attention to asset visibility. Item identification, which includes source of manufacture, lot number, and a unique DoD identification code (DODIC) for each type of munition is the basis for asset visibility. RFID technology provides the first opportunity to automate source data in the distribution process. It was especially useful during Operation Iraqi Freedom in allowing the selective discharge of the afloat pre-positioned munitions ships. Unlike munitions storage during Operation Desert Shield/Desert Storm, in which thousands of tons of munitions were put into large storage areas just in case the items were needed, in Operation Iraqi Freedom the ability to quickly identify munitions containers and selectively discharge those needed to meet requirements limited the amount of munitions on the ground without sacrificing timely delivery to DSUs in the battle space. The use of RFID technology from source to DSU and operating unit provides asset visibility to commanders and logisticians and enables battlefield redistribution to an extent never before possible.

The bulk fuel supply chain is also quite different from that of other commodities in that DoD taps into a global network of suppliers of refined fuel. DESC contracts for specific formulation needed for military use. The most ubiquitous, JP-8, which is used for both aircraft and ground vehicles, results from successful fuel standardization efforts of the 1980s, which have greatly streamlined bulk fuel distribution in the theater. DESC contracts now provide for timely delivery within the theater to multiple air forces' forward operating locations, to ISB distribution sites for the land forces, and to forward naval bases for loading aboard shuttle tankers to refuel naval auxiliary station ships with the maritime component forces. DESC elements operating with the combatant commands also manage some bulk fuel inventory for the service component commands.

Distribution to the land force DSUs typically is by pipeline and tank truck. Airlift, through use of either fixed-wing internally loaded fuel bags or the aircraft wing tanks ("wet wing"), has been used successfully when the fuel demands were modest. Helicopter-borne fuel bags (e.g., five-hundred-gallon "blivets") are used to replenish helicopter rearm-refuel points. The heavy brigade task forces' consumption of 150,000–200,000 gallons per day requires 30–40 tanker trucks traveling an LOC from the ISB or fuel distribution points at the end of pipelines.

21ST-CENTURY BATTLE SPACE SUSTAINMENT SCENARIO

In order to summarize the force sustainment concept, let us create a land forces sustainment scenario. As the campaign unfolds, the JTF has established several noncontiguous engagement areas into which Army brigade task forces (with a slice of combat support organizations in the same footprints), special operations forces, and a Marine air-ground task force have deployed and are engaged in their missions. Each task force has an associated task-organized DSU that operates an air access point (or several)—airfield or VSTOL landing zone (the MAGTF). One brigade's area of responsibility includes a shallow-draft port. Its support unit is augmented with a cargo-handling unit. The MAGTF is supported by VSTOL aircraft from its ARGs and C-130 tankers from land ISBs. The Army brigade task forces are supported from two ISBs. One ISB provides bulk fuel to both U.S. and coalition land forces; it can receive direct pipeline or tanker deliveries and has fuel storage facilities. Its use reduces the air traffic at the other ISB, which also is one of several air component command operating bases. The other ISB contains component repair centers and a joint distribution center for the remaining sustainment needs of the JTF land and air components.

Task force DSUs continually update the supply status of their consumables such as food, water, munitions, and fuel so as to maintain the three days consumption status they are equipped to carry. Much of this updating can be done automatically through algorithms capturing what ammunition is fired or POL, food, and water consumed by the task forces; these data are automatically fed to the ISB distribution centers and their service theater logistics organizations. The distribution center builds the log pac resupply packages for supported task force DSUs with the help of the DSUs' liaison teams and the service theater logistics organizations, then schedules the airlift or theater support vessel sorties to deliver to the DSUs.

The airlift and sealift schedules are necessarily flexible and require a "call forward" by the DSUs so that they do not become overloaded nor run short of supplies. The DSUs and/or combat units then arrange the addition to the log pacs of special items (e.g., a pair of size 18 boots), repair teams, and replacements for repair parts inventory or other parts not stocked—all this through a Web-based order fulfillment knowledge process.

That process originates in the combat unit with supply status and system availability reports from unit elements. Individual combat vehicles are programmed to automatically transmit fuel and ammo status and systems status to the unit's operations officer, logistics officer, and the supporting DSU, e.g., a support company of a combat battalion. The Web-based information process combines combat element information with the status of supplies carried in logistics vehicles (if any) and periodically transmits it to the brigade/MAGTF command cell and DSU, along with a predicted status based on operations for the next eight to twelve hours.

With such a Web-based process the brigade/MAGTF logistics operator, the command cell, and the ISB distribution center (and their DSU liaison teams) can share the information in real time and, through conferencing, make changes to the next log pac. The distribution center's log pac load descriptions (with destinations, inter-engagement window information, and other instructions) are automatically relayed to the airlift or sealift load planning systems to be combined with requirements for other cargo and passengers in their loading models to create the load plans and update flight schedules.

Intra-Theater Airlift/Sealift Control

Managing the intra-theater airlift and sealift arriving in the battle spaces presents yet another coordination challenge. The JTF's intra-theater transportation management authority books the sustainment missions as well as missions carrying replacements, repositioning units, humanitarian supplies and workers and the evacuation of casualties, prisoners, and system components.

There is a joint/combined battle space movements control organization to de-conflict missions in both the air and the sea environments in the battle space, especially at ports and airfields with limited capacity.[8] It also regulates common user land transport and road space between subordinate units. This sustainment organization operates in a close relationship with the land, air, and maritime component commands to assure the coordination with operations and force-protection organizations (air defense, military police, chem-bio defense, etc.).

Continuously Shared Knowledge—Key to Sustainment

This scenario dramatizes the demand for continuously shared knowledge—what has been called a common operating (and logistics) picture. At any one time there are multiple engagements in the several brigade/MAGTF battle spaces. Because of the changing threat conditions, some airfields are usable only at night. Roads between organizations may make it difficult for one brigade to use another's airfield or port. The changing threat environment and operational tempo require constant alertness by the logistics operators in the DSUs and movement control organizations as well as the ISB distribution centers and JTF transportation authority.[9] They all need a robust set of information about the operational and intelligence parameters as well as logistics status to make informed decisions—and change them when neces-

---

[8] The joint/combined air component command (J/CFACC) exercises air space control to separate the lift sorties from others.
[9] The last three organizations should have a single parent: the joint/combined theater logistics management organization as later described.

sary. Collectively the logisticians manage a flow of supplies and people that can be only partially programmed but must be sensitive to the changing environment and customer organization needs, so that each resupply window produces the necessary sustainment resources for the combat organizations to be able to carry out their missions.

Thus far, the scenario has followed the generation of requirements changes through the planned launch of the airlift or sealift vehicles. We should not think that air-landed and sea-delivered log pacs are the only transport means from ISB to the direct logistics support unit's distribution points. If conditions permit—or require—some replenishment may come from the port to the task force DSUs by truck over land, by helicopter, by VSTOL, by unmanned aerial vehicle (UAV), or even by parachute. Some log pacs may be delivered by para-sail—a cargo delivery means (still in R&D at this writing) potentially capable of releasing packages from aircraft at stand-off ranges, e.g., twenty-five miles and twenty-five thousand feet altitude, that could power-glide to designated landing points at *remote* combat units' locations. The special operations forces in this scenario usually meet the test of remoteness and frequently must depend upon parachute or para-sail delivery of their log pacs. (Such was the case in both the Afghanistan and the Iraq operations.)

Distribution to Combat Units

The normal log pac delivery to combat units from the DSU's distribution point is timed and executed so as to fit the operational situation: between engagements and arranged to minimize force-protection risks. Rearming and refueling (as well as accepting other resupply) on the move has long been a characteristic practice of battlefield resupply. But the techniques require training to maintain proficiency. The GPS has made the most difficult earlier problem—marrying the supplies with the customer at night in strange terrain—nearly an anachronism. However, land force DSUs have had to develop proficiency through rigorous training for the "marrying" event just as the Navy's station ships and combatants must train for underway replenishment. The delivery of log pacs to both land and maritime combat organizations requires planning and attention to the myriad details and continuously shared knowledge of times, locations, and precise descriptions of supplies being transferred.

The inter-engagement periods also allow the maintenance technicians to mount replacement components that arrived in the log pac (assisted perhaps by other technicians who came with the components from the ISB repair centers).

Distribution means within Army brigades and Marine task forces include trucks and helicopters. The choice of transport means to deliver log pacs to combat units depends on threat and operational conditions. In this scenario, packaging of consumables such as food, water, medical items, ammunition, and packaged POL products into the scheduled log pacs is arranged at the ISB distribution center to permit cross-docking at the DSU and rapid breakdown to the combat units' subordinate elements in order to minimize the time required to transfer the supplies from the DSUs' trucks/helicopters. Bulk fuel may also be included in the log pacs in fuel bladders or containers on twenty-foot platforms, e.g., PLS flat rack or Marine six-con containers or through wet wing delivery.[10] The DSU delivery vehicles/aircraft also pick up system components needing repair for transport back to the DSU and then to an ISB repair center.

A parallel system exists to evacuate casualties from the combat units' aid stations and trauma team sites to the DSUs' patient stabilization elements and by returning airlift to the ISB hospital. Both ground and air ambulances are used within the battle space. The intra-theater airlift assets rig modules for patient evacuation for the trip to the land or afloat ISBs. Interservice integration is especially important for moving critically wounded patients to operating facilities, so Army patients might be lifted by air ambulance to Navy ARG vessels—a process managed by the JTF's medical regulating center. Those ambulances also return to their field positions with medical supplies—an important supplement to the supplies included in the log pacs.

Scenario Conclusions

The purpose in providing this scenario at the beginning of the sustainment section of the book has been to offer a context for the more detailed discussions of processes to follow in chapters 6–10. The scenario helps to show how the processes for weapons system and people sustainment are integrated

---

[10] Using the wing tanks of the airlifter pumping into the DSU fuel carriers.

at the ISB, using the log pac mechanism to minimize the sorting out of supplies and other support within the battle space.

The glue that makes this complex sustainment effort work is the Web-based information process that produces continuously shared knowledge of this critical sustainment effort—its load composition, departure, and arrival programmed times and any special instructions from the battle space movement and terminal controllers. All—including each combat unit's logistics officer—share a common understanding. That logistics officer may be tracking a particular component or piece of equipment in order to schedule a repair task for a subordinate element's combat system and must arrange the subordinate element's rendezvous with the trucks or aircraft bringing the log pac. Continuously shared knowledge makes it possible to alter the plans if enemy action or other operational or environment conditions change—and keep all the participants aware of the changes throughout the replenishment operation. Making this footprint-reducing scenario work in combat operations will also require superb training within all the logistics organizations to go along with the continuously shared knowledge illustrated here.

SUMMARY

We can see through the battle space sustainment scenario how continuously shared knowledge enables a replenishment process that does not depend upon large inventories of supplies nor large logistics units. Rather it depends upon discrete, timely flows of mutually agreed packages—the log pacs—tailored by the ISB distribution center under the watchful eye of the Army and Marine DSUs' liaison teams and delivered either directly to the combat units or through the Army brigade/Marine task force DSUs. The effect is to minimize the logistics footprint in the battle space while maintaining effective sustainment. The process depends upon the rapid reaction of the ISB, its distribution and repair centers, and intra-theater lift assets. Although the support configurations are different for the AEF and the naval fleet, the process characteristics and objectives are remarkably similar. All three service logistics elements strive for timely delivery of support with a minimal logistics footprint in their sustainment missions.

CHAPTER 6

SUSTAINING WEAPONS AND SUPPORT SYSTEMS: THE PROCESSES

BATTLE-READY SYSTEMS OBJECTIVE

We have described sustainment of the forces in the battle spaces and partially unfolded the two sustainment categories: systems and people. In this chapter we turn to examining the processes within each category more closely, from the customers in the battle spaces through the chain of organizations and processes that contribute to keeping both people and their weapons and support systems battle ready. The principal objective of these processes is just that: *battle-ready systems and people*. Another objective, as in any endeavor with limited resources, is to achieve the "battle-ready" objective for the least expenditure of resources.

Combatant commands can employ well over a thousand different combat and support systems to achieve their campaign objectives. Many of these systems can contribute multiple capabilities. For example, an F-15 fighter can perform a counter-air role or interdict enemy forces by dropping bombs. Destroyers can be used offensively to provide support to forces ashore or to protect CVBGs and ARGs from submarines, surface vessels, or air threats. Support systems, likewise, serve several functions; amphibious force ships provide both a strategic transport means for Marine expeditionary units and a sea base during MEU operations in the battle space. These systems range in complexity from the relatively simple single-purpose systems, such as trucks, to immensely complex "systems-of-systems," such as an aircraft carrier or the Global Command and Control System.

THE PRODUCT SUPPORT SUPPLY CHAIN

In this discussion of the sustainment of systems, the term "product support" describes the set of processes necessary to sustain battle-ready systems. "Product support" is a useful term because it characterizes the same processes we find in civilian commerce. It allows us to compare the processes of sustaining civilian systems, from our own automobiles to airliners or cruise ships, with the processes used for sustaining military systems. They are remarkably similar, and one message of this book is that the military should recognize the similarities, understand the best practices developed and used in the competitive commercial environment, and adopt those that will improve the effectiveness and efficiency of military product support.

The chain of product support processes and organizations is described in the current literature as a "supply chain" or, more recently, a "value chain," the latter to connote the value-yielding properties of viewing these supply chain processes as interdependent rather than stand-alone activities. The term "supply chain" will suffice for our purposes. A typical product support supply chain is depicted in Figure 5-1. Let us travel along this chain to understand the interdependent activities that take place to produce a battle-ready system.

Our journey begins with the deployed combat or support unit customer. The first step is to describe the roles of the operator/crew and the direct support maintenance organization—or "DSU", one of the direct support logistics organizations described in chapter 5—that deploys and lives in the battle space with the customers. The next step back in the product support supply chain is the intermediate support base(s). The processes there provide needed replacement components (and systems) as well as back-up technical assistance that is beyond the capability of the DSU technicians. Next we will discuss the CONUS (including in this term forward stations and home ports or bases outside CONUS) sustaining base support to describe product support management and the processes that link the sources of replacement parts and components, system overhauls, and product improvements to the battle space customers.

Chapters 7 and 8 will examine these processes through the framework we adopted in chapter 1 to assess their effectiveness, then suggest a direction of improvements that would increase battlefield readiness and/or reduce costs in the processes. I will conclude this section on sustaining weapons and support systems by suggesting a scenario of 21st-century product support incorporating the proposed improvements—using the scenario as an integrating device to suggest the operation of a 21st-century product support supply chain.

ROLE OF OPERATORS/CREWS IN PRODUCT SUPPORT

Well trained operators or crews will accomplish many of the critical activities of product support. There are two principal groups of activities: preventive maintenance and servicing. Typically, the crew/operator accomplishes the "before," "during," and "after" operations preventive maintenance checks described in the system technical publications to assure that the system is functioning properly. If it is not, a DSU technician is brought into the picture. Secondly the operator/crew performs some services for the system, e.g., refueling and changing bulbs and filters. Such services also are described in the system technical publications. The aircraft crew chief takes care of some of the services, although refueling and other services also are performed by a refueling crew from the parent wing or the DSU. For land-based military aircraft as for civil airliners, pilots do "walk-around" inspections before takeoff, following a detailed checklist. They do not service the aircraft with fuel or other consumables, but must affirm that those tasks have been done before takeoff.

For naval vessels, the crew/operator *is* a technician. For example, the sonar operators on a naval vessel are sonar technicians trained to operate *and* maintain the sonar system aboard the vessel. Thus vessel crews carry out not only the preventive maintenance and servicing tasks outlined in this section but also the direct support maintenance tasks described in the following section.

ROLE OF THE DIRECT SUPPORT MAINTENANCE ORGANIZATION

The second group of major players in battle space maintenance for air and land systems are the organizations that directly support the system-owning organizations. These DSUs exist to keep combat and support systems ready to fight or support. They have two primary tasks: preventive maintenance and fault diagnosis and repair, frequently by replacement of components on the system. Restoration of system availability can take other forms, from adjustments to wiring, welding, or other repairs that can be accomplished in the battle space in the time available.

Preventive Maintenance

Working back from the user through the supply chain, the next stage of product support is *preventive maintenance services*. The process for military systems is similar to that for automobiles—periodic engine oil and other fluid changes, lubrication of moving parts, and periodic inspections by trained technicians. The approach to preventive maintenance and services differs according to system. Typically, some tasks are allocated to the owning organization's maintenance staff, others to the DSU. Because of the complexity of even 1980s' technology systems and the depth of maintenance skills and productive time available in owning organizations, there has been a migration of technicians from owning organizations, especially in the Army's tank, mechanized infantry, and aircraft organizations, to their DSUs. For a time, the Air Force put all its technicians in wing maintenance squadrons, which allowed apprentice technicians to gain valuable experience working with senior skilled technicians in an organizational context that afforded depth and more productive use of available time. Subsequently crew chiefs were transferred to the flying units, reducing the number of technicians in the DSUs, although a reversal of that policy now may be in the offing.

Fault Diagnosis and Repair

DSMOs (as well as maintenance staffs of some system-owning organizations) are responsible for fault diagnosis and repair when systems fail. Their technicians perform initial diagnoses from trouble reports made by operators/crews and their own inspections. Using appropriate test equipment, the technicians determine the appropriate repair—adjustment or replacement of a malfunctioning component or other tasks such as rewiring or welding. Using the DSMO tools, diagnosis, and repair aids (electronic or paper technical publications, built-in test-equipment or fault diagnosis software, etc.), the technician removes the faulty component, orders a serviceable replacement, makes adjustments, and installs the replacement component.

We should keep in mind from our discussion of battle space logistics that direct support maintenance technicians for land, naval, and some air systems operate in the same battle space as their war-fighting customers. On land they are subject to the risks of indirect fire, guerrilla/terrorist attack, and ambushes. At sea they live and work in the same space as the combat systems they support.[1] They are the military component of the product support chain

---

[1] This discussion considers the DSU tasks to be those that can be accomplished in the battle space. Some vessel component replacement tasks cannot be accomplished in the sea battle space. The vessel must be taken to a port repair activity and the repair accomplished by the shore intermediate maintenance technicians and/or a contractor along with the vessel's crew.

because we do not usually place civilians in the battle space environment. The maintenance technician's major task is to return failed systems to battle-ready status as soon as possible in order to maintain combat power at designed levels—levels on which the war-fighting leaders depend. Therefore, if the system's design facilitates accurate, rapid fault diagnosis, ease of access to platform components, and ease of removal/replacement, the DSU technician can accomplish the task of restoring system battle readiness quickly. And if the process of obtaining the replacement component results in timely availability, the total time to regain battle readiness can be minimized.

Critical Dimensions of Direct Support Maintenance

Four dimensions of direct support maintenance define the core of the process of sustaining systems in the battle space:

> - design for ease of diagnosis and component replacement or adjustment
> - off-system test equipment and maintenance aids
> - serviceable component order fulfillment cycle (called most recently and aptly "customer wait time")
> - technician skill at diagnosis and component replacement and repair

Their interrelationships are apparent. The simpler the diagnosis and removal/replacement tasks permitted by the design, the less skill is required of the technician. That reduction in the skill requirement can also be attained by careful design of maintenance aides, e.g., fault diagnosis via built-in or off-system test equipment, repair instructions in accessible electronic media (such as mobile wearable or handheld computers), and limitation of the number of tools required for removal/replacement of fasteners. Such maintenance aids can also partially make up for supply process lags by facilitating the process of making one ready system out of two or more failed systems. Ideally, system program managers (PMs) and direct support maintenance organizations set their sights on doing their best along all four dimensions—the PMs through insisting on the design objective, providing the test equipment and maintenance aids and a responsive supply chain for components, and insisting on high standards of technician training. The DSUs' tasks are to insist that their technicians attain the necessary diagnosis and repair skills and manage effectively their portion of the supply chain process for replacement components.

This process description applies also to naval vessel maintenance. The DSU for naval vessels is embedded in their crews. They are operator-maintainers who are trained to accomplish all the tasks noted above, who are technically qualified and resourced, and who can make selective component repairs on board vessels. Generally the vessel systems, including combat and navigation systems, power plants, command and control, and hotel equipment, are maintained by the crew, a policy that follows the general prescription that maintenance/product support in the battle spaces should be the task of the military.[2] Increasingly there are exceptions in which contractor field service and civil servant technicians are aboard to provide needed technical expertise to crew members—especially for new items of equipment.

COMPONENT REPAIR

The next node is the location(s) of *component repair* processes. Most component repair activities for land and land-based air forces are sited outside the battle spaces since they are not required immediately to maintain system availability. The products of these processes, serviceable components, are supplied to the DSMOs in the battle spaces for their component replacement tasks.

Many naval vessel and air system component repair processes are located aboard carriers and large amphibious vessels. For example, aircraft carriers house repair facilities for components that experience failures sufficient to justify making space available for repair fixtures, tools, test benches, and technicians. Jet engine test stands are carried aboard to allow repair and test of engines. These facilities illustrate how naval forces bring their intermediate support bases with them into the battle spaces.

In earlier times one could find repair shops for generators and other small components in an Army division's area in the battle space, but the drive to achieve a smaller logistics footprint, plus the increased reliability of these components, has pushed such activities out of the land battle space and into the ISB—or even to the CONUS base. Similarly, the AEF's component repair "back shops" that deploy to forward operating locations have been

---

[2] "Hotel equipment" is the equipment that supports the crew's living accommodations.

significantly reduced, a major contributor to a reduced deployment footprint. Those back shops are now placed in regional forward support locations accessible to the deployed AEFs and shared by several.

The location of component repair facilities for any given system depends upon a number of factors, the principal one being the ability to provide serviceable components to direct support technicians in the battle space when needed. If there is ample inventory of a low-failure-rate, inexpensive components, a repair facility may be unnecessary. On the other hand, as in the aircraft carrier repair facility example, a higher-failure-rate component with low serviceable inventory (which happens in peacetime with very expensive components) will require a repair facility if the flow of serviceable components is to meet demands. This is an issue of trade-offs—assessing the risks of stock depletion and consequent readiness shortfalls against the practicability of deploying the repair facility. The system PM and the service component commander's logistics staff should agree on the strategy since the PM will know the supply chain's ability to sustain the supply of the component to the DSU.

Component Repair at the ISB

The value of having a "nearby" repair facility at an ISB comes not only in reducing the repair cycle time (measured from the time of removal of the unserviceable carcass to its return to stock at the ISB), but also in providing skilled technicians who can render technical assistance to direct support technicians in the battle space through e-mail, teleconference, or personal visits between engagements. For example, early in the Gulf War the Army deployed the Eighteenth Airborne Corps Signal Brigade newly equipped with the battlefield cellular communications system—mobile subscriber equipment (MSE). However, even before most of the brigade's MSE shelters had arrived in Saudi Arabia, the component repair center manned by the contractor's technicians had set up and ably assisted the brigade's soldiers in activating the system. Since there was no ground combat for nearly five months, the center technicians could extend their technical assistance as well as repair components. The system's availability regularly stayed at 98 percent or better. Once the ground operation achieved its objective and the enemy threat had disappeared, the technicians made the rounds of the MSE units, checking on or assisting the soldier technicians in replacing components to assure the continuation of highly reliable communications.

Repair of naval vessel components usually takes a different tack than described above. If diagnosis shows that the component can be repaired on board, then parts and technicians can be brought aboard if necessary. Otherwise the technicians in the crew can replace the component and evacuate it via the shuttle ship to the appropriate forward naval base and eventually to a repair site. Also, unlike other systems, failure of some major components such as engines or generators may require a shipyard availability to replace or repair them.

Component Repair Structure in the ISB

There may be several repair facilities for a particular weapons/support system, or a single facility may serve several systems. The logistics elements of the service component command and PMs determine how best to meet the component repair requirement, ideally during the preparation of the logistics plan because the deployment space/weight demand of each component repair activity must be captured in the overall time-phased flow into the ISB. The activity must move not only the technicians who repair the components (as well as platforms), their tools, and test equipment, but also the necessary piece parts (shop-replaceable units) likely to be required. They should also move and manage the serviceable component inventory to support the services' deployed systems and manage the unserviceable inventory as it develops—for induction into the repair process. These repair activities, a system's chief support resource in the theater, also manage a "float" of direct support test equipment and maintenance aids and, as in the MSE repair center example, provide technical assistance to the direct support technicians in the battle spaces. Service component commands may also position a set of extra, or "float," equipment in the ISB. That equipment can replace equipment that requires lengthy repair or that was lost in battle. When we add together such facilities for all the services' deployed systems, we see a significant footprint—a necessary cost of maintaining the battle readiness of the deployed force, yet a cost that attracts efforts to further reduce its size through system reliability and survivability advances and through more compact, transportable support equipment.

Technical Assistance for Direct Support
Maintenance Technicians

The link between the direct support technicians in the land battle space and the component repair facilities in the ISBs is a "lifeline." The battle space DSU technicians order replacement components from their own limited stockage and send the failed item to the ISB or other repair site. The repair site's serviceable inventory is the normal source for replacement components for the DSUs. Its ability to provide the necessary supply of serviceable components of reliably high quality is perhaps its major contribution to strengthening the DSUs' ability to maintain system availability.

The link also binds together the two geographically separated groups of technicians. It strengthens the capabilities of the DSU technicians, who can secure back-up assistance with diagnostic or repair tasks, and it makes the repair center technicians aware of in-service problems. We will explore this lifeline process further in discussing the value of continuously shared knowledge. It is apparent that the battle readiness of combat and support systems depends heavily on that lifeline link to the ISB (or CONUS) component repair center both for the flow of serviceable components and for backup technical assistance.

PRODUCT SUPPORT IN THE CONUS SUSTAINING BASE

In this section we will both describe the product support processes that enable the system-owning organizations and their DSMOs to maintain system readiness standards and describe the two approaches to managing the sustaining base processes.

Sustaining Base Processes for System Support

The third major locus of product support processes (after the battle space and the ISB) is found in the CONUS (and/or forward-stationed) base. Here one finds the nodes in the supply chain critical to the life cycle management of the weapon or support system. The product support processes that operate at these nodes provide the foundation of support for the equipment-owning organizations and their DSUs. As one can tell from Figure 6-1, they are the source of replacement components, technician diagnostic and repair proce-

FIGURE 6-1   Sustaining Base Processes

+ Configuration management
+ Component inventory management
+ System overhaul and major repair
+ System modification
+ Sustainment engineering
+ Financial management

dures, and replacement systems when owned systems must be overhauled—the most critical support resources for the DSMOs and their system-owning unit customers in their efforts to maintain the operational availability of weapons and support systems. A brief description of the significant processes illustrates the role of the sustaining base.

Configuration management is the process for deliberately managing the form, fit, and function of the set of components in a weapons or support system. It is the foundation of all in-service technical and logistics support for a system. The configuration consists of the model, serial number, and other markers that describe the technical characteristics of each subsystem mounted on the platform. The system's configuration database is the essential part of the configuration management process, allowing the PM or system/ commodity command to exercise configuration control.

Why is this management process so important? Production of systems may stretch over many years, during which technology evolves. For example, an avionics component installed in an aircraft in the first year's production may evolve several times even in initial production. And, since services retain platforms for twenty to forty or fifty years, the component may be replaced with a new version several more times. Quite obviously all the component replacements are not made at the same time, so it is necessary to the effective support of the platform that managers in the customer unit as well as inventory and repair managers know which model goes into the particular platform when a failure requires it be replaced. There may be a dozen different models of the same functional component in the inventory or in use, but only the one with its own particular technical characteristics may fit in with associated components.

Therefore, it is best if an operating unit is equipped with all platforms in a single block configuration to simplify diagnosis and repair procedures, to avoid multiple components with the same function, and to facilitate "controlled substitution" from another platform when a replacement component is not immediately available. Configuration management is therefore one of the most important processes in helping organizations sustain battle readiness and control maintenance costs.

Component inventory management is the process of managing the supply of reparable components and consumable parts so that the direct support, component repair or the overhaul/remanufacturing technicians needing a replacement can obtain it as quickly as possible even when neither the direct support maintenance organization, the ISB, nor the local storage activities have the item. The inventory manager's task is to

> forecast demands for components and parts
> decide which—and how many—to keep in the national inventory
> acquire them from industry and arrange for repair of unserviceable reparable components
> fill the demands of the DSUs, component repair activities at ISBs, and other repair facilities around the world
> manage the related financial resources.

Demand Forecasting

Each part of this task itself involves several processes and complex interrelationships. Demand forecasting makes use of computer models based in historical demand experience, but such forecasts need to be tempered by engineering judgment, based on clear understanding of failure modes and causes. In one example, demands for an expensive component increased abruptly, causing the inventory position to drop dramatically as the automated system sought to satisfy the requisitions. Had there been no human intervention to discern the cause, the requirement to acquire the component from industry would have shot up, putting more stress on an already constrained acquisition budget. However, the system PM's staff members noticed the phenomenon while they were visiting the affected customer units and direct support organizations. They found that the demands were caused not by the failure of the component, but by a failure of the test process. When the supposed unserviceable components were inducted for repair, the repair activity found "no evidence of failure" in many. Thus, the forecasting system depends on technical judgments as well as the raw data demand. While this is only one example, it is by no means rare. The conclusion should be that sudden demand increases need that human intervention to look for causes before allowing an automated inventory management system to generate what may well become excess inventories once a root cause is found.

Another very difficult problem for inventory managers is deciding when an item has had too few demands to meet the service or agency criterion for retaining it in the inventory. Frequently items are bought for inventory based on engineering estimates of failure rates at the time of system fielding. Yet the item may not fail at the expected rate, and the result is insufficient demand to meet the retention criterion. Therefore the inventory manager authorizes the Defense Reutilization Management Service (part of DLA) to dispose of the item, usually at a fraction of its original cost. Then comes the surprise. Failures appear, and there is no stock to meet the demand, requiring either re-procurement of the item from the buyer of the disposed of stock or new production. Both are expensive propositions; the latter also requires lengthy lead time. A recent analysis of this phenomenon led to DLA's lengthening the period of holding without demands to seven years from only three years, with expected savings of nearly $100 million from avoiding the need to re-procure.

Deciding on Stockage

Determining whether to stock an item, and in what quantities, also requires useful computer algorithms and technical judgments. It is a risk management process since the budgets may not allow stockage of all the items forecast to be needed. Inventory managers are aided by a process of arraying the expensive components by their contribution to system availability, with the algorithm allocating budget in proportion to each component's likely impact on fleet readiness during the period. The Air Force does this calculation to cover all of its component inventory, including that kept in CONUS distribution depots as well as at bases. The Army and Navy have similar readiness-based stockage determination processes.

A part of this stockage decision is the *positioning* of the stock—the closer to the demand source, the better, so that customer wait time can be minimized. Careful examination of excessive wait times in 2001–02 led DLA and the services to direct repositioning of new stock to reflect changed demand patterns—or simply heretofore unrecognized patterns. Likewise, the allocation between direct support organization, ISB, and national storage locations should follow similar logic.

Component Acquisition and Repair

Reparable component or consumable part acquisition involves another set of processes. Inventory managers are more concerned with depot-level reparables than those customarily repaired at installations because depot reparables, e.g., engines, are usually far more expensive. They use reparable forecasting algorithms to compute the likely yield of serviceable components from unserviceable carcasses. Since there are always "washouts"—those components found to be uneconomically reparable—the repair process will cause inventory reduction. Repair facilities typically meet much of the forecasted demand. The balance must be met from buying newly manufactured components. Inventory managers must update their forecasting algorithms periodically, since as the components age, the yield of serviceable components from the repair activities is likely to decline. And as noted earlier, inventory managers must also watch for spikes in failure rates, which should trigger a failure mode analysis and perhaps redesign.

Repair of depot reparable components in the CONUS sustaining base is performed at both the service's (or another service's) depots or shipyards and by contractors. Over the last ten years the service's source-of-repair analyses have assigned increasing amounts to industry. For example, the General Accounting Office noted in 2001 that the Air Force assigned forty-eight of sixty-six systems and components to industry as a result of its source-of-repair analyses.[3] Also, since the introduction of the policy for charging customer units for depot-level reparables, many commands began repairing them at their own installations or with contracted repair in an attempt to obtain serviceable components at less cost—a practice we shall revisit.

Build-to-Print and Diminishing Manufacturing Sources

Since reparable components usually are the most expensive, new buys require special attention from the PM as well as the inventory manager. One issue is whether to buy "build-to-print," i.e., simply use the existing techni-

---

[3] General Accounting Office, "Defense Logistics, Actions Needed to Overcome Gaps in the Public Depot System," GAO Report 02-105, Oct. 2001, p. 16.

cal specification drawings and either complete the purchase, as has been an earlier practice, or add other purchases to an existing multiyear contract that the supplier holds. Buying build-to-print often commits investment to old technology. This is an especially critical issue for electronic components, where the technology changes more rapidly than in mechanical or hydraulics components, creating obsolescence. Unless large purchases with healthy profits are foreseen, the supplier may be unwilling to fill an order.

More than one inventory manager in recent years has been confronted by a previous supplier's unwillingness to keep the jigs and fixtures to produce expensive but technologically obsolete components, especially for low-density systems. This phenomenon, known as "diminishing manufacturing sources," has been growing as systems are kept in the force longer than the commercial technology cycles and in progressively fewer numbers as force structure reductions have reduced the system populations. In spite of their wish to continue to support military systems, these manufacturers often cannot afford the costs to bridge between infrequent orders. They must make productive use of the manufacturing facilities in which they have invested, because their stockholders demand that they seek business with adequate return on investment. Buying build-to-print components that must mesh technically with other components also is a high-risk proposition since engineering drawings often fail to describe how the component fits with others. It is particularly risky when software is embedded in the components.

Component Technology Upgrades

The decision to buy new components is also the opportunity to upgrade the technology, perhaps improving performance, maintainability, or reliability (reducing the failure and life cycle costs). If such is the decision, then the PM must use the configuration management records to decide to which platform owners the new component can be sent. This usually is not a time-critical process; there will likely be several months' lead time to permit production of the first articles, to test them, and to accumulate enough to begin the installation process at the first unit. The PM normally will arrange for installation of each unit's new component while taking possession of the older model it replaces, putting it—if serviceable—back into inventory. The PM and inventory manager will then synchronize the acquisition of the new model with the overall component inventory position. If the procurement of the new model exceeds the washout rate of the old model, then the inventory manager may dispose of reparable carcasses rather than spend the money to repair them and create stock that may never be used.

Lead Time

A major complicator of an inventory manager's life is the lead time between deciding to buy or repair an item and the manager's ability to send it to a customer. The services' inventory managers have long been faced with two kinds of lead times: administrative lead time (preparing the procurement package for the buying organization to compete it) and production lead time.

A major component of administrative lead time is the time required for retrieving and reviewing engineering drawings of the component—sometimes a bureaucratically tortuous process. For example, DLA's defense support centers (DSCs) in Columbus and Richmond manage consumable repair parts for the services' systems. The DSCs must go to the service system or commodity command that manages the weapon or support system for which the part is to be purchased in order to validate the drawings it might have or to get new ones. (Drawings for many parts were not provided to DLA when the services accomplished the OSD-directed transfer of consumable repair parts in the early 1990s.) This inter-organization process adds even more administrative lead time. The remaining time is required for preparing the "procurement work directive," as it is sometimes known, and securing the funding and necessary administrative approvals. After the procurement package is assembled, it may be competed—and protested—further adding lead time.

The second type of lead time is the actual production lead time. The chosen supplier will need lead time to work the item into its own manufacturing process, including subcontracting for subcomponents with their lead times, acquiring raw materials, and conducting, in parallel, its own engineering reviews and development of manufacturing instructions.

In reality, the drawings provided often do not contain all the detail necessary to manufacture. Firms that developed the original item may have what they consider to be proprietary manufacturing processes, the descriptions of which they may exclude from drawings provided to the government and used to compete the re-procurement. Thus, the new (or even former) supplier must tailor the production instructions to match its own production process. A first article test and certifications usually are needed if the component is to be used on an aircraft. Lead time further increases if there must be changes to adjust the production process required by test results.

The component acquisition process, as it exists in most service inventory management activities, is a lengthy "heel-to-toe" process, with the sum of the administrative and production lead times frequently exceeding *two years* from the time the process is initiated when the inventory management model shows that a reorder point has been reached. While the process appears to be expensive (in terms of two-plus years inventory required to cover the lead time), inefficient (it is), and certainly not consistent with industry's best practices even twenty years ago, the necessity for the services to comply with acquisition laws and the political give-and-take behind them must bear a share of the responsibility. (We will turn to that issue as part of a discussion of the influence of public policy on product support.)

Order Fulfillment

The inventory manager's next task is to fill the orders of the DSMOs and the CONUS and ISB repair facilities. The services use issue priority designators (IPDs) that combine a force activity designator with a need designator. An IPD #1, for example, would denote a combat unit in the battle space needing a part that will restore one of its mission-critical systems to an operational condition. Such an IPD would generate high-priority handling and expedited shipment to the organization making the system repair. Orders for normal inventory replacement at DSUs and other repair/parts-stocking activities carry a lower IPD and allow standard handling, which may still mean air shipment outside CONUS.

Parallel processes are used to manage truly exceptional items, for example, to allocate between many organizations using IPD #1, where inventory is short and/or the item is a high-cost component. In such cases the service component command would allocate the items based upon the priority of the system owning units. An example of the order fulfillment process follows.

"Desert Express"

During the first Gulf War, each of the services had critical needs for expedited delivery of components. TRANSCOM allocated one C-141 sortie a day (designated "Desert Express") to fly direct to Saudi Arabia from

Charleston Air Force Base with its 463-L pallet positions allocated to the services, five to each service.[4] Continuing dialogue between the service logistics staffs in the area of operations and their service logistics commands in CONUS usually resulted in moving components via FedEx, UPS, and similar carriers from CONUS repair facilities and storage locations to Charleston, where service liaison officers worked with the aerial port to prepare the pallets for the daily flight. In the case of Army components, in many instances a component for an Apache helicopter or Patriot missile battery was ordered through INMARSAT from the Saudi Arabian desert by an Army Materiel Command logistics assistance representative to the inventory manager, and the component was placed on that or the next day's Desert Express flight from Charleston, was picked up on the ramp at Dhahran, and was flown or driven immediately to the DSU for the repair task. Not only did these critical components receive expedited handling, but the process allowed the positive tracking of the components through the whole supply chain. While it required dedicated people and lift, it produced urgently needed components critical to major weapons systems operability.

Sourcing from Production

The inventory manager has other resources to tap to meet critical needs, especially for systems still in production. To fill critical parts shortages on newly fielded systems, PMs have long pulled components awaiting assembly into new platforms. With increasing visibility of the inventories of DSUs and repair facilities around the world, the inventory manager can arrange for the purchase or loan of components and their air shipment to the organization needing them. A similar practice has always been common at direct support level. This practice is institutionalized as a best practice by commercial firms engaging in worldwide product support. For example, Caterpillar's inventory system gives its dealers, and even its major customers, visibility of component assets on its Web site, which includes a purchase order form for any dealer or customer to buy the component from another—a process that

---

[4] See James K. Matthews and Cora J. Holt, So Many, So Much, So Far, So Fast: United States Transportation Command and Strategic Deployment for Operation Desert Shield/Desert Storm (Joint History Office, Office of the Chairman of the Joint Chiefs of Staff, and Research Center, United States Transportation Command, 1995), pp. 59–62.

clearly provides mutual advantage in keeping expensive construction machinery in operation.

Resourcing Inventory Management

Finally, the inventory management task requires a significant resourcing effort: developing a program and budget to cover the resource requirements and juggling ever-changing requirements for component repairs or procurement, using the working capital fund obligation authority with the available funds. For the most part, inventory management does not use annual appropriated funds such as operation and maintenance or procurement. Rather it uses the service or agency working capital fund—a type of revolving fund. The customers "buy" components from the inventory management activity using their appropriated funds, which then add to the cash position of the working capital fund, allowing it to procure or repair other items. But the cash position of the working capital fund can put a limit on purchases of components, parts, and repair services from industry as well as repair services from DoD repair facilities. That cash position can be affected by the services' financial management actions, too. The inventory management process has been disrupted too frequently by transfers of "cash" (revenues from sales of components to operating forces) to pay other service bills not related to product support, leaving the inventory management process without sufficient funds to replace depleted inventory.

PMs and inventory managers also face the normal problems in justifying their funding requirements for new obligation authority to buy from industry and to obtain component repairs from DoD repair facilities. Theoretically, there should be sufficient revenue gained from sales to the operating forces plus a small increment to cover inflation to pay for replacing "washed out" components and to pay for repairs. The theory is based on the pricing of serviceable components, which includes factors for repairing components and replacing washouts and for inflation. However, the recent history of increasing failure rates of older components and older platforms, coupled with large price increases (frequently for small lots of components with obsolescent technology), causes overall costs to grow even faster than the normal inflation factor. Each of the services has run into billion-dollar-plus shortages of obligation authority—which have led to shortages of components and lower system readiness rates for some major systems.

Such situations can be remedied only with additional obligation authority, and that can come only when the services, OSD, and Congress trust the estimates of needs. Many of the service and OSD financial managers and congressional overseers thought that providing the operating forces more operations and maintenance funding would solve the problem. That reflects a lack of understanding of the fundamental fact that if inventory managers cannot buy serviceable components from industry vendors or industry and DoD repair facilities, they will have insufficient stocks for the operating forces to buy, no matter how much funding the operating forces have been given. This is but one of the financial management issues that bedevil the product support process.

System Overhaul and Major Repair

The next major process for which the CONUS sustaining base is responsible is the major repair or overhaul of the platform or other end item. Many, if not most, weapons and support system platforms will require a periodic trip to a shipyard, DoD depot, or contractor facility to undergo a lengthy period of disassembly, inspection for structural wear and tear (e.g., fuselage, hull stresses, corrosion effects, wiring age and wear, etc.), and the necessary repairs to restore them to serviceable condition. There is "periodic depot maintenance" for aircraft, "shipyard availability" for vessels, and overhaul programs for land vehicles and many components, e.g., aircraft engines, which are treated like end, or "principal," items. For the major platforms, these overhaul periods are quite lengthy. Refueling a nuclear carrier takes about two years, and the depot maintenance periods of aged B-52 bombers and KC-135 tankers have gone well over a year because of the extensive work packages involved.

The Overhaul Process

A true depot overhaul process is much akin to the commercial remanufacturing process. The facility is a "factory" with the normal production planning and control processes. It has a disassembly and inspection process in which all or most components are removed from the platform and sent to auxiliary or "back shops," where they may be tested and disassembled, and new or reconditioned shop replaceable units incorporated to produce a serviceable or "like new" component. The stripped platform is itself reconditioned through removal of accumulated corrosion, resurfaced and/or repainted, rewired, and made ready for the reassembly of its components. That process, which closely resembles original manufacturing, is accompanied by various inspection regimes and testing to affirm the equipment is ready to issue to the forces.

Periodic depot maintenance and ship availability activities are normally scheduled several years in advance; and replacement aircraft, vessels, or vehicles are provided to the operating forces to maintain the normal force availability. The services' programs and budgets reflect the estimated costs of these overhaul activities, and the funding is an operations and maintenance budget line, directly appropriated by the Congress (although not tied to particular systems). In the cases in which major repair is required—e.g., the repair of the extensive damage to the USS *Cole* from the terrorists' bombs—the Congress appropriates the funds in a "supplemental" appropriation, a legitimate action to cover an unforeseen event.

As in the case of depot-level reparable components, overhauls take place in government or industry facilities, sometimes in both for a single system, where the relatively new depot partnerships are at work. Also as in the case of reparables, most of the newer or modified systems depot overhauls or maintenance periods are being assigned to industry, reflecting DoD and service judgments that the best value repair source is industry, since the existing industry facilities and workforce already are trained to perform the tasks as a result of producing the systems and performing maintenance during the initial fielding process.[5]

Product Improvement

Periodic overhaul periods present opportunities to install improved components or new subsystems. Much of the installation costs of product improvements are associated with the labor of opening up the platform, doing rewiring, and so on—the same activities that are required in an overhaul. Thus, the PM can save labor costs by combining the product improvement and the overhaul work packages. Increasingly, the services are combining major upgrades and overhaul into programs variously named "service life extension" or "recapitalization," both reflecting the decreasing availability of many of the aging systems that remain critical to war-fighting missions.

---

[5] GAO Report 02-105, p. 16.

Sustainment Engineering

The *sustainment engineering* part of product support is—or should be—the process by which the PM and service determine how to maintain a system's performance over its life and to control the growth of operating and support costs. I say, "should be" because the services' funding of sustainment engineering frequently has been parsimonious. Sustainment has none of the glamour of engineering new technology. It involves collecting and analyzing performance and maintenance data on the system, its related test equipment, and even the maintenance technicians and operator crews, in order to determine the causes of component failures or other factors that are responsible for failures to meet the designed or expected standards. Funding is needed to analyze the many factors that can contribute to unexpectedly high failure rates—from inherent technology problems to insufficiently skilled technicians. Once the causes of the failures are known, funding, usually for engineering staff or contractor tasks, again is needed to develop solutions. These solutions can range from the simple improvement of training, diagnostic, or repair procedures to the redesign of the offending components or the manner of their integration into the system.

Unfortunately, over the last decade or so, the pressures for cost reduction in the DoD have resulted in funding levels that are only a small fraction of that necessary to pursue many of the improvements that could be made to aging fleets of systems. In industry, many such improvements would be looked upon as capital investments, with the payback in fewer component removals and repairs. No such mechanism is available in DoD because of the structure of the financial management and appropriation processes, as well as the illusion that military technicians' services constitute a "free good." On the other hand, the various life extension and recapitalization programs that have been funded show that some sustainment engineering is accomplished and, perhaps, demonstrate the potential for payoffs were more resources to be allocated for that process.

Management of Financial Resources

Funding Stovepipes

Our final stage in this survey of product support processes in the CONUS base is a brief overview of the financial management processes that enable all the other processes to work. We previously referred to the working capital fund (WCF) and the operations and maintenance (O&M) appropriation funding components—the two most frequently thought of in product support. Research, development, test and evaluation, and procurement appropriations are used in conjunction with development and acquisition of new systems and product improvements. The military personnel appropriations fund the military participants in the product support process; however, these funds are not available to other parts of the product support process, even if a significant improvement in the reliability or maintainability of the system could be achieved that would reduce by half the number of technicians required to support the system. In a rational process of making capital investments to reduce future costs, these different funding "stovepipes" should not matter. However, in the congressionally mandated budgetary processes, the investment funds, a combination of R&D and procurement that would yield large operations and support cost savings, compete in each funding category with other service initiatives. Although the payoff may be in reduced costs to the forces (O&M savings) and fewer technicians (military personnel cost savings), the investment's justification frequently does not find supporters since it may not result in any war-fighting capability improvement. In the competition for available investment funding, reduced costs and manpower seldom trump improved capabilities.

Customer Transactions

We noted in our discussion of inventory management that the operating forces "customers" were allocated O&M funds to carry out their operational and/or training missions. Those funds are used in the product support process to buy components, to pay for supplemental contractor technical support and services, and to buy consumables (fuel, lubricants, filters, and the like). They buy most serviceable components from either their service's, another service's, or DLA's inventory management activities—a purchase that is reflected as revenue to the service's or the DLA's WCF. Revenue—or "cash"— is the normal means of buying repaired or replacement components to put back into inventory. The price of a component, generally established once a year to reduce accounting turbulence in the operating forces, includes both the estimated repair cost of that component during the next year and its estimated share of the cost of washouts. Repair costs since the end of the Cold War have climbed precipitously—a phenomenon whose rationale one needs to understand, because it has been, and probably will continue for some time to be, a driver in the high cost of reparable components—"sticker shock," if you will.

More importantly, these increased costs have been partly to blame for the dysfunctional behavior within the services for the last decade or so, causing installation and force commanders to search for lower cost component repairs from commercial repair sources, frequently without adequate quality controls and acceptance testing. Use of those sources has led to much lower reliability as well as reduced demand for services' organic repair facilities and to the creation of artificial excess capacity, which cannot be easily disposed of. Thus the services find themselves in these situations paying for both a commercial repair *and* the organic facilities and workforce that could repair the item—further increasing the costs that must be recovered through the price mechanism.

Surcharges and Full Cost Recovery

An additional contributor to the repair costs sticker shock of the last decade has been the added "management" surcharges. In 1990, OSD changed the working capital fund process to require full cost recovery in rates. Therefore, the cost of all the activities necessary to the provision of the part or component to the operating forces was to be recovered through the price mechanism and the revenues gamed. It was thought that this would be an incentive for more efficient operation of those product support management activities, such as inventory, configuration, and funds management, that were not already under the full cost recovery regimen as the depots and shipyards were. The added activities are generally thought of as overhead functions that are necessary to product support but are not directly involved in component repair or platform overhaul. The salaries of the civilian managers and staffs and most other costs of those activities are added together to become the surcharge that is added to the price of a new or repaired component.

The question is, "Has the effort to improve efficiency of these management activities worked?" An economist would quickly recognize monopolist behavior—a largely captive customer base who must buy from the one supplier, who is in turn free to set prices in a noncompetitive way. Not only is there little or no competitive incentive for the depot repair organizations, product support managers, or transportation providers to reduce costs and price, but there is every incentive to maximize revenue to pay people who are in the workforce. And these activities cannot regulate the size of their workforces because of the various laws enacted over the years to limit the President's ability to reduce the civilian workforce. Various programs were initiated to find savings in the processes of inventory management and repair but few—outside of the attrition-and-hiring-freeze policy, with all its inequitable and dysfunctional consequences—have made much difference, and prices continue to rise. Only the base realignment actions, the last in 1995, have enabled significant reduction in excess facilities. Yet force and weapons system reductions continued after that time, with no commensurate ability to pare down the support infrastructure. The next opportunity comes in the scheduled 2005 base realignment process.

The Credit System and Counterproductive Incentives

One other feature of the new full cost recovery system deserves mention because it reflects how operating forces respond to the economic incentives that face them. The designers of the 1990 working capital fund policy thought that credit should be given for the turn-in of carcasses—the unserviceable components. In earlier years when components were procurement funded, many units would dispose of the reparable items rather than be inconvenienced by having to turn them in for repair. They were "free," so the unit bore no penalty for not turning in the unserviceable but reparable items. Therefore, a separate transaction was introduced, and a pricing policy for carcasses was established to "pay" units for these carcasses. The predictable happened. Many system-owning and direct support maintenance units of an entrepreneurial bent "cleaned the carcasses," removing serviceable shop-replaceable units to repair other like components, and turned in stripped carcasses. Repair activities then found that their previous repair estimates never considered the possibility of stripping, and the stripping actions required them to replace many more shop-replaceable units, resulting in much higher average repair costs. Secondly, some units made a habit through much of this time of drawing out of the DLA property disposal sites uneconomically reparable carcasses cast off by repair facilities and turning them in to get the credits. Of course, the stripping activities added incalculably more maintenance hours for the mostly military DSUs, another cost of this efficiency goal. In response to these perverse incentives, to avoid the resulting high cost of serviceables many installations contracted the repair directly with local civilian repair firms, at prices sometimes considerably lower than those set by the services' inventory management activities.

Of course, the net effect of these "gaming" ventures is that the product support process costs have been higher than they should have been, and the quality of the repairs deteriorated in many cases. The services have had to pay for the unused depot and shipyard repair capacity as well as for the work diverted by the local installation. (Later we will examine how the application of our *simplicity* principle might produce more effective system availability results, and at a lower cost than the present system of surcharges and credits.)

Management of Sustaining Base Processes

There are two distinct approaches to managing the sustaining base processes, and indeed, the life cycle support of weapons and support systems. The most prevalent approach is the traditional functional management, in which the responsibilities and authority for supporting a service's systems are divided functionally. The second approach, now in use mostly by systems fielded since 1995, is management by the system PM, usually with a contractor-integrator and some participation by organic DoD activities.

Functional Management

For the most part these processes operate under the shared responsibility of a service system command and a major force command. For the Army, process responsibilities are divided between the subordinate "commodity" command of Army Materiel Command (Tank Automotive and Armaments, Aviation and Missile, and Communications and Electronics commands) and the system-owning commands (Forces Command, U.S. Army Europe, etc.). The processes are divided functionally within the commodity command— e.g., teams manage the inventory of engines, fire control sub systems, transmissions, helicopter rotors, and other reparable components—across systems. Other organizations within the commodity commands manage depot overhaul planning, sustainment engineering, and configuration control. DLA inventory control centers manage most of the consumable repair parts of Army systems as well as those of Navy/Marine and Air Force systems. The system-owning commands that are allocated the operations and maintenance funds both buy and arrange the repair of many reparable components; others, depot-level reparables, are tasked to the maintenance depots or contractors by the commodity commands but "bought" by the system-owning commands. Depot overhaul of platforms is funded through Army Materiel Command and managed by the commodity commands. No single individual—short of the commodity command commander—is responsible for the sustaining base support of the systems themselves.

The Air Force functional management approach is similar. The Air Force Materiel Command's subordinate commands, the air logistics centers at Warner Robins AFB, Georgia; Oklahoma City, Oklahoma; and Ogden, Utah, house the functional process managers. They also are the depot maintenance sites. The Air Combat Command plays a much more active role than its Army counterparts in managing component and depot maintenance; it is given all of the operations and maintenance funding for the systems. It not only buys components from the air logistics centers and some contractors, but it also schedules—and buys—periodic platform depot maintenance from them.

The Navy's functional management approach to sustaining base product support has more in common with the Air Force's central role of its force providing command. Like Air Combat Command, the Atlantic and Pacific fleets are given the operations and maintenance funds and have a central role in managing the maintenance and overhaul of ships through the type commanders, i.e., aircraft carriers, submarines, and surface ships such as cruisers, destroyers, and amphibious ships. Naval Sea Systems and Space and Warfare Systems commands have more of a technical oversight role in the platform maintenance activities but manage, along with Naval Supply Systems Command, the reparables inventory in support of the fleets and the sub-system and platform configuration control and sustainment engineering functions. Sea Systems Command also commands three of the Navy's shipyards (Portsmouth, New Hampshire; Norfolk, Virginia; and Puget Sound, Washington); the fourth, Pearl Harbor, is under Pacific fleet.

Since the mid 1990s, the management of surface ships has been evolving to a "regional maintenance" concept in an effort to reduce excess maintenance infrastructure and costs and lessen the maintenance and overhaul periods. The intent has been to have the fleet control the industrial infrastructure in the regional centers, to keep them at level work loads, and to contract for the work over those levels. Assets formerly under Sea Systems

Command, such as the fleet technical support centers and some of the supervisors of shipbuilding (who contract for repair in commercial shipyards), as well as Pearl Harbor Naval Shipyard, were transferred to the fleets. Regional maintenance commanders are to assume the responsibility for shore maintenance under the fleets' oversight, using both organic and commercial assets, including the shore intermediate maintenance activities (SIMA), the organizations that employ sailors during their shore-duty tours. Port engineers would continue to integrate all the work packages of an individual platform during its shore maintenance period.

Early in the evolution of this concept, the General Accounting Office and the Naval Studies Board noted that the Navy had to meet several challenges before the concept would meet its objectives. Among them were the resistance caused by the elimination of organizations (and jobs), the lack of visibility of maintenance-related costs (including the costs of the military personnel), unconnected management systems of the legacy infrastructure, and the larger number of shore positions needed to support sea-shore rotation than are needed for the maintenance functions.[6] As of this writing aircraft carriers and submarines are not included in the regional maintenance concept.

For Navy and Marine aircraft under the functional management approach, the Naval Air Systems Command plays a more involved role as the technical authority for all maintenance repair and overhaul, and it controls some of the funding. In addition, like other systems commands, Naval Air Systems Command manages the reparable components as well as the sustainment engineering and configuration control and commands the naval air depots. Still, the fleet air commands are directly involved in ashore maintenance, operating the air station intermediate maintenance activities and placing work beyond the air station capabilities in the naval aviation depots or with contractors.

With only a few—but important—exceptions, and as in the other services, no single individual involved in the Navy's sustaining base product support, i.e., the program manager is responsible for a given weapons or support system that was placed in operation before 1995.

---

[6] Naval Studies Board, National Research Council, Recapitalizing the Navy (Washington, DC: National Academy Press, 1998), pp. 36–37.

Program Management of Sustaining Base Product Support

The functional management model described above has been supplemented—some say replaced—by an integrated weapons system approach to sustaining base support. This model was born in 1994 with a change to the major DoD acquisition policy that requires program managers to continue their systems management responsibility for the life cycle of the system. This approach to management has been employed in conjunction with contractor support as its core, rather than the organic support characteristic of the functional management approach described earlier. Program management of systems such as the Navy's ICBM fleet, the Air Force KC-10 aerial tanker and F-117 fighter, and the Army's MSE battlefield cellular communications system preceded the new directive. Since that time, new systems, such as the C-17 and the Navy's F-18 E/F, have gone into service under PM life-cycle management.

During the 1990s, the Defense Science Board and other advisory groups strongly recommended that the PM life-cycle management model replace the functional approach and be complemented by contractor logistics support. The May 2003 edition of the DoD capstone acquisition policy statement, DoD Directive 5000.1, has moved partially in this direction. It states:

> *Total Systems Approach. The PM shall be the single point of accountability for accomplishing program objectives for total life-cycle systems management, including sustainment. The PM shall apply human systems integration to optimize total system performance (hardware, software, and human), operational effectiveness, and suitability, survivability, safety, and affordability. PMs shall consider supportability, life cycle costs, performance, and schedule comparable in making program decisions. Planning for Operation and Support and the estimation of total ownership costs shall begin as early as possible. Supportability, a key component of performance, shall be considered throughout the system life cycle.*[7]

---

[7] U.S. Department of Defense, The Defense Acquisition System, DoD Directive 5000.1, May 12, 2003, ¶ E1.29.

A more detailed explanation of the responsibilities of the PM is found in DoD Instruction No. 5000.2,[8] but it is not prescriptive and does not even discuss PM authorities or funding that would be necessary to carry out what one would reasonably conclude were "responsibilities." Those words were certainly a casualty of the negotiations with services that did not want to change their management of legacy systems and, perhaps, that wanted to retract the PM authorities for new systems in the interest of accommodating those organizations that lost authority over functions.

Implementation of this policy for systems already fielded is an open question. The likeliest opportunities are at the time of a major system upgrade, such as occurred in the Army at the time of the modernization of part of the M1 tank fleet to the M1A2 configuration. The PM did assume responsibility for sustainment management and tasked the integrating contractor with managing system-unique components as well as other product support functions, including some five thousand consumable repair parts transferred from DLA management. Quite clearly, transferring other legacy systems to PM management entails major reorientation of the system and commodity commands from their functional management roles to contractor management roles—oversight versus direct management. The likely results would be a significant reduction in the number of civil servants who do the functional management tasks. Such a change has large cultural and political impacts, far greater than what a commercial firm would experience, because of the inevitable involvement of the Congress.

---

[8] U.S. Department of Defense, DoD Instruction 5000.2, May 12, 2003, ¶ 3.9.

CHAPTER 7

ASSESSING THE PRODUCT SUPPORT PROCESSES: PART I

FRAMEWORK FOR ASSESSMENT

In chapter 1 we adopted a conceptual framework (Figure 7-1) for assessing process strengths and opportunities for improvements.

We now employ this conceptual framework to examine the product support supply chain processes that operate in the battle spaces, the ISB, and the CONUS base. Since both logistics objectives—making timely delivery of support to customers and minimizing the logistics footprint in battle spaces—depend to some extent upon effective application of the supporting principles, we will begin this examination by assessing how well these principles are followed and then propose changes to the processes so that they

FIGURE 7-1 Framework

♦ How well do these processes contribute to the two logistics objectives named in chapter 1?
1. Timely delivery of forces and support to customers of logistics activities
2. Minimized logistics footprint in battle spaces

♦ Supporting Principles: How well do the processes measure up to the following principles?
- Accountability for process performance
- Continuously shared knowledge of asset status, campaign requirements, customer status, and process barriers
- Maximized commercial contracting of logistics activities in CONUS and ISBs
- Allocation of logistics tasks to coalition partners based on a principle of comparative advantage
- Simplicity in management, resourcing, and sourcing

better enable the accomplishment of the two logistics objectives. In this chapter I will cover the first four principles. In chapter 8 I will turn to the task of simplifying product support management and funding and propose a far-reaching change in the management of the funding process. I will also describe how risk management can be improved through adoption of the proposed process changes and discuss the inventory ownership options that go with contractor logistics support. A discussion of how this management change would contribute to achieving timely delivery of support with a minimum logistics footprint in the battle spaces will demonstrate how the proposed product support changes promote logistics effectiveness. This section ends by showing how logistics efficiency can be a major by-product of the process changes.

ACCOUNTABILITY FOR PRODUCT SUPPORT PERFORMANCE

Clear Accountability in Operating and Direct Support Maintenance Organizations

Accountability for system performance, and, therefore, for the outcome of the product support process, is clear in the system operating organizations that must employ the weapons and support systems to accomplish their missions. They frequently report system availability in peacetime and war and must answer to their chains of command for attaining availability objectives. Likewise their DSUs tasked with the responsibility for maintaining a high degree of operational availability for those systems, are as accountable for their work to the same chain of command. Both organizations know the operational status of each system and, for those not available for missions, what is required to make them mission ready. The DSUs perform the vast majority of the work to assure system availability.

Accountability for Product Support outside the Battle Spaces

To achieve the operational availability objectives, the DSU depends upon resources that must come from organizations further back in the product support supply chain, principally these five types of resources:

> - replacements for failed components
> - updated and calibrated test equipment and diagnostic aids

> technical publications and updates
> special tools
> technical assistance

At this writing, accountability for providing these resources, except for a few systems, is so dispersed as to be practically meaningless. The DSU must order replacement components from different supply sources. Rarely is there any single activity with the mission to assure that the DSUs are continuously supplied with components to replace those used in repair. Diagnostic aids and test equipment updates usually are distributed to DSUs automatically by activities in the services' system/commodity commands; however, these can easily be misdirected, so the DSUs must always be certain they have the latest. These practices are not so difficult in a normal training environment where there is adequate time and good communications and the DSU is in familiar surroundings, utilizing a familiar resource network. But the lack of a proactive resourcing arrangement can have devastating consequences when the DSU is deployed into battle spaces, moving in unfamiliar territory away from its familiar resource network, and relying upon uncertain communications. Diagnostic aids and special tools can be lost, orders for replacement components can be lost in transmission, or the components can be misplaced or misdirected in the distribution process. Thus the risk is high that some DSUs will make poor diagnoses, or repairs will not be made because of the lack of replacement components, updated test equipment, tools, or technical procedures. The result is reduced operational availability of the weapons systems for which the DSU is responsible.

Operation Iraqi Freedom provided just the latest example of the failure to provide adequate resource support to DSUs in Army forces. After-action reports of the operation to capture Baghdad and other objectives indicated that not a single unit received replacement components during the three-week operation. Marine forces appeared to fare little better.

The reason for this state of affairs has much to do with the services' traditional ways of acquiring and sustaining systems. For many years the services have appointed program managers to manage the development, acquisition, and fielding of systems. The PM organizations contract with industry to produce and deliver the systems along with their initial sustainment resources to their service's operating force. During this period, the system operating organizations and DSUs experience the supportive, customer-focused attention of a PM organization with its support contractors committed to assuring that the customer organizations are provided the proper tools, diagnostic aids, ample technical assistance, and training and rapid response to replacement component needs. The PM organization and system contractor care deeply that the initial stages of fielding go well and go to great lengths to assure that problems are recognized and dealt with promptly. There is no question about who feels accountable for assisting the customer organizations in achieving the required operational availability of the newly fielded system. The PM and contractor team have many incentives to have the fielding go well.

Post-Fielding Dispersal of Accountability for Supporting DSUs

However, once the initial fielding phase had passed, problems discovered in operational evaluations had been corrected, and the system was fielded in "full rate production," the PM's responsibility for oversight of those fielded systems largely ended. The PM then turned to the product improvement phase of the life cycle, overseeing the development of (usually) capability improvements and their incorporation into the platforms. The responsibility, authority, and funding for sustainment support of DSUs and operating organizations shifted to the services' forces and systems/commodity commands. In the systems/commodity commands, responsibility, authority, and funding were further dispersed to component and functional managers. The DSUs and operating organizations lost the single point of contact for sustainment support they had experienced in initial fielding.

The forces commands, depending on the service, do have a system focus and responsibility, authority, and funding to sustain the systems, but they lack the PM organizations', the contractors', and the systems commands' technical expertise to identify causes of failure and other factors that affect availability. Their focus is necessarily restricted to meeting short-term operational readiness objectives and is limited to the part of the system fleet within their commands.

Within the systems/commodity commands, component managers look after the inventory of similar components of several systems. Managers assigned to different functional activities within the commands plan periodic depot maintenance, perform sustainment engineering on components within very limited resources, and manage technical data, special tools, and diagnostic aids for many systems. The component and functional managers are responsible for fulfilling the DSU's orders for the resources noted above. However, these managers are not even part of the same national-level organizations. For example, fulfilling orders for the major reparable components of a single system may be managed by several service national inventory control points and the consumable piece parts of the system managed by one or more of the DLA supply centers.

DLA's responsibility, authority, and funding for consumable repair parts build in organizational obstacles, because the services manage the technical data required for DLA to prepare the procurement package each time a new procurement is necessary. Thus it is no surprise that the administrative lead times necessary to buy the piece parts are so lengthy. In this dispersed, "stovepiped" process, the DSU must order consumable parts from the DLA source, reparables from the service inventory management organizations, and technical publications from another source, and must report a major repair (beyond its capability) to yet another.

The result in most cases in this traditional functional method of product support management is that *no single manager* performs the oversight, anticipatory, integrative role as a fleet manager.[1] The DSU knows only what happens to its part of the system fleet; it cannot sense trends in component failures or aberrant test set performance—in startling contrast to the situation during initial fielding, when the PM and system contractor would be attuned to watching for those trends, informing the DSUs, and finding remedies. Under the traditional management process, those symptoms can be uncovered only by the individual component or functional managers, sometimes long after the trends are evident. Since they must manage similar components of several kinds of systems, it is no wonder that these trends escape attention for so long. Where many organizations have authority over functions, accountability is a meaningless term. If all are "responsible," none is.

PM-Led Contractor Supported Systems—Clear Accountability

The deplorable state of sustainment accountability beyond the operating organization and DSU, as described above, applies for most fielded systems

---

[1] I will use the term "fleet" to refer to the population of individual systems, e.g., tanks, F-16s, cruisers. Fleet management is a commercial concept for sustaining and replacing individual equipment or platforms in the fleet.

but stands in stark contrast to the few that have had PM life-cycle management after fielding. All of those systems also have been contractor supported rather than subjected to post-fielding dispersal into stovepipes. They have benefited from a consistent single major source of sustainment support ever since their initial fielding. They were not subjected to the typical dispersal of responsibilities, authority, and funding. The PM's role has been to manage the contracted sustainment support—in addition to developing the product improvements. Frequently organic logistics activities participate as subcontractors to the integration contractor. Inevitably that role has required oversight of the health of the fleet and accountability, responsive as a very visible single supporter to the operating organizations and their DSUs.

Systems such as the Navy ballistic missiles—from Polaris through Trident—the Air Force F-117, and the Army mobile subscriber equipment (MSE) battlefield cellular communications system have been sustained through this PM management method for a decade or more. More recently, the Air Force's C-17 and the Navy's F/A-18E/F have joined the operational forces. These systems were among the most technically complex in their services at the time they were acquired and have served vitally important operational and support functions.

The result of these *fleet management* approaches has been responsive support of the necessary resources to DSUs and operating organizations, early recognition of trends in failure modes, continuous focus on improvement in all parts of the product support process—usually because of the contract incentives and the opportunity to sell product improvements. The contractors' motivation has been tied to system availability, with rewards and penalties to undergird the need for high availability. Likewise, the service PM is clearly accountable for providing the external resources required by the system operating organizations, assisting both the DSUs and the operating organizations to maintain a high level of availability, catching the inevitable systemic failures that arise through an adequately funded sustainment engineering effort, and developing and distributing the "fixes" to deal with the failures. In other words, the PM and the support contractor provide that necessary single point of integrated systems support outside the battle space. They are accountable for support to the operating and direct support maintenance organizations in maintaining the operational availability objective.

Barriers to Implementing PM Management of Fielded Systems

Yet, the transition of the fielded systems to fleet management is proving perilous. Not until May 2003 did the Secretary of Defense issue the change to DoD Directive 5000.1 (described in chapter 6) mandating PMs to assume system life-cycle support responsibilities for all systems, some eight years after directing it for new systems. The barriers to organization and process change found in both the government and the private sector are so much more difficult to surmount in government than in private industry. Because change inevitably involves uncertain consequences for the current organizations and workforces, they resist. Their jobs and very livelihoods are at stake. And they are all constituents of members of Congress, who must be seen by the civil service workforce, their families, and their communities as zealously protecting those jobs. Chapter 6 described some of the congressional efforts to protect constituents' jobs. That protection is attempted through the legislative process, notably the efforts of the "depot caucus" and like-minded senators to restrict DoD's ability to make changes seen to be threatening to their livelihoods.

Opposition to converting to PM management of fielded systems also has come from within the services over concern about "lots of PMs running around the battle space looking after only their systems." This concern seems to arise over the service theater support commanders' ability to integrate their efforts to achieve ready systems. This worry is a red herring. Certainly one would expect the PMs of most major systems to establish repair centers in the ISBs for critical components and to provide technical support to the DSUs. But the PM activities should be part of the service component logistic support organization. In that way, each PM's efforts can be integrated into the overall sustainment operation. For example, Army or Marine task forces may have fifteen to twenty major system PMs in support of their DSUs. The Army theater support command and Marine force service support group should ensure the integration of their PMs' efforts to provide parts and other resources to the DSUs and to retrieve component carcasses for repair. The PM activities would rely upon the support commands to arrange transport and to combine their filled orders with other commodities in the periodic log pacs transported to the task forces from the theater distribution centers.

Several attempts have been made to place fielded systems under PM-led contractor support to fix accountability and to save resources. Early in the 1990s, the Air Force's ICBM fleet was converted partially to contractor support. The major function withheld was the inventory management of components and repair parts. One supposes that the loss of "business" to the Air Logistics Centers (and the related surcharge funds) was too much for them to tolerate. Yet some expensive subsystems such as aircraft engines have been converted to contractor-depot partnership support within the Air Force and the Army. Also, within the Army, the PM for the product-improved self-propelled howitzer, "Paladin," made a convincing case for conversion to contractor support by the integrating contractor (with ample depot participation) who built and fielded the system. The loss of business again defeated the attempt. The last major effort was Boeing's proposal to assume the support responsibilities for the Apache helicopter, initially with the D-model product-improved version and then for the remainder of the fleet. The contractor guaranteed the Army significant savings, along with the assumption of risks by buying out the component inventory, a billion-dollar proposition. The issue was vigorously debated at the most senior levels of the Army leadership, eventually failing because of the impact of withdrawing so much of the Army's working capital fund revenue sources—the loss of business to the organic infrastructure.

Overcoming the Accountability Barriers

In spite of all the barriers to instituting effective PM life-cycle management for legacy systems, *the service secretaries can break the dam* by giving system PMs, through the program executive officers and service acquisition executives, the responsibility for fleet management and sustainment beyond the capabilities of the operating organizations and DSUs. Breaking the dam of opposition will require courage on the part of these leaders. They can be roundly criticized by members of Congress whose constituents feel threatened and even by some military leaders who fear such a major change and a loss of control, in spite of the improvements in effective sustainment that are available at lower cost.

Implementation of PM-led product support should begin with the services' major systems, both platforms and major subsystems such as aircraft engines. Transforming the major systems offers the opportunities for achieving significant improvements in both long-term availability and costs. The services should perform business case analyses to establish as good estimates as feasible of present sustainment effectiveness metrics and costs in order to establish a baseline. These analyses should evaluate the options for competitive sourcing, including both contractor and organic sources of the sustainment functions.

The product of the business case analysis should be an approved transition plan with the necessary funding, authorities, and implementation milestones to allow the PM to employ an integration contractor that will manage the provision of components, repair parts, and the other resources described earlier that are necessary to achieving system availability objectives.[2] Each legacy system likely will have a different plan, reflecting its particular situation. Most plans should include effective teaming with organic facilities and workforces, a practice that has been growing in subsystem support.

The management changes will need a transition period to work out inevitable kinks. For example, costs of the present management process, as the business case analyses will discover, are only imperfectly known, so the first phase of the transition should provide for a cost-plus-incentive-fee contract for a year or two, with emphasis on gathering the cost data during that period. After that period the contract could include more fixed-price elements, perhaps with an award-term incentive. There are useful lessons to be learned from the experiences of the PM management teams of the past decade or so. The transition plans should take advantage of those experiences.

Arranging funding is key to the success of implementation. As one wise observer of bureaucratic process has noted, "A plan without resources is an illusion." Accountability can work only if the PM commands the funding and authority necessary to support the DSUs' and operating organizations' efforts to achieve system availability objectives through the system contractor team in the same way that the C-17, the F/A-18E/F, and the older PM-managed systems have been supported. (We will cover the funding issue in more detail in chapter 8.)

Once these plans are in place, one will see accountability rise to the level normally seen in private sector management and in the few DoD systems already operating under the fleet management model. The section on

---

[2] Some observers suggest that a commodity/systems command can act as the integration contractor. That arrangement leaves the PM with ambiguous authority and in a situation little different from today's process. A contract with incentives and sanctions is simply not feasible with organic activities.

simplicity in management and funding in chapter 8 will propose a management process for the services to implement life-cycle management under the PMs' leadership.

CONTINUOUSLY SHARED KNOWLEDGE

The second critical principle for achieving product support effectiveness is *continuously shared knowledge*. We established early on the criticality of this logistics attribute and its centrality to both effective, timely support of the war-fighting elements and to minimization of the force's logistics footprint in the battle spaces.

Current State versus Commercial Practices

The current state of continuously shared knowledge in product support processes simply does not measure up to needs, although visibility of assets in stock and in transit is clearly improving. While commercial firms can utilize their own enterprise resource planning systems for asset visibility and the information resources of third-party logistics providers for in-transit visibility, the services are still far from that capability.

The principle of *continuously shared knowledge* for the military product support processes seeks to create actionable knowledge for all the participants in the processes and should be designed to aid in attaining system operational availability objectives. The process participants require the continuous feed of knowledge about asset status, the status of the "customers"— the system operating units and their DSUs, knowledge of barriers to the smooth flow of resources to customers, and campaign requirements.

Asset status translates in product support to knowledge about each individual system or platform, its particular configuration, including principal components with their serial numbers, and its maintenance record. That knowledge should be easily available to the operating organization, its DSU, the PM fleet manager, and the parts of the supply chain that can influence the readiness of the system. For example, the continuously shared knowledge process would record component removals and replacements by serial number so that the DSU and fleet manager could spot "bad actor" components that fail more often than they should.

Asset status should be rolled up by particular configurations (models) and in a fleet-wide form, accessible to all parts of the supply chain and to command and audit activities as well. While systems have long had individual log books in which operators and technicians record configuration changes, periodic services, major component replacements, and the like, those have been paper records with varying degrees of fidelity, as they are dependent upon frequently disappointing human input and are not visible to the supply chain. Major commercial operators of aircraft, truck, and other fleets have such asset status knowledge, some for a decade or more. While most condition data is still entered by technicians, it usually is entered only one time (touch screen on a personal data assistant [PDA] or notebook computer) and updates the fleet asset record.

Rather than rely on human input to monitor system health, commercial firms operating large complex systems have sought self-reporting, or "autonomic," means of reporting component performance deviations. By incorporating sensors into the major components, linking them into a data base, and transmitting out-of-tolerance data to an external monitoring system, these firms have been able to anticipate failures, usually in time to replace the component before failure. The number of sensors per system has increased over time as the technology has improved. For example, the Boeing 777 (a mid-'90s aircraft) has over two hundred sensors that continuously monitor the health of the many subsystems, notifying the operating airlines and Boeing's maintenance control center of performance deviations. Boeing and the airlines made the considerable investment in that health-monitoring system in order to warrant *98 percent availability-at-the-gate.*

Customer status knowledge would enable the supply chain participants to know the location (important for frequently moving operating and DSU organizations), the number and skill level of technicians (highlighting particularly critical skill shortages so that tech assistance can be dispatched), and even the times individual technicians require to complete maintenance tasks; with this information, training can be adjusted to improve diagnostic or repair skills. Status of DSU test equipment and other diagnostic aids should be part of the customer knowledge base so that the PM/integration contractor can replace or repair shortfalls in those resources. Knowledge of changing campaign requirements for employment of the combat and support systems would help in assessing the need for additional maintenance resources or system replacements.

Operation Iraqi Freedom Experience

Emerging evidence from Army experience during Operation Iraqi Freedom in the spring of 2003 illustrates the glaring differences between commercial firms' use of information technology for product support knowledge and what the Army was able to provide to its major combat unit engaged in the campaign. Reports indicated that although there were pre-positioned components for the major combat and support systems in Kuwait, the order fulfillment process didn't work. DSUs and operating units had only what they carried with them on the 325-mile, three-week drive to Baghdad and what they could cannibalize from inoperable systems. Reports also indicated that several units had such little faith in the order fulfillment process that they left their ordering computers (both unit-level logistics systems [ULLS] in the operating units and standard Army retail supply systems [SARSS] in the DSUs) in Kuwait. There are reports that even those units that brought the computers could not use them for lack of communications. The communications means supporting ULLS and SARSS in the Army's combat divisions relies nearly completely on terrestrial systems, which could not be established while the units were moving continuously. In contrast, medical units in the divisions used tactical satellite or the Iridium satellite to order aero-medical evacuation and medical supplies (frequently transported on the evacuation aircraft).

The conclusions of an Army study group looking into the situation included the following:[3]

> ➤ heroic efforts by CSS soldiers and leaders
> ➤ "just in time" logistics—wasn't
> ➤ no maneuver brigade received any Class IX; CS/CSS similar
> ➤ cannibalization only parts source in Iraq
> ➤ poor in-transit visibility; units sent parties out to forage for parts/supplies

The DODAAC Problem

A principal reason for the loss of visibility is the continued existence of a major "self-inflicted wound" even after repeated "lessons learned" reports from operations as far back as Vietnam. One culprit is the method of as-

---

[3] Author(s) unknown. Several independent sources have verified these perceptions/conclusions.

signing DODAACs. Normally each battalion, squadron, or ship and separate smaller unit that independently reports its own logistics status, holds its own equipment on property records, and is authorized to use the supply request system is assigned a separate DODAAC. The DODAAC is used for both supply and financial management. There is a central DODAAC registry in each service, which records the assignment of a particular DODAAC to an organization, using the service's means of identifying its organizations, e.g., the Army's unit identification code (UIC). The registry also records the location of the DODAAC of the organization's supporting DSU.Thus an item that fills an order from a unit assigned the DODAAC can be sent to the proper DSU for delivery to that unit. Therefore deploying units and their DSUs must notify the central registry of the new location to which they are deploying so that material release orders will reflect the deployed location, and CONUS and theater distribution centers can ship to it.

The "wound" occurs when units do not report the location change, so that the item is shipped to the home station of the unit even though it has deployed. The location change process requires human intervention in this automated central registry. Even if changes are submitted, they may not alter the routing of supplies until after deployment because of the time it takes for the registry to record the changes. Also, apparently many units do not submit the changes until after they have deployed, so that anything they ordered prior to deployment has to be forwarded from their previous station— which may never happen. Another common problem occurs when only parts of battalions, squadrons, or separate companies deploy as part of tailored task organizations with support provided by a different DSU than the one providing home station support. In this case, the new task organization must secure a new DODAAC—and that seems to be a lengthy process.

This administrative lead time is completely incompatible with 21st-century campaign planning's need to adjust task organizations. This process practically guarantees that organizations will have great difficulty receiving repair parts and other individually ordered supplies and equipment—just as the organizations in Operation Iraqi Freedom have experienced. And there were multiple Army and Marine units that deployed without a DODAAC of any kind. Erroneous DODAAC information led to problems that were not easily corrected. Canceling and/or reinstating thousands of requisitions that have already been shipped elsewhere, although possible, was frequently too little, too late.

These problems are not of recent vintage. They have existed for years, at least from Vietnam days. Yet, because the DODAAC process seems to be regarded as "administrivia," its dysfunctional impacts tend to be quickly forgotten in the so-called lessons-learned process that follows each of the nation's conflicts. The consequences of this "lesson forgotten" from the many conflicts of the 1990s was apparent in Iraq. The land forces organizations'—both customer units and DSUs—response to this flawed system was to take with them as many parts as they could manage, which in the future could compromise the goal of minimizing the amount of accompanying supplies in order to provide for as much combat power as possible. The customer units and DSUs would bring the traditional "iron mountain" if they could, because of their distrust of the resupply system.

Clearly the DODAAC issue is one that cries out for early resolution. The need for rapid deployment and the modularization of battalions, squadrons, and other units is a fact of life in 21st-century campaigns. All the services are task-forcing: the Air Force's AEFs are composed of parts of squadrons, depending on their missions. Army combat and support battalions frequently are split, with their line companies placed under task force headquarters, often with different supporting DSUs than their home station alignment. Similar situations exist for Navy construction battalions and Marine air-ground task forces. DoD can no longer afford the anachronism of the present DODAAC arrangement if it expects to achieve the level of continuously shared knowledge critical to 21st-century campaign success.

Impact of Iraqi Freedom Knowledge Vacuum

Knowledge of replacement component and technical assistance requirements, asset status, and customer status was not available to the land forces support organizations outside the operating unit–DSU battle spaces. There was a knowledge "vacuum." Thus all the resources of the supply chain supporting DSUs could not be brought to bear because of the abysmal communication and information-handling systems these otherwise potent combat forces possess.

The consequence of the lack of a supply of replacement components in the land forces, to no one's surprise, was a serious deterioration of the operational availability rate of both combat and support systems by the end of the three-week drive—to a reported level of about 50 percent. But even this data point is suspect because of the difficulty in obtaining reports on operational availability. One example of the recognition—at long last—of the effect of the communications inadequacies was evident in an interview that *Sea Power* magazine held with Gen. Michael Hagee, commandant of the Marine Corps. *Sea Power* asked, "In what way did Operation Iraqi Freedom highlight supply system challenges?" Gen. Hagee replied:

> *"We need to work on the ability to get supplies quickly to a requesting unit. We did a good job during Operation Iraqi Freedom; we never ran out of ammunition and fuel. But we could do a whole lot better. We moved at unbelievable speed compared with past operations. We also moved units around the battlefield. Our system, the communications infrastructure, was not set up to quickly identify where the requesting unit had gone so that the parts could get to the right location. We are going to work on that.[4]"*

The one exception to this grim picture was the movements tracking system (MTS), a militarized commercial system relying on satellite communications to communicate with transport units in convoy operations. It was a major facilitator of the distribution of combat support commodities such as ammunition and fuel and of vital troop support supplies of food and water. MTS provided an effective command and control capability to manage the numerous distribution convoys on the road nets between the Kuwait base and the forces.

There is no evidence that either the Navy or the Air Force had such difficulties, but, of course, neither had the communications challenges experienced by the Army and Marine land forces. What would have been the situation in the land forces if the campaign had not been so successful and ended so quickly? Given the difficulties in maintaining system readiness, would there have been a serious deterioration in combat power had the campaign required another three weeks? Even if the question is unanswerable, the Operation Iraqi Freedom story does point to the great need for DoD to invest in continuously shared knowledge processes if the combatant forces are to maintain combat effectiveness for the duration of future campaigns.

---

[4] Marine Corps Commandant, Gen. Michael Hagee, interview, "Projecting Power Faster, Better," *Sea Power*, November 2003, p. 27.

A 21st-Century Model

Probably the boldest effort to design a product support knowledge approach is being undertaken for the Joint Strike Fighter. Although it probably will not be operational before 2010, its design includes double or triple the sensors found on the Boeing 777 when it was put into service. It will become the model of an autonomic health-monitoring system. Its example is being followed in the *Virginia* class of new submarines, the CVNX carrier, and the Army's Future Combat system. The challenge is to bring what autonomic monitoring is possible technologically and affordably to presently fielded systems so they can substantially improve their *availability-at-the-gate* mission readiness. An even greater challenge is to integrate this health-monitoring system into a supply chain–wide continuously shared knowledge process.

Process Architecture

This knowledge process also should allow system "health" records to be visible, with appropriate need-to-know safeguards, so that such deviations from the readiness standard as high removal rates of components, long customer wait times for parts, and longer-than-standard diagnosis and repair times—all characteristics that reduce system availability—can be readily seen both for the individual system and for all or portions of the system fleet. Such a process has been partially designed and tested for the Army's CH-47D cargo helicopter as the lead system. An important part of the design has been applied successfully to one of the Army's heavy truck models.

Rapid Diagnosis and Automatic Component Ordering

As the battle space scenario of chapter 5 illustrated, a major product support objective is the rapid diagnosis of each potential or actual system failure in order to restore it to operation as quickly as possible. Thus, the knowledge process should highlight the health record change made by the system's health-monitoring process or the technician to signal the anticipated or actual fault and the diagnostic results (including expected time to repair) and automatically order any necessary replacement components. If replacement components are not available at the DSU, the knowledge process records the order number and receives and displays status reports of the progress toward providing that replacement component to the DSU, the owning unit, the system's ISB repair center, and its CONUS control center.

If the component is normally stocked at the DSU, the knowledge process linking the system supply chain elements tracks the DSU's component stockage status and previously would have ordered the replacement component automatically from the closest source in order to restore the approved stockage level. The knowledge process would have automatically upgraded the priority of the stockage replenishment order when the system failure generated the new order in our example. If the DSU had the replacement component in its stock, its issue would trigger the automatic demand for back fill—much like commercial cash register sales trigger the back-fill order for products.

Continuously Shared Status Reporting

The knowledge system would then record closure on that fault when the replacement component was installed and tested. Some of these events should be automatically reported into the operational chain since the combat power represented by the system requiring repair would not be available until the component replacement is completed. That platform would be carried as "not ready," but the knowledge process would carry also a projected time when the system would become "ready," a projection that could be automatically updated in both the supply chain and the operational chain as the replacement events occurred—or were delayed. Therefore, all those who need to know, i.e., the system's crew/operator, the supporting DSU that is managing the component replacement action, the operating organization and its parent organization(s), and the PM's system repair center in the ISB and CONUS management activity, would be able to track progress on the corrective action and intervene to influence the events, if necessary, until availability was restored. In addition, the PM and integration contractor would provide for automatic asset visibility to major component suppliers (for their own components) so they would know the real-time status of the inventory of the components they supply and thus know when to increase (or decrease) production to meet demands. The suppliers' contracts can reflect this knowledge, requiring them to maintain certain levels of shelf stockage, but allowing them to use their own production algorithms to meet the stockage requirements. Likewise, the diagnostics data would allow continuous root cause analysis and would thus improve the ability to propose or make reliability-enhancing changes to the component and/or to send technicians to repair centers and DSUs to assist them in diagnosing system failures and restoring availability.

The DSU Node in Continuously Shared Knowledge

The performance of DSU technicians is critical to achieving system availability targets. Too often the services have expected much of them while failing to provide essential tools. They are the "first responders" to signals of actual or potential system failure, and they provide the critical first diagnosis. The services must recognize that these "first responders" must have readily available all the necessary technical information about the particular "tail number" of the system they support as well as diagnosis procedures, special tools required, and the parts ordering, test set, and calibration instructions. And they need that information as they begin to work on the system. If their work is to be productive, e.g., making an accurate first diagnosis, correctly ordering the right parts, and using the correct repair procedure so that minimum available time is lost, they must be equipped with the proper knowledge tools. Commercial firms facing the same availability pressures have exploited knowledge technology—both software and hardware—to equip their technicians to achieve the same high productivity standards that DSUs require.

Equipping DSUs for Knowledge Sharing

An example: FedEx has equipped its aircraft technicians with "wearable computers" with wireless communication links to its maintenance control center at its principal hub in Memphis, Tennessee. In the FedEx system, aircraft deliver cargo from their outlying terminals, e.g., Newark and Washington-Dulles, to "hub-sortation" centers at night and then pick up loads to go to outlying terminals within several hours. The time allowed for the aircraft technicians at the hubs to check on trouble reports and to do their own required inspections is very short. Yet aircraft safety demands thoroughness in maintenance checks. There is the efficiency factor as well. FedEx naturally wants to staff the technician activity with no more people than it needs, so each technician's time—and the technical accuracy of the technician's work—is valuable. The wearable computer with a wireless communication link to the hub's maintenance control center allows the technician to receive trouble reports from the flight crew and any relevant maintenance history, as well as the maintenance check procedures for that type aircraft, as he/she travels along the flight line to the aircraft. If in the course of diagnosis a part must be replaced before the aircraft can fly, the technician can check its availability in the parts center and, if available, can have it delivered planeside. Repairs not required for flight safety can be reported, and the maintenance center can schedule them at an appropriate time, along with parts delivery and technician assignment—all with the center's own continuously shared knowledge system.

The wearable computer further allows the technician hands-free conduct of maintenance checks. Voice recognition software further enhances the hands-free feature. Such a system would have the same payoff for all DSU technicians, not only for aircraft support. AEF maintenance elements could adopt nearly the same system as FedEx employs on each of their operating bases. Land force DSUs could use this technology with satellite-enabled wireless links even when the technicians' "contact teams" are several kilometers removed from their maintenance control locations. Navy technicians could use wearables with a vessel's wireless local area network as they become even more ubiquitous. The value of such a capability is that it equips the "first responder" technician with a tool that not only enables the technician to do his/her job right the first time but also provides accurate timely data for the knowledge system to be shared with all the affected parties, as described above. Whether wearable computers are the best solution for all maintenance first responders in need of an accessible knowledge tool can be determined for each system. As their price comes down with increasing volume of purchases, it is hard to argue against their utility, as compared with carrying a laptop.

The land force and AEF DSUs and the naval vessels should combine the technician's wearable or other computer with satellite communications that would link the technician's orders for components and other resources to the DSU's maintenance control center, parts supply activity, and the other nodes in the supply chain of the system the technician supports. In that way each of the system's supply chain nodes would gain information about the resource needs of its principal customer, the DSU.

Lack of communications was a major cause of the failure of the land forces' order-management process during Operation Iraqi Freedom. While the medical elements of the DSUs used Iridium satellite terminals to call for medical evacuation (and replenishment supply) support, the maintenance elements could use only terrestrial means, which failed because of the long distances between the ISB and the DSUs with the fast moving forces. Satellite communication is the only alternative means of supporting widely dispersed and mobile DSUs. Without it, the combat forces pay the price of reduced availability that was paid during the latter stage of the drive to Baghdad. Terrestrial communications will work only as an exception because of the dispersed nature of the land forces' battle space, AEF base location, and naval expeditionary task forces.

The major stumbling block in achieving this capability is likely to be the "communications expert" community, if past experience is any guide. They have long protested that there is insufficient bandwidth to support the kinds of logistics information transmissions implied by the process described above. And they have protested that the proposed knowledge architecture would require encrypting transmissions so as not to compromise the security of operational campaigns, and that so much encrypting would be unaffordable. However, proper use of "store-and-forward," database update and data compression techniques should minimize bandwidth demand. Commercial firms of all sizes now manage their supply chains with the same knowledge processes described. The need for massive encrypting of information also is a red herring. With the exception of the links to the operational chain that carry system availability knowledge, the other data would be practicably unintelligible to an enemy, even if it could be intercepted.

It should be noted that Army logisticians have had some success in making the case for satellite communications since the conclusion of major combat operations, and they are deploying it to the DSUs in Iraq. They had failed to convince the "communications experts" or the senior commanders before the operations began, with the unfortunate consequences noted earlier.

Value of Supplier-in-the-Loop: Reaction to System Failure— A Vignette

The proposed knowledge architecture, as outlined above, would link the CONUS sources, the vendors, with the theater nodes, so that failures of components reported by the DSU would be communicated to the components' vendors so that they could decide when to ship replacements and when to initiate new production lots, and could compile failure mode data for later improvements in the components or in failure diagnoses and repair procedures.

A vignette from the Gulf War will illustrate the value of knowledge sent early to the supplier. Early in Operation Desert Shield (October 1990), during the buildup of forces in Saudi Arabia, the U.S. Army deployed two Patriot anti-aircraft missile brigades from Germany. Those were the earliest Patriot systems acquired, having been fielded in 1986 and 1987. Soon after their deployment to Saudi Arabia, they began to experience failures in power generation, which made whole firing batteries inoperative. The power generation system, a government-furnished component of each missile battery, had a turbine engine to drive the generator. The Army had bought that particular turbine engine from one well-known turbine manufacturer only for the first set of Patriot systems and then had re-competed and awarded the next quantity to another firm. There was no current supplier to provide that particular model engine, nor had the Army engaged the original engine manufacturer to perform life-cycle support. Rather, support was provided by the DoD depot system and the Army/DLA commodity commands. It was believed that Tooele Army Depot could handle the major repair/overhaul of the engines and that Cherry Point Naval Air Depot could repair several of the key turbine components.

The problem arose when neither Tooele nor Cherry Point could fix the engine problems, and failures kept occurring in the harsh desert environment. The concerns about an inoperative anti-aircraft and missile defense system rose further as more forces poured into Saudi Arabia. The problems were finally resolved when the CEO of the original supplier was called and immediately dispatched the engine's chief engineer first to Cherry Point, then to Tooele Army Depot, to instruct both sets of technicians on repair procedures. The chief engineer then took a team of his technicians to Saudi Arabia to check each engine and to improve the diagnosis, preventive maintenance, and repair processes.

How much simpler would correcting the problems have been had the supplier been made aware of the failures in the beginning by a deployed field service technician, who also would have been able to anticipate the environment-caused problems—perhaps with the help of the supplier's engineers in CONUS—avoiding the inoperable engines (and the inoperative missile batteries). Continuously shared knowledge of the first indications of engine failures certainly would have brought immediate technical help from the supplier rather than a delayed response to the sequential passing on of partially understood problem descriptions—information that took weeks to get to the supplier. In retrospect, it is fortunate that the Iraqis did not launch their missiles into Saudi Arabia when these batteries were inoperative. Certainly neither the CENTCOM commander, the President, nor the Saudi king would have understood why the affected Patriot batteries could not have responded.

Supplier-in-the-Loop: Anticipated Failures—Vignette 2

At about the same time, a potential environment-caused major system failure to the UH-60 helicopter was averted. This case points up the value of continuously shared knowledge when it is used to anticipate, and make changes to avoid, system failures caused by environmental or other conditions. When the deployment was ordered in August 1990, Sikorsky (the UH-60's manufacturer) and the UH-60 PM established an operations center at the Sikorsky plant to collect and analyze information about the effects of the hot, dry, blowing sand environment. Sikorsky was able to access a large store of knowledge about system changes that would be necessary to cope with the environment since it had built a number of commercial UH-60 derivatives for the Saudis and had accumulated a vast storehouse of experience and lessons learned. Even though Sikorsky and the UH-60 PM had access to the same information technology as did other system manufacturers and PMs, they had established an especially strong cooperative relationship throughout the ongoing UH-60 production, fielding, and interim product support processes. The deploying organizations became part of this network as soon as their deployment orders were announced. And Sikorsky field service technicians deployed with them, maintained regular contact with the operations center, and were continually updated by the operations center as to the required system modifications or changes to maintenance practices. That continuously shared knowledge existed throughout the campaign and influenced the manufacture, product improvement, and support of subsequent aircraft.

Lessons Learned

Both vignettes illustrate the critical need to tie together not only the operational and direct support players in the system availability venture but also the product support technical and management players, especially the most knowledgeable technical player, the system contractor (e.g., Sikorsky for the UH-60 and Allison Gas Turbine, the original turbine engine supplier, for the Patriot). The UH-60 problems were anticipated because of the knowledge continuously shared by operational and product support players. The turbine engine problem was not anticipated nor easily remedied because the most knowledgeable technical player was not a sharer of the knowledge about the failures and maintenance difficulties. Given the increasing technical sophistication of defense systems, the services have no choice but to keep their system contractors well positioned in the continuously shared knowledge loop for the entire life cycle of the systems they produce. The nation should never again risk the potential disasters of system failure that the Patriot system faced in the fall of 1990. The DoD management decision to place PMs in charge of the total life-cycle support of systems can facilitate the structuring and maintenance of the continuously shared knowledge network—a "community of practice" in the lexicon of knowledge management.

MAXIMIZED COMMERCIAL CONTRACTING OF PRODUCT SUPPORT OUTSIDE THE BATTLE SPACES

Background of Organic Product Support Outside the Battle Spaces

This principle raises more controversy than all the other aspects of the product support process because satisfying it requires an immense cultural change on the part of the services, the traditional CONUS logistics workforces, and their elected representatives in the Congress. Historically, the services have operated their own product support processes as organic activities with little contractor support. From the earliest days of the Republic, naval shipyards both built and repaired vessels. The Army's arsenals manufactured and repaired cannon—and still do so. When aircraft were introduced, the air arms of the Army and Navy established repair depots; and with the advent of tanks, trucks, and the like, they created more such industrial facilities, until by the end of World War II there was an elaborate organic defense industrial base employing several hundred thousand military personnel and civil servants. Several generations of the same family might have been employed at naval shipyards beginning in the 1700s, and more recently at Army, Air Force, and Naval Air Depots. These defense establishments have often been the most important job sources in their communities. Even in the early

21st century, the Warner Robins Air Logistics Center near Atlanta employs over twenty-six thousand people.

Senators and representatives are always interested in bringing jobs to their constituents, the more highly paid the better, for the economic well-being of the state or district. Thus they are vitally interested in preserving federal jobs and installations in their states and districts because, unlike their relationship with private sector employers, they do have leverage with the DoD. They can support or withdraw support for other defense programs. A not-so-long-ago example concerned one congressman's threat to derail a major service program if the local depot appeared on a base closure list. (The depot did, but rather than attempt to carry out his threat he chose to run for governor—unsuccessfully it turned out.) DoD leaders take the congressional protective relationships seriously because they understand the influence a particular legislator might have.

And when groups of congressmen who have the organic depots and shipyards (or their workers) in their districts come together, they represent an even more effective influence on service and DoD programs. Since they have deep constituent interests, their legislative initiatives or opposition to DoD proposals can carry the day, in both houses of the Congress. In fact, the "depot caucus"—a bipartisan group who are mostly members of the Subcommittee on Readiness of the House Armed Services Committee—has been one of the most effective of the many caucuses in the Congress. There are no members of Congress more zealous in protecting their constituents' current employment and in making efforts to add to the facilities in their districts. The addition of facilities or programs results in both new program-related jobs and construction work for local contractors and their employees. While employment at the defense depots and shipyards is the primary focus of the depot caucus, its members also represent constituents who work at the system and commodity commands.

Therefore, efforts to strengthen industry's role in life-cycle support conflict with the depot caucus members' efforts to preserve and enhance defense employment. No matter how many benefits—such as improved quality of support or cost reductions—are anticipated by the Defense Department as a result of enlarging the industry role in product support, the political barriers must be dealt with. Since the early '90s, DoD has attempted to draw down the organic acquisition and logistics workforce to a size appropriate to the significant reduction in forces that occurred following the Cold War.

Some depot and other logistics activities were closed in the 1988, 1991, and 1995 base closure processes.

Yet many DoD advisory panels have recommended that DoD establish a policy of "contracting logistics support" for each weapon system, major subsystem, and support system.[5] The exception would be for support inside the battle spaces, which military DSUs would provide since the contractor technicians would normally be at risk of hostile action. The advisory panels repeatedly recommended that outside the battle space—ISBs and CONUS or forward bases—contractors should perform the product support tasks that we have discussed earlier in this chapter, under the management oversight of the system program managers.

Four Reasons for Contractor Product Support

The common rationale for the advisory panels' recommendations was a combination of the following—all having to do with extending industry's role in system development and improvement to a major role in system support. The benefits, seen already in those few systems following the fleet management model, are *better quality support delivered* to DSUs and owning organizations *more quickly at less overall cost.* There are four principal reasons for these recommendations: system technical knowledge, integration of product improvement, accountability, and workforce flexibility.

System Technical Knowledge

First, the range and depth of technical knowledge required for increasingly complex weapons systems and their subsystems is to be found in the firms and their subcontractors that build the systems. These firms can do a far better job than the DoD in attracting the necessary technical talent. Better pay and greater technical challenges all play a role. Because of civil service

---

[5] Three such panels were especially important:

> ➤ The Defense Science Board (DSB) 1996 Summer Study, *Achieving an Innovative Support Structure for 21st Century Military Superiority: Higher Performance at Lower Costs,* September 1996
> ➤ Report of the Defense Science Board Acquisition Workforce Sub-Panel of the Defense Acquisition Reform Task Force, *On Defense Reform,* March 1998
> ➤ Presentation of the Panel on Commercialization in the U.S. Defense Establishment, June 1999

rules, attracting enough talented people into positions in the civil service has proven extremely difficult. For example, civil service employment was reduced (as was military strength) in the post–Cold War drawdown. Where "reduction in force" procedures were followed (in accordance with the law) as in the cases of the base closures and the position reductions at the services' logistics commands, the result was too often to eliminate the "last hired," with little or no regard for technical skill. And the few new positions have been filled through the seniority-based "bumping" rules or DoD's "priority placement program" for displaced employees, again with little or no regard for technical qualifications. Such a policy discourages those technically skilled people who might want to work in DoD since successive administrations have continued the workforce reductions. The result is a civil service workforce averaging around fifty years of age, only nearing retirement and with little stomach for the necessary training to update or learn new skills. There are, of course, exceptions to this broad characterization. They are the dedicated, competent few whom the services have had to deploy repeatedly to support systems in the many post–Cold War operations.

Integration of Product Improvement

Second, industry's role in life-cycle sustainment would also contribute to better integration of product improvement with product support. Sustainment technicians and engineers would be motivated by their firms (through bonuses and salary adjustments among other incentives) to search for product and process improvements that could improve performance and/or reduce operating and support costs—typical incentives for fleet management contractors seeking to increase revenues and profits. Until civil service reforms are implemented, such incentives can't be offered to the government workforce. Of course, the opportunities for product and process improvements need to go through the PM and the PM's supporting staff's analytical and resourcing reviews to ensure that they make positive and affordable contributions to the system's effectiveness and cost.

Accountability

A third reason for the advisory panels' recommendations for contractor logistics support was the desire to fix accountability for providing product support resources to the DSUs and their owning-unit customers. Since the services' organizational arrangements allocated different support functions to separate organizations, there is no accountability for the performance of a system fleet until one reaches a three- or four-star general or flag officer or even the service secretary. No single individual responsible for the health of the system fleet could speak to the operating forces customers in the same way that a Boeing or Caterpillar PM could speak to airline or construction company customers. Part of the solution has been for DoD to direct the services to place a PM in charge of life-cycle (product) support in addition to responsibilities for acquisition and product improvement. But PMs have deliberately limited staffs, so who can integrate the multiple functions discussed above? There is no obvious service organization. The existing functionally organized logistics organizations are not structured to do so, and one doubts that the bureaucracy's culture and existing civil service rules would give a PM sufficient personnel management authority to hold such an organization accountable for "better-cheaper-faster" results. But defense firms are used to doing project management in developing and producing the systems. The advisory panels recognized—as has DoD—that industry management structures, relatively unfettered by legislation and regulation, are adept at pulling together the talent necessary to manage the disparate product support functions either from within their own organizations or through subcontractors. In the system acquisition process, there is normally a system "integrator" who is responsible for delivering the complete operating system to the service force customers. The integration contractor executes these tasks through a variety of subcontractors and groups within its own firm. The same contracting arrangement is at work in the systems already being supported by contractors.

A contract between the PM and the integration contractor can be tailored to whatever the situation requires. It would include incentives to meet responsiveness objectives, e.g., customer wait time for parts, repair-cycle time objectives, in fact all of the process metrics essential to providing operating forces the support they need to achieve their system availability objectives. It has also been recognized that the service's organic functional activities, such as depots and shipyards, can play a significant role as subcontractors, enabling the POM and the integration contractor to make use of DoD-owned assets such as dry docks or engine test facilities. This arrangement can be attractive to the integration contractor when the depot capabilities provide a best-value opportunity such as a skilled workforce, lower labor rates, and the indemnification for environmental issues that comes from work on a government installation. This depot partnering strategy helps ameliorate the political difficulties of implementing contractor logistics support.

Workforce Flexibility

A fourth reason for the advisory panels' advocacy of contractor logistics support was to allow DoD more flexibility in sizing the workforce to meet changing needs. The panels recognized the great difficulty in shrinking jobs for a system being retired while increasing staffing for another with different skill requirements, perhaps in a different place. One example from the 1990s illustrates the point. There was a major reduction in the Navy's submarine fleet, and thus in its requirement for shipyard support. At the same time new aircraft were entering the naval aviation force, requiring skills that could not be met by shipyard employees. Even though there were several submarine shipyard closings during the period, the Navy was still left with large excess capacity and could not use the funds from eliminating that excess in order to staff the aviation requirements. It is the normal practice in industry that as programs contract, firms eliminate jobs, and those former employees move to new jobs, usually with other firms and frequently at new locations—a strength of the U.S. economy. Government workers only rarely do so, and then only at great delay and expense.

Those four reasons for recommending contractor logistics support outside the battle spaces provided ample reason for the DoD to move more vigorously toward the model that features an integration contractor who then employs a variety of subcontractors, including government depots and, perhaps, other service or DLA functional activities, to provide product support resources under the PM's authority. It may be easier to start off a newly fielded system with contractor support; it is far more difficult to alter the entrenched arrangements for supporting the 250 or so legacy systems, although the advisory panels foresaw more effective support and estimated cost savings on the order of $10–$20 billion a year. Business case analyses for specific systems are needed to pin down the benefits—including cost savings—and costs of adopting contractor logistics support in order to establish a baseline for measuring both performance and costs of their life cycle sustainment programs. They should be the basis for working out the contract metrics and incentives to assure effective support to the DSUs and system-owning organizations.

The problem of convincing legislators and other skeptics is that until DoD converts several presently fielded systems to contractor support, we will only see estimates, not comparative data. There are hard data, however, supporting the decisions to contract for the support resources for new systems such as the B-2 and the C-17. In these cases, the Air Force faced a several hundred million dollar investment for depot facilities and hiring and training the workforces in order to adopt an organic support approach. The B-2, with over half of its depot maintenance requirement in software support, was a particular challenge. The system contractors in both cases already had both facilities and trained workforces and required little or none of that investment.

Revival of the Historical Preference for Private Sector Performance

In this contentious area of contracting, we should keep in mind the basic philosophy of the relationship between the private and public sectors in this Republic. Historically, we Americans have limited the reach of the public sector in our society to those activities that relate to governance—such as defense, law enforcement, and revenue collection—and education. Even though government has funded road building and other major infrastructure construction such as rural electric power and airports and seaports, it has contracted with the private sector or local authorities to build, operate, and maintain them. Generally, where the private sector would invest in economic activity, our political process has encouraged it, realizing the societal benefits of free economic activity. Thus government, generally, has chosen not to compete with the private sector. These policies have been articulated in executive orders and other directives dating back to the Eisenhower administration. One of the clearest descriptions of the policy is found in Office of Management and Budget Circular A-76.[6]

The preference for private sector performance of those government-owned activities has been resisted most strongly when activities such as shipyards, factories, and other major employment centers were created under government control. The rationale for their creation was a conclusion by political leadership at the time that they were "inherently governmental"— a necessary extension of the Navy's need for ships and their maintenance

---

[6] Office of Management and Budget, *Circular No. A-76*, May 29, 2003, para. 4, p. 1.

(shipyards) or the Army's need for guns, ammunition, and combat vehicles (arsenals). Thus, throughout World War II these industrial activities were thought to be a necessary part of a service's functions. But World War II demonstrated that the better source of innovation and production expertise lay in U.S. industry, which mobilized quickly and took over the lion's share of defense production.

Slow Cultural Change

But cultures change only slowly. Thus over fifty years later, DoD still operates arsenals that build parts of guns—and manufacture other parts for DLA. Naval shipyards no longer build vessels, but they share overhaul and repair with a vigorous private shipyard industry. Maintenance depots of all three services continue to do overhauls and component repair but increasingly share that work with defense industry. Thus, the advocates of government's continuing performance of these activities in competition with industry have had to resort to dubious rationales such as the need to maintain a "core" capability for this product support work (having long since given up on production) in government-owned facilities and performed by the federal government workforce.[7]

All parties realize that there is no persuasive logic to the rationale. Industry builds virtually all and maintains some of the most critical weapons systems in our armed forces. Thus the argument that these core systems cannot be trusted to defense industry is only a thin cover for preserving jobs in those DoD employment centers that remain. Even the most avid legislator- advocate of private enterprise falls in line with those arguing to preserve these employment centers—if such a center or a number of its federal employees are located in the legislator's congressional district or state. A cynic might call such core-activity claims mere job protection. It is hard to argue otherwise.

Conversion of Product Support Activities to Contract Performance

The gradual evolution of these organic defense industrial activities seems bound to continue no matter which political party wins the presidency or

---

[7] There remains a critical requirement that the services have in their civil service and military workforces the technical skills to develop requirements and performance specifications for system support and to oversee the contractors—all clearly "inherently government" functions.

controls the Congress—although the party less beholden to the public employee unions certainly has more freedom to dispose of or outsource them. And perhaps that is the only politically acceptable way to complete this now half-century-old transformation: the combination of consolidation and closure of some of those activities that have glaring excess capacity, continued natural attrition of the aging workforce with only limited hiring, and the more recent adoption of industry partnering may help hasten the transformation.

There is evidence that this evolution is under way. In the past several years all the services have made progressively more arrangements for industry and depot partnering. One recent example is the large partnering contract awarded to Sikorsky to support Corpus Christi Army Depot for critical component overhaul and repair parts. GE engineers team with that depot for engine overhauls, as well.

Another step in that evolution would be to transfer all of the facilities that house the organic maintenance depots and shipyards to local development authorities in their states and allow the services to lease those portions of the sites where government or government-contractor-operated activities are still necessary. This action should be part of the 2005 base closure commission's recommendation. The local authorities can then put the remaining excess facilities on their tax rolls. Such a step would reduce the current cost of upkeep of excess facilities and present an opportunity for business case analyses to determine the most effective and efficient combination of contractor and government support. DoD's analysis of what parts of these organic facilities to retain can follow the base closure decisions to allow joint community-DoD planning.

The DoD overhaul and repair activities are not the only organizations in the supply chain in need of transformation. As we have noted before, the whole set of service- and DLA-operated product support activities are undergoing this needed transformation. The budget-driven attrition of employees has been forcing the leaders and managers in system and commodity commands to bring in contractor staff to help the organic staff accomplish the product support workloads. Both DLA and the Army are engaged in major efforts to outsource the modernization and operation of their inventory management information systems for as long as they may be needed. Also several Army system commands have turned over most life-cycle product support activities for some low-density systems to consortia of contractors.

Transformation of Component and Consumable Repair Parts Management

DLA has been attempting to contract for the inventory management of large segments of its nearly 4 million consumable repair parts since the mid 1990s. While it has been hugely successful in contracting for the commercial items that it supplies, e.g., pharmaceuticals, clothing, and food, in "prime vendor" programs, unique defense repair parts with no commercial use pose a greater, and perhaps insurmountable, challenge. DLA's difficulty simply points up the huge problem of managing these individual parts of systems as some sort of commodity, like fasteners or housekeeping supplies. They are unique parts of systems, only occasionally interchangeable between systems. Better to manage them in an integrated way with the larger components or assemblies of which they are part to ensure that the performance of the component does not suffer from a piece part that is not interchangeable with the part it replaces. This can be a particularly difficult problem with consumable circuit boards managed by DLA and procured from a new supplier. Compatibility of form, fit, and function are subject to acceptance testing, but test failures and re-procurement or rework prolong the lead time, exacerbating any backlogs that may exist.

The transformation of product support to the fleet management model would pull the inventory management of those unique piece parts from DLA supply centers and of the reparable components from the service ICPs, and assign it to the fleet manager, along with the configuration management, component repair, sustainment engineering, overhaul, test equipment, technical data, and publications functions. That transformation would allow the services' logistics commands to change roles from directly managing those inventories and functions to supporting the PMs' management of fleet product support, performing such "inherently" government-unique tasks as programming and budgeting, planning for product improvements and contract formation and management. Eventually DLA would lose most repair parts management responsibilities and focus on its common-commodity prime vendor management relationships. The service inventory management activities and related functional managers would provide the functional expertise and contractor oversight for the system PMs, just as they do early in the acquisition process for systems. There would be a fundamental shift of the services' system and commodity commands' core competencies away from managing supplies to managing suppliers, with all the planning, budgeting, and resource management that entails.

Some who oppose the change to PM-led product support have argued that DoD would give up the synergies possible with managing high-cost subsystems across platforms. Yet there is no need to give up the value of subsystem management when moving to PM-led contractor support. For example, Navy subsystem PMs can operate in combination with the ship-type (e.g., cruisers) system PMs under a program executive officer for surface combatants or carriers. Since vessels have many different major subsystems, such as the Aegis combat management system or the engines, pumps, and missiles systems that are common among different vessel types, having subsystem PMs responsible and adequately funded for the life-cycle support of the major subsystems should create focus on both maintaining needed subsystem availability and containing ownership costs.

The proponents of subsystem management have a valid point in emphasizing the need for cross-platform management in cases of very high cost subsystems. Thus provision should be made for PM fleet management of major subsystems where the benefits of such management are significant. In any event, it will be necessary to closely integrate the contracted support for the subsystems with their host systems to avoid ambiguity in accountability for overall system performance. The service benefits by the higher level of attention to critical subsystems and the opportunity to spread its investment in technology upgrades across several platforms.

Control of On-System Maintenance

There is one fly in the contracting support ointment that DSUs, PMs, and integration contractors need to keep in mind. At home station and ISB locations, there will be a tendency for the military DSU technicians to "let the contractor do it." The field service representatives, with all their expertise and incentives to contribute to high system availability, will work hard to keep the systems they support operable. That well-intentioned intervention can result in a failure to develop the military technicians' skills for diagnosing and repairing faults. There needs to be a disciplined approach by military DSU commanders and PMs to control on-system maintenance, lest the DSU technicians not be capable of the required support while in the battle spaces—*without the field service representatives.* Structured, monitored, and measured improvement and maintenance of military technicians' proficiency must be a documented requirement in the contracting arrangement with the integration contractors.

Change of the Product Support Paradigm

This book argues that the best alternative for DoD product support in the 21st century is to drop as quickly as possible—and well before the ten-year implementation period now planned—the whole traditional paradigm of functional support, with its responsibility for a system's support divided among many defense activities. Placing a service PM in charge of overseeing the fleet management of system and major subsystem product support, equipped with the funding and empowered to contract with an integrator for all the product support activities outside the battle spaces, is a far better paradigm. It accomplishes the objective to engage industry more completely in the life-cycle management of defense systems, so that industry partners have a financial stake in maintaining the required availability of systems at least overall cost. It transforms the services' roles to managing the providers of support and eliminates their attempts to imitate commercial firms that provide such support.

PM-led contractor support allows the services to shrink their logistics management activities to the inherently government functions of program management, and it allows the services' PMs to concentrate on ensuring that the operational forces and their DSUs receive all the support necessary for readiness. It demands of the PMs strong leadership in the life-cycle management of systems, a clear customer focus, and the communication skills and ability to work with the operating-force owners of the systems and their DSUs. PMs will need budget discipline and persuasive skills to balance sometimes conflicting requirements for operational tempo and maintenance time, as well as to obtain for their systems a fair share of resources in competition with other PMs and service requirements. The PM and his/her team will also need competence in planning, scheduling, and programming and, importantly, the ability to form and maintain a constructive relationship with the integration contractor and others that critically assess performance. But these are all skills that successful PMs have required for development and acquisition. We should expect no less when dealing with the in-service part of the system's life, the period that will consume around 80 percent of its total life-cycle cost and deliver the combat power so critical to campaign success.

COALITION PARTNERS' ROLE IN PRODUCT SUPPORT

We turn now to discuss the application of the principle of *comparative advantage* with respect to allies/coalition partners in the product support of systems.

The Search for Interoperability

Interoperability of weapons systems among coalition partners has been a dream, sometimes an objective, since its usual absence created often severe operational problems in World War II. Even such minimal degrees of interoperability as aircraft radios sharing the same frequency band have been always difficult to attain. Results have been generally disappointing. In all our fellow democracies, weapons systems are lucrative public works programs, and designs of systems are as often as much the result of the democratic "spoils" process as any militarily logical criteria. The U.S. and NATO allies, especially, have tried hard in their military planning to achieve interoperability and the opportunity to use components in other nations' systems. However, the only results have been produced (and they are significant) in aircraft systems where a nation has bought U.S. high-performance aircraft because their own industry lagged so far behind the U.S technologically. In land and naval systems as well as helicopters and less sophisticated fixed-wing aircraft, national producers have prevailed. Thus, with the exception of the high-performance aircraft and some high-technology target acquisition components, the opportunity to get product support resources from other nations is limited. That is not to say that interoperability goals are useless—quite the contrary, since software can now help bridge previous communications gaps. Process standardization such as the NATO Standardization Agreements (STANAGs) also helps enhance interoperability between forces. But we should not expect much progress in opportunities for product support beyond the high-technology content systems and subsystems.

Contractors as Agents for Interoperability

Especially in the case of high-performance aircraft, the contractor who builds and supports its aircraft in a number of partner nations is the best agent for realizing advantages in all parts of the product support supply chain. For example, component repair to support deployed U.S. forces might easily be accomplished by the integration contractor in a facility supporting the same aircraft in a partner country nearer to the battle space. Even less complex systems have benefited, and may continue to benefit, from contractor-led efforts to involve allied sources of components, repair, and distribution. A U.S. truck manufacturer, for example, might incorporate significant component manufacture and product support activities of allied countries in its business planning and production in an effort to win production contracts for similar trucks for their forces. Similar arrangements for communications and other equipment could provide product support sources closer to ISBs, all under the management of the integration contractor. PMs can influence those product support interoperability activities as long as the integrator's cost and performance incentive structure supports them. Attempting to direct such "comparative advantage" activities without incentives would be self-defeating to the overall system availability and cost objectives.

CHAPTER 8
Assessing the Product Support Processes: Part II

This chapter completes our assessment of product support processes with an examination of the application of the principle of *simplicity* to product support management and funding. We also will examine two important product support issues that do not fit directly into our principles framework: managing risks and inventory ownership. I then will show how the improvements recommended in applying the principles to product support processes will enable DoD to better achieve the logistics objectives of timely delivery of support with minimized logistics footprint in the battle spaces. While these two objectives promote logistics effectiveness, the proposed product support process changes also will promote efficiency, as the last section of the chapter will relate.

SIMPLICITY IN PRODUCT SUPPORT MANAGEMENT AND FUNDING

Two product support processes benefit from simplification: management and funding.

Product Support Management Responsibility Assigned to PMs

Implementation of the policy change in the May 2003 revision of DoD Directive 5000.1 has been an important first step in simplifying product support management. It should resolve the question of who manages life-cycle product support of the services' weapons and support systems. There is a long road between declaring that system program managers will assume life-cycle support responsibility and making it happen. The bureaucracy moves slowly to realign funding and organizations and to overcome the opposition of those who see their organizations losing resources and status because of this policy change. That said, just making the policy change in the environment that chapters 6 and 7 described is a signal accomplishment.

Presumably the leadership of the Office of the Secretary of Defense and the services will press forward with implementation.

How this policy change is implemented is the key. The concept of "responsibility" is empty of meaning unless the PMs are given the same kind of resources and authority for the many facets of life-cycle support that they already have for development and acquisition. With such implementation, the PMs would provide the system-owning organizations and the DSUs one organization—"one face to the customer"—that integrates all the product support activities for a particular system, to replace the multiple functional activities they now face. Implementing this directive will bring a much simplified management structure as well as accountability for the performance of the product support tasks.

Simplifying ISB Product Support

However, there remains a gray area of responsibility and authority for product support between the land force DSUs in the battle spaces and PM-managed sustaining base support activities: product support in the ISBs. The issue is who will be responsible for these four capabilities:

> ➤ stocking necessary repair parts to send to the battle space DSUs
> ➤ performing component repair and evacuating other components to CONUS repair activities
> ➤ providing technical assistance to the DSUs
> ➤ providing management of the system contractors that increasingly accompany deploying forces

The gray area is a consequence partly of the change in life-cycle system sustainment responsibility to the PMs and partly of the relocation of support activities out of the battle spaces to minimize the logistics footprint, thus creating geographical separation between the DSUs and the above four capabilities. For the deployed naval forces and the AEFs there is not the same geographical split between battle space and those back-up support functions. The AEF carries those capabilities and the necessary management structure with it to the main operating bases or relies upon CONUS or forward-based sources of support. These bases are serviced by the common theater assets, but any unique ISB product support activities, for example, back shops, are co-located with the direct support logistics organizations at the base or are located at forward bases, e.g., Ramstein AFB in Germany.

The situation is similar for the naval forces. They carry some component repair capabilities and parts aboard their combatants and additional spares aboard combat logistics force ships. For their intermediate maintenance needs, the ships would need to return to a forward base, e.g., Bahrain in the Persian Gulf since the 1990s, or maintenance teams can bring repair capability on board the ships.

The issue of responsibility for the four ISB capabilities is a particular challenge for Army and Marine forces, which traditionally have relied upon several echelons of support to their systems and now face the necessity for geographical separation of battle space support from the support capabilities listed above in order to reduce their logistics footprints. The MAGTFs and their combat service support detachments ashore must rely upon the force service support group elements and system contractors aboard the ARG or ashore for the set of ISB support capabilities listed above.

Heretofore, the Army brigade task force and support organization DSUs have had a complex set of assisting resources, principally division and corps materiel management centers within the battle space, which have provided product support resources such as processing requisitions for repair parts. They bring a sizable footprint of people, vehicles, and their own support into the battle space. There also has been a theater support command at the ISB with a materiel management center, distribution, and some component repair capabilities. With the development of logistics communications to support continuously shared knowledge, there is no reason why the division and corps materiel management functions cannot be combined with those of the theater support command, thus eliminating their battle space footprint—and simplifying and facilitating ISB-centered product support of operations.

Adapting to PM-Led Product Support

PM-led product support demands the presence of a representative of the PM in the ISB to manage the weapons system's theater spares inventory, component repair centers, technical assistance, and system contractor personnel. The PM representative in the ISB extends the one-face-to-the-customer commitment to the service theater logistics organization and to the DSUs in the battle spaces that support the PM managed systems. PM leadership simplifies the management of product support in the ISB, allowing the system-focused management of the four product support capabilities described earlier, and it provides an authoritative source of knowledge on system availability issues for the service component command and its logistics organization. This management approach worked well in Operation Desert Shield/Desert Storm for the Army's MSE system and was expanded in Operation Iraqi Freedom to several more Army systems, the Marines' new eight-ton truck, and the Navy F-18 E/F. Each of these system PMs employed support contractors to perform the majority of the four ISB functions.

Service Component Command Integration and Oversight

System PMs' assumption of ISB product support responsibility removes the gray area of responsibility for the four ISB support capabilities for each system, but it presents for the service component a problem of "managing the managers," assuring that their needs for common resources are balanced with those of other claimants. The service component commander needs to make sure that all of the systems within the combat and support organizations are maintained at a high level of availability. Thus the service component commander must be able to integrate the many ISB-located product support activities, both those managed by the PM and those managed by the current logistics structure, through an arrangement that provides oversight of their efforts. Allowing each system PM representative and support contractor free rein to introduce into the ISB whatever resources they believe necessary could harm the overall campaign effort. Management simplicity argues for a structure that provides oversight—requiring, for example, the PM to go through the service component command or its logistics command to add contractor or other personnel and to acquire common services such as transportation, real estate, and contracted (non-system) support services.

Army Logistics Support Element Example

In Operation Desert Shield/Desert Storm, Army Materiel Command deployed a management structure to oversee much of the component repair, modification, and field technical assistance functions. AMC created and deployed to Saudi Arabia a logistics support element (LSE) that was placed under the operational control of the Army component commander's theater logistics organization (which had been organized specifically for the operation).

The LSE then integrated the various AMC product support activities, so that they had adequate resources to accomplish their tasks and the theater logistics organization had one accountable leader—the leader of the LSE—for those critical system support functions. The strength of this approach lay in the concentrated focus it allowed for the Army component commander, who could readily keep track of system availability and progress on the numerous modification programs during Operation Desert Shield. Also, the AMC commander and the Army headquarters in CONUS could monitor the LSE's needs for resources and support from CONUS and respond quickly. AMC continually deployed and redeployed technicians, both organic and contractor, with the approval of the theater support command. The LSE managed the work of these technicians and their support, providing local transportation and facilities. The LSE, as part of the theater support command, was the "face" to the supported commander for system support.

A service component LSE organization offers great benefits to the service component commander through its role in arranging common support needs such as distribution, work space, and local transportation for the PM's support activities, through the joint theater logistics manager. The LSE also can act as a mediator between the service's DSUs in the battle spaces, the PMs and their support contractors in the ISBs and CONUS, and the joint theater logistics manager. Such a function is especially critical to timely and reliable transport of required supplies and people to the DSUs. Through its constant contact with the DSUs, the LSE can build a relationship of trust that what the combat and support forces need will be delivered when needed—and there will be no need to build just-in-case inventories in the battle space. The LSE also could play the same role it played for the Army in Desert Shield/Desert Storm for those systems not under PM management, bringing CONUS-based capabilities to the ISB when necessary.

The theater support organization would then contain the service commodity or system command elements such as munitions managers and the PMs' ISB repair centers under its operational control producing the arrangement that proved so successful for them in the Gulf War. This concept was partially implemented in Operation Iraqi Freedom by adding to the AMC LSE an ad hoc organization composed of representatives of PMs who had contractors in support of the weapon systems. This organization kept track of the contractors, and the PM representatives had an entity that could assist them in obtaining the needed support for their efforts to sustain the systems for which they were responsible.

Application of the Simplicity Principle to Sustainment-Base Ship Support

One potential application of both the management and the financial aspects of the *simplicity* principle is to the CONUS (and forward naval base) ship maintenance process. PM-led product support would replace the current regional maintenance process adopted by the Navy in the early nineties but only recently fully implemented. This application of PM-led contracted product support would include shore-based maintenance and overhaul as part of the PMs' life-cycle support responsibility. The present arrangement gives this responsibility to the Atlantic and Pacific fleet commanders and their "type" (e.g., cruiser-destroyer) commanders who, as force providers to the operating fleets, are responsible for the ships' readiness to meet deployment requirements. The commander of the Atlantic fleet is dual-hatted as commander of Fleet Forces Command and oversees all the dimensions of fleet readiness. Former Sea Systems command planning and repair activities were reassigned to the Atlantic and Pacific fleets, which were given authority to integrate the efforts of the naval shipyards into their regional maintenance processes.

One can surmise that the hesitancy in implementing the regional maintenance arrangements might have a lot to do with the fact that long-term ship maintenance is not a core competence of the leadership of the two commands, whose background and focus have been operations, training, manning, and other resource dimensions. This leadership experiences frequent turnover, as is the case in the other services, and therefore is likely to see commensurately frequent changes in ideas on how best to perform the complex tasks of ship maintenance in a resource-constrained environment. One of the consequences of this prolonged deliberation, through numerous task groups and studies of maintenance concepts is that the fundamentals of product support get neglected. The basics of determining what items to stock, with all the analysis of demands, failure rates, and so on that effort requires, and the most basic task of keeping configuration data up-to-date, all seem to have been partially neglected, according to a General Accounting Office analysis.[1] The GAO report summary stated:

---

[1] General Accounting Office, *Opportunities Exist to Improve Spare Parts Support Aboard Deployed Navy Ships*, GAO:03-887, Washington, D.C., August 2003.

What GAO Found:

In typical 6-month deployments at sea, Navy ships are generally unable to meet the Navy's supply performance goals for spare parts. GAO's analysis of data for 132,000 parts requisitions from ships in 6 Atlantic and Pacific battle groups deployed in fiscal years 1999 and 2000 showed that 54 percent could be filled from inventories onboard ship. This supply rate falls short of Navy's long-standing 65 percent goal. When parts were requisitioned, maintenance crews waited an average of 18.1 days to get the parts—more than 3 times the Navy's wait-time goal of 5.6 days for ships outside the continental United States. The Navy recognizes it has not met its supply goals for over 20 years.

Two key problems contribute to the Navy's inability to achieve its supply goals. Its ship configuration records, which identify the types of equipment and weapons systems that are installed on a ship, are often inaccurate because they are not updated in a timely manner and because audits to ensure their accuracy are not conducted periodically. In addition, the Navy's historical demand data are often out-of-date, incomplete, or erroneous because supply crews do not always enter the right information into the ships' supply system databases or do not enter it on a timely basis. Because configuration-record and demand data are used in models to estimate what a ship needs to carry in inventory, inaccuracies in this information can result in a ship's not stocking the right parts for the equipment on board or not carrying the right number of parts that may be needed during deployment. . . .

While precise impacts are not always well defined, the Navy's spare parts supply problems can affect a deployed ship's operations, mission readiness, and costs. GAO's analysis of data on 50,000 work orders from 6 deployed battle groups showed that 58 percent could not be completed because the right parts were not available onboard. More complete reporting of work orders identified as critical or important would have resulted in a more complete assessment of ship mission readiness. In addition, the Navy expends substantial funds—nearly $25 million for 6 ships GAO reviewed—to maintain large inventories that are not requisitioned during deployments.

In addition, the type commands are necessarily concerned with near-term fleet readiness, a focus that can rationalize postponing technology insertion and necessary, but longer term, shipyard availabilities to maintain current operational availability. The PM, as the Navy's agent for life-cycle product support of the platforms, could balance current availability with the needs *for service-life capability preservation* and make the best use of O&M, WCF, procurement funds, and infrastructure availability to produce that result.

The need to better integrate current readiness requirements with sustaining system capability over its service life was one of the reasons that led to the DoD policy change that directed management of life-cycle product support be placed in the PEO/PM chain.

In the proposed process, platform PMs and subsystem PMs working under the PEOs can provide the technical expertise to update each vessel's configuration database and, using readiness-based spares stockage models, revise and monitor the on-board spares inventory list. The PM's team could conduct component failure-rate analysis across the platform fleet to upgrade, over time, the reliability of components. The PM's team can also develop and implement the work packages for tasking to the organic repair activities and contractors. They can integrate maintenance and technology insertion in coordination with the vessel and type commands to meet objectives for availability for operations and training. PMs could choose the most effective and efficient mix of contractor and organic support for particular work packages. They could work with the fleet commands to make the best use of the shore intermediate maintenance activities, which provide the shore rotation base for sailor-technicians, integrating them into the work packages so as to preserve and improve their technical skills and reduce the labor costs of the work packages. Placing the PMs in charge of the support would provide the type commanders and the Navy with the DSU resources for the crews identified here (and the previous chapter as well) as simplified, accountable vessel repair, overhaul, and upgrade support under performance agreements specifying availability targets within available resources. It would allow fleet and type commanders to focus more on their training, manning, and operational preparation tasks, maintain the critical balance between current and service-life capability, and forgo the harmful and embarrassing consequences of sacrificing needed maintenance. (This occurred with the aircraft carrier

John Kennedy a short time ago; the roots of that case probably included the long-standing problems of configuration management and inventory inadequacies identified in the GAO analysis.)

Simplifying Financial Management

Simplifying the financial processes for product support is vastly more difficult than simplifying the management arrangements. The complexity and opportunities for mismanagement are major impediments to providing needed product support to the combat forces. The present process is a complex bureaucratic concoction that is frustrating and wasteful—a perverse incentive for effective, efficient support. The issue revolves around two major process characteristics: managerial/cost accounting and funds management.

Absence of a DoD Cost-Accounting Process

First, there is no adequate managerial/cost-accounting process comparable to that found even in private sector nonprofit organizations, e.g., cost centers where managers monitor project and activity expenditures against budgeted costs. Few defense activities outside working-capital-funded organizations charge the costs of their people to their work projects. Since people costs are such a large share of defense logistics costs, there is no way to know how productive these activities are and could be.

The present financial accounting process obscures the ability to track costs to their purpose, e.g., sustaining weapons system "X." There simply is no DoD-sanctioned process to account for these expenditures across organizations except in the functional categories used for budgeting, e.g., salaries, materiel, etc. (Some organizations have invented their own activity-based cost processes using best estimates of budget expenditure data.) While an individual depot might have visibility of its component repair costs for a system, the accounting process doesn't add that depot's cost elements to other depot work on that system or the costs of contracted repairs, DSU costs, sustainment engineering expenditures, or other life-cycle support costs. Efforts are made in all the services to extract budget execution data to estimate operating and support costs, but these historical cost estimates are only marginally useful for managing current system support.

Dysfunctional Funds Management Process

Secondly, the funds management process for product support aids and abets inefficiencies—and sometimes fraud. To understand how funds management can be so dysfunctional to effective product support, some background will be useful.

Operations and maintenance (O&M), procurement, and research, development, test, and evaluation (RDT&E) appropriations and the working capital funds (WCF) can fund different product support sustainment activities, although the two principal funding sources are O&M and WCF. Customer units and DSUs spend O&M funds allocated for training (or operations) to buy parts and some contractual services. Those funds are paid to the services and DLA inventory management organizations for reparable components and consumable parts and supplies and to local sources for some supplies and services. O&M funds paid to the inventory management organizations are converted into "cash" in the WCF activity account. That cash replenishes the WCF's obligation authority and is then used to buy parts and repair services from industry, component repairs from depots and shipyards, and distribution services from industry and DLA. The WCF also pays the salaries of a number of management personnel in the commodity and system commands through surcharges on the parts sold to the forces, the perfect setup for monopoly behavior. Since O&M funds expire at the end of each fiscal year, organizations funded by the O&M appropriation need newly appropriated funds at the beginning of each fiscal year in order to buy supplies and services and to pay civil servants. WCF cash has no time restriction and thus becomes a vehicle for insulating logistics activities from the O&M limitations.

Converting War-Fighters to Financial Managers of System Readiness

One example of the dysfunctional consequences of funds management has to do with the efforts to force financial management into combat units, ostensibly to make them more "efficient." Some financial management clearly is required for consumable supplies, including bulk petroleum products, to promote responsible use of public funds. The addition of product support was overkill. A policy change in 1990 required customer units to pay for depot-level and other reparable components (in addition to consumables and field-level reparables). Most of these reparables are expensive, many over one hundred thousand dollars.[2] Army DSUs—on behalf of their supported units—receive O&M "credits" for reparable component carcasses as an incentive for recovering them—which creates another set of transactions in addition to the purchase of serviceable components for these operational units to deal with. Often what the amount of credit is or whether it is granted at all, based on subjective judgments of the condition of the carcass, is a matter of major conflict between organizations—all of whom believe they have too few resources. In numerous instances customer units have retrieved components from DLA's disposal sites—where they had been sent after repair centers classified them as uneconomically reparable. The customer units then turned them in for credit in order to gain funds for base support or other activities. As one can readily guess, this credit activity absorbs enormous management energy, detracting from the management attention needed for the important task of maintaining system availability. In addition, credits often cannot be matched with turn-in documents; errors in the paperwork are routine and frequent. If funds run short due to a higher than budgeted rate of failures of expensive components, system availability will suffer. The funding process forces the organization with the least flexibility to bear the risks of unpredictable failure rates.

Distorted Incentives in Working Capital Fund Management

In addition to the credit issue, the financial process has distorted both customer and organic repair and inventory management activities' incentives. The latter two activities, as noted above, receive customer O&M funds in payment for reparables and consumables. They use their service WCF to buy serviceable components from organic and contract repair centers and supplies and consumables from industry suppliers. The WCF pays the salaries and other management expenses of their staffs to comply with the "total cost recovery" policy. Thus the price to the customer includes not only the cost of the item supplied by industry or the defense repair center but also a surcharge to cover the defense inventory management process overhead.

---

[2] This change resulted in large additions to operation forces O&M budgets—a cornucopia compared to previous levels of funding. It created veritable "cash cows" for financing other not-so-well resourced activities such as quality of life and family support.

This practice should yield the same kind of price that a customer would pay a commercial distributor. But unlike the commercial distributor, which can adjust the size of its workforce and its facilities to match its market demand, DoD's ability to adjust the size of its defense facilities and workforces is controlled by congressional actions, severely limiting its ability to reduce either workforce or facilities when the workload no longer justifies the resources. As we saw in chapter 5, those operations with large excess capacity hang on until the occasional base-closure political event can be launched (the last in 1995, the next scheduled for 2005). From 1990 until only recently, the ever-increasing costs of this large excess of both workforce and facilities had to be covered by an ever-decreasing volume of products and services sold to the ever-diminishing number of unit customers. The result, of course, was outrageously high prices to the customer. The customer's response in many cases was to use its O&M funds to contract with commercial enterprises "outside the back gate" for component repair, rather than use the organic system with its high surcharge. (Operation Iraqi Freedom reversed the ever-decreasing production trend as a result of the extraordinary wear and tear that the land forces systems experienced.)

Therefore, the service had to pay twice for the needed products and services; it still must support its organic activities, with their consequently lower workloads and increased excess capacity, while its units have paid the outside repairer—certainly conserving their own O&M funds but denying needed revenue to the organic repair and inventory management activities. Moreover, the quality of repairs produced by the local repair shops has frequently been poor, requiring even more removals and repairs.

The financial management process thus distorts customers' behavior, incentivizing them through the pricing structure to make do with lower quality components, adversely affecting readiness. The organic repair depots, with few options to reduce their costs, face even greater excess capacity and must charge even higher prices under the total cost recovery policy. Representatives and senators are reluctant to allow DoD more ability to close unneeded facilities and/or reduce workforces because the legislators are punished by their workforce constituents (and families, friends, and local businesses) for not protecting those government jobs. Customer organizations become cynical about the monopolistic supply sources in the face of ever-increasing prices, and the organic repair and inventory activities face the continuing shortage of revenues and the pressure to make cost reductions that they cannot accommodate because of the legislative and financial constraints.

Time to Abandon Bad Practices

It is time to leave behind the decade-long, poorly conceived experiment in business management we have just reviewed. Subjecting operating forces and their DSUs to surcharge-burdened high prices for their most critical mission components, when they have only limited influence on the failure rates and no authority to use alternative legitimate repair sources, amounts to little more than a façade for transferring operations and maintenance funds from combat organizations into the services' working capital cash accounts. The full cost recovery policy for reparables has allowed the services to raid the WCF cash accounts in order to pay for unbudgeted expenses (rather than replacement parts) without the inconvenience of having to go to the Congress for supplemental appropriations. This distortion of the working capital fund system, moreover, has proven itself to be a major distracter from combat unit training effectiveness because of the forces' incentives to find ways to conserve their O&M funds.

Present Financial Management Process Undermines PM Management

The funding issues with which we have been wrestling lie at the heart of the biggest challenge in implementing the new policy of life-cycle support: defining precisely *what is* the PM's product support responsibility—and authority—within his/her overall life-cycle responsibilities. Various management options have been tried, others debated. One difficulty is defining the differences in responsibility between the PMs, acting as the services' system managers, and the operational chain of command over the system operating units—the Air Force wings, Army corps and divisions, Navy type commanders and fleets, and Marine divisions and wings. Historically, most of the funds to maintain system availability have been allocated through the operational chain of command for parts and intermediate and depot maintenance, and to the services' and DLA inventory control points, which buy parts and serviceable components to resell to the DSUs/operating units. (In the Army, depot overhaul funding is allocated to AMC, rather than to the operational chain of command, and then to its subordinate commodity commands for centrally approved system overhaul programs.)

This funding allocation leaves PMs with no means to manage the product support part of their life-cycle system responsibilities. To execute their responsibilities for system R&D and acquisition, PMs have RDT&E and procurement funds. For the recently acquired life-cycle sustainment responsibilities, PMs have neither WCF obligation authority to purchase spares or component repairs nor sufficient O&M funds to obtain contractor support or other resources necessary to provide the DSUs and customer units with the support they require. (Some PMs apparently have been allocated sustainment engineering funds—perhaps a small step forward.) The result of this lack of sustainment resources is to vitiate the policy of PM life-cycle management responsibility. Without funding, PMs have no real authority to influence the course of life-cycle support. It is hard to see how the PMs can be accountable for any results or achieve the objectives of the DoD policy change.

Product Support Financial Management for the 21st Century—A Transformation

The beginning of this section on simplifying financial management of product support cited the lack of a DoD managerial/cost-accounting process and unnecessary complexity in managing O&M and WCF funds. A new financial management process will remedy those defects. Transformation is essential![3]

The first task is to develop a financial management structure to illuminate product support costs by system at a level of detail that enables managers to allocate resources to activities, measure results against costs, and be able to reallocate funds in response to unexpected demands. DoD has begun an ambitious effort to restructure its entire financial management process. A capability for activity-based cost accounting is promised. Such a

---

[3] The services already have begun to disconnect operational funds from base support funds. In 2002 the Army created the Installation Management Agency and placed all its bases under it. Funding for base support now is allocated to the IMA from the headquarters. No longer can operational commanders move funds between mission and base support accounts. The Navy recently announced the formation of a similar organization.

structure will be a large part of the foundation for more meaningful financial knowledge and management of life-cycle product support. An activity-based costing system would facilitate discipline without the chaotic financial management processes of today. The services would continue to use the working capital fund system for component and parts inventory. Each PM could manage a system activity group to allow management of the working capital funds without running into the appropriations time limits, since it is advantageous for the service rather than the contractor to own the inventory of reparables and consumable repair parts (as we shall discuss later).

The new life-cycle management policy also demands a new fleet management approach—rooted in a new philosophy about "ownership" of systems and the linking of funding authority with life-cycle support responsibility. This new philosophy assumes that the systems are all owned by the service, and *not* by its subordinate commands. The service's objective is to maintain each fleet of systems in the highest state of readiness that resources will permit. This fleet is allocated to the services' combat and support organizations, who become *custodians* of their allocated systems, much like an airline operating a leased fleet of aircraft. These allocations of ships, aircraft, fighting vehicles, or other equipment can be transferred by the service to other organizations. The task of these custodians, then, is to operate and maintain the availability of the systems so as to be able to perform their organizations' missions, with the knowledge that the systems may be transferred to other organizations at any time. By establishing the understanding that the service owns all the systems, the service can logically designate the PMs as the service's agents for managing the system fleets. DoD Directive 5000.1 by itself will not cause the change in culture necessary for implementation of PM responsibility for life-cycle support. Changing the concept of ownership will help.

Product Support Funds for the PM

The services then need to back up their designation of the PM as their agent for life-cycle support of the system fleets with the authority to manage that support. It is unreasonable to expect that the PM can fulfill the product support portion of the life-cycle support mission without the same kind of authority and funding that he/she possesses in R&D and production. Therefore, under this proposed implementation, all funds for maintenance of system availability would be allocated to the PM.

This implementation of life-cycle product support enables the services' operating forces to focus on the real purpose of military organizations: to prepare to fight, and to fight, the nation's wars. The system operating units and their DSUs still are responsible for maintaining the targeted availability of their systems and managing their resources, ordering parts and technical assistance as necessary. But PM-managed life-cycle support, implemented along the lines described here, allows them to stop the practices that grew up over the last decade or so of trying to act like businesses. It does so by changing the resource allocation and funding processes of the services so that the operating forces are allocated op tempo levels—flying hours, steaming days, operational "miles" (for ground vehicles) or hours based upon their missions and the budgeted operating funds.

Deployed operating forces might be allocated sufficient operational flying hours to support missions and training during the deployed time and a reduced rate when redeployed. Similar allocations would be made for all major systems and those support systems for which annual costs are sensitive to use. The budgeting process would allocate O&M funds to the PMs to support the op tempo allocations and commensurate WCF obligation authority (if the inventory is government owned), using separate WCF activity groups for each major system or group of small systems to finance the inventory of reparables and consumable repair parts.

That funding would support the system contractor(s) and organic repair, distribution, and management organizations in managing the service-owned inventory, repairing components, acquiring replacements, and providing the technical support required for the system fleet. The only O&M product support funding that would be allocated through the service operational commands to the owning organizations would be for petroleum products. (Similarly, O&M funding would also be allocated to the DSUs for items such as support of common test equipment, POL, common hardware, etc.)

As provided in DoD's implementation plan for PM-managed product support, the PM would enter into "performance agreements" with the operating commands, specifying availability objectives based on budgeted resources to support the op tempo allocations for the system operating units within the commands. The PMs' performance agreements with customer organizations also would be the basis for synchronizing support with operations and training events, e.g., scheduling periodic depot maintenance or shipyard availabilities.

Impacts of the Transformation

This new funds management process removes the onus of most financial accounting for product support from the operating forces and allows them to focus on their training or operations mission and still act as responsible custodians of the equipment they operate. DSUs and customer units would order parts as necessary to maintain system availability. The costs of parts and other services (contractor technical support, for example) would be captured (by the DSU) as part of the repair actions and reported by individual system, its custodian unit, and its DSU for management review. The only financial transaction would be the "selling" of the parts from the PM's WCF activity group account to the O&M expenditure account. Reparables would be managed by direct exchange of broken components for serviceable components (with the appropriate costs captured). The problem of control of reparables (failure to return the broken component) would be dealt with through RFID serial-numbered tracking of the change in accountability between the distribution centers and the DSUs.

Thus the operating units' and their DSUs' management challenge is to stay within the budgeted usage, including gaining approval for adjustments based on changed missions or circumstances. The PMs would oversee contractors' performance and adjust their level of effort as the budgeted allocation changes. They would also work closely with the contractor teams to monitor DSU effectiveness and capture the system operating and support costs. These costs are essential ingredients for measuring contractor performance and for future budgeting. Increasing the accuracy of costs per flying hour/steaming day or operational miles by capturing those costs for different operational modes would be a major help in improving the validity of budget estimates.

Through the knowledge system shared by all participants in fleet management, there would be visibility of system configurations and both requirements for parts and the status and location of the assets, enabling as quick a response as can be given by Boeing or Caterpillar to their customers. System operating organizations and their DSUs will see the proposed process as a clear improvement over the present situation, where they face the problem of trying to get prompt response to their parts orders with little help other than what attention their angry e-mails and phone calls can attract. Under the proposed process, problems with system availability are the service's, not just a wing's or division's, and a PM is on the hook to deliver support according to the service's priorities and resources.

The proposed transformation of the funding mechanism would also allow organic commodity/systems management organizations to be taken out of the WCF and funded like other government organizations—through direct O&M funding—removing the decade-long fiction that only their expenditures, and not those of the training and operational command organizations, should be included as part of the full cost of readiness.

Creating cost centers in those management organizations and recording work time distribution by employees (including military) can allow productivity measurement and adjustment to workload changes, including charging such efforts to the appropriate weapons/support system. As the transformation to contractor-supported systems continues, the management roles of these organic commodity/system management organizations shift to supporting PMs. It is in everyone's interest (except those who wish to conceal the real costs from the public's, or even the leadership's, eyes) to make these management costs visible. Competing for direct O&M funding with other service readiness management organizations would expose the excess management costs caused by congressionally imposed rigidities, stripping away the disguise from the relationship of those costs to product support.

Organic repair centers, as legitimate industrial-type activities, should continue using the working capital funds with extended use of activity-based costing to illuminate support and overhead activities as well as direct labor and materiel. As transformation of product support proceeds, some parts of the depots and shipyards will become subcontractors to the system integrators, forcing more focused overhead management—if the Congress will permit. Observing the *simplicity* principle can "de-thatch" the complex array of funding arrangements and allow management to focus its resources on system readiness and operations.

Two Side Benefits

This 21st-century funding process has two significant side benefits that remove sources of irritation and dysfunctional behaviors described earlier.

ELIMINATE CREDIT TRANSACTIONS   The first benefit is the elimination of the confusing credit transactions. The new funding process eliminates this source of irritation to logisticians and operating forces. While the policy had the purpose of assuring that DSUs turned in reparable unserviceable carcasses for repair when they bought serviceable replacements, in practice it set off the gaming of the system to maximize the credit flow to use for other unit purposes. With the new process, each PM can calculate once a year a standard cost of repairing each component, using the cost of the previous year's repairs (requiring activity/project costing) plus the cost of replacing washed-out components and the necessary transportation and handling, divided by the projected demand. As noted above, the DSU is expected to turn in a carcass in exchange for the repaired/new component. Some components will be damaged through combat or accident, both costs of operations. If the carcass has been discarded or deliberately damaged beyond fair wear and tear, it can be treated like a lost or stolen end/principal item in accordance with DoD and service regulations, grounds for appropriate disciplinary action. Thus there is no need for credit transactions.

END THE PRACTICE OF CHARGING OPERATING UNITS FOR MAINTAINING READINESS   Secondly, the new funding process attacks the heart of the assumption that military organizations can be operated as businesses. But even businesses don't charge their operating units on a transaction basis for the maintenance of their aircraft or construction equipment, although costs are captured and reported. Establishing training parameters—flying hours in different modes, field training days, and ship steaming days—should provide sufficient guidelines for resource management for the combat and support forces. Under the proposed funding process, services would have their DSUs and PMs capture the materiel, labor, and other costs so that budgets can be prepared, operations costs compared—and op tempo adjusted. Costs would still be attributed to the system operating organizations via their DSUs and the PMs' analyses. Even cursory analysis of cost data can reveal abuse of the systems or poor management by operating or support units. Root-cause analysis of seemingly premature component failures can reveal improper operation of systems. In these cases action can be taken to improve management or operational use.

Two Objections to Funding PMs

There are two major objections to shifting the allocation of O&M funds and working capital fund obligation authority to the PMs. The first comes from the operating forces commands that are accustomed to allocating the

O&M funds during the budget execution year to meet ever-changing requirements for both product support and other needs. Clearly, withdrawing product support O&M funding from those commands reduces their funding flexibility. Yet it also responds to continued (valid) congressional criticism that the services justify their product support budgets before Congress but too often divert funds from product support to other uses, such as installation/quality of life support, that have not been adequately funded in the approved appropriations. The Army recently removed some of the diversion potential by transferring installation support management and related funding from its major commands to a central agency reporting to the Army headquarters directly. The Navy is in the process of doing the same.

Yet the change in policy to life-cycle fleet management argues that the fleet manager must have funding to manage the fleet of systems; otherwise the whole policy would be a sham. The implication of the policy is that the service allocates portions of the fleet to the different operating commands, an allocation that can be changed by deployments or stationing changes of the system operating units. The service has a great interest in assuring the highest level of availability of the whole fleet consistent with resources. The service influences availability through the allocation of budgeted op tempo—flying hours, steaming days, and so on—to the commands, an allocation that becomes the basis of the periodic performance agreements between the commands and the PM and governs the allocation of support for the system between the customer units. The result for the operating unit should not be very different from today's process. An F-18 squadron returning to its shore station from deployment might have a lower availability objective placed on its aircraft than it was assigned while deployed, an objective agreed to in the PM's performance agreement with the operational command. The op tempo assignment would then be increased as it begins to prepare for the next deployment. The op tempo requirements and budgeted O&M funds will generally set the parameters for the system availability objectives, objectives that will change, as they do now, depending on operational and training requirements and shifting priorities.

The major difficulty will be the effort required to shift funds during the budget execution year between systems. However, since there are no organizational boundaries (U.S. Army Europe versus Forces Command, for example), such O&M funds transfers between PMs should be manageable under the direction of the service headquarters. The big problem would occur, as now, with a major increase in funding required to greatly increase the op tempo, e.g., for C-17 airlift. Even if the O&M was transferred to the C-17 PM, there might be insufficient parts within the whole supply chain to sustain the higher op tempo. Shifting op tempo funding from one command to another would be managed by the PMs involved for their systems, mirroring the service headquarters' transfer of op tempo allocations between the commands.

The second objection to allocating the funding to the PMs is the services' financial managers' loss of flexibility for funds management. The objection is that allocating the funds to so many different activities—the hundred or more PMs—makes it very difficult to retrieve funds to pay pressing unanticipated bills during the budget execution year. There is even greater concern when one adds the contracted support legal obligations to the funding allocation process. The argument says, in its simplest form, that the government will have to obligate the budgeted system product support funds early in the fiscal year to meet contract terms, leaving no ability to reduce those funds for reallocation to another system that might have higher priority and more immediate needs.

The objection would be valid if the contract for product support provided for the contractor to deliver a level of system availability with relatively no involvement by other support providers. This concept has been discussed as one option, but it is *not* what this book has proposed. Rather, this book proposes a *partnership* between PM, contractor team, DSU, and operating units. The contract should give the service the flexibility to make op tempo and budget changes during the year. The only issue should be the magnitude of the changes. The contractor provides a set of services, some of which will be a fixed cost for management of the repair and supply chain processes, the inventory, and a core of field service technicians. The component repair and overhaul activities have a significant element of variable costs; repairs can be postponed. Thus the contract should have both a relatively fixed management cost element and a variable cost element that can be altered during the year if necessary. The other large part of the PMs' O&M funding goes for the consumption of components and piece parts—issues from the government-owned inventory for the DSUs and the contractors for use in repairing systems and components. These funds remain under PM management. They could be held at the program executive officer (PEO) level, reducing the number of funded activities. Cost reports from the DSUs and contractors would facilitate more responsive financial management than now is possible with the allocation to the operating forces, where system identity of the funds is frequently lost. With such greater visibility, the impact of re-allocations can be judged far better than at present. Op tempo consequences can be weighed; and the operating forces, the PM/PEO, and the service head-quarters can make better informed decisions when those reallocations must be made.

These two objections certainly require thoughtful planning and imple-mentation, but they do not pose any barrier to implementing the funda-mental change in policy to make the PM the responsible life-cycle support manager, with the authority and funding to carry out those responsibilities. Some rice bowls inevitably will be broken, as happens any time change over-takes organizations. People adjust under firm, positive leadership.

This implementation proposal for PM-led contracted product support satisfies both the *accountability* and the *simplicity* principles. It gives the PM the authority and resources as well as the responsibility for the product sup-port element of life-cycle system support. The integration contractor is given incentives for supporting the DSUs and operating units in achieving op tempo and availability targets. The operating unit, motivated to attain those targets, has a greatly simplified structure to deal with—as does the DSU, both having been freed from the complicated "business management para-digm and able to concentrate on execution of the current campaign or prepa-ration for the next.

IMPLEMENTING CONTRACTED PRODUCT SUPPORT: TWO CRITICAL ISSUES

Risk Management

With this understanding of the proposed financial implementation of PM-led product support, let us return to the critical issues in forming and man-aging the PMs' contracts with the product support integrators and their team members. Chapter 7 proposed performance-based, incentivized contracts to support the service objective flying or operating hours, steaming days, and availability at a price. How can a contractor (as well as the PM) *manage the risks* that the DSUs and operating organizations will fail in properly operat-ing the system, accurately reporting faults, promptly and accurately diagnosing the causes of failure, ordering parts, and making prompt repairs? Four features that should be included in a PM's management strategy can mitigate these risks: creating a partnership, developing a performance-based contract, selecting appropriate performance and cost metrics, and including contractor field technicians in the integration contract.

Partnership

PMs must understand first that the concept behind this support strategy should be a partnership between the PM, the integration contractor and its team, the operating units, and DSUs. It is the first step for managing risks. A partnership among these stakeholders cements the understanding that they all benefit from achieving the availability targets for their systems. The whole incentive structure within military organizations is focused on achieving mission goals—in this case, available systems. The DSUs want to be successful, and they take great pride in keeping high availability for the systems for which they are responsible. In fact they will go to great lengths via scrounging for parts and cannibalization to restore systems to full operational capability. PMs are graded on how well they attain both operational availability and resource use targets. The incentives in contractors' performance-based contracts should be linked to the principal availability and cost metrics. Everyone in the chain is motivated. This partnership is expressed in a variety of ways in planning support and reviewing performance. At the operating level there should be periodic performance reviews between the operating unit, the DSU, the contractor's field technical representative, and the PM's representative to review performance in meeting the availability and cost objectives and other metrics that are included in the performance agreement between the operating force and the PM, as well as to adjust to changed op tempo or other requirements. That team should be able to resolve most issues that might impede performance and is certainly able to elevate the remaining issues through the operating force and program management chains of command. The partnership approach in this team formation should allow a unified effort to recognize and minimize the risk that the inherent problems in achieving product support objectives will be ignored. Both the customer and the support provider would engage in the effort to attain the availability and cost objectives, alert to problems, and able to anticipate or react quickly to solve them.

Performance-Based Contracts

One of the challenges facing the program managers as they further develop their plans for competitive product support is forming the performance-based contract itself—the vital second part of the risk management strategy. Life-cycle product support contract vehicles are still relatively new. They are unlike the R&D service contracts with which the acquisition people have experience, so training for the PM and acquisition team is necessary. One of the better techniques is to use existing contracts as models, coupled with interviews of PMs who have employed them, in order to incorporate lessons learned. The PM and acquisition team can then construct draft requests for proposal (RFPs) to gain industry comments on the metrics, terms and conditions, and the like. Also, because of the frequent lack of good baseline cost and performance knowledge, it would be fruitful to begin with a cost-plus type contract (with incentives) for perhaps a two-year period, followed by a fixed-price performance contract to be negotiated during the first contract period. That would allow the PM and the integration contractor the necessary time to develop the baseline and to understand other issues in the transition from organic to contractor-managed product support.

Metrics

One of the most important facets of performance-based contracts is the set of metrics that describe required performance. System availability is a principal subset of the metrics; cost metrics are the second principal subset.

PERFORMANCE METRICS   The availability targets should be focused not upon total operable days in a month—a historical and traditional measure that says nothing of the critical times when systems must operate at their maximum. Such metrics create perverse incentives to apply unnecessary resources simply to meet an end-of-month target. Rather, like the airlines, PMs and operating forces should focus on "availability-at-the-gate" metrics, i.e., availability for operations and training events—a meaningful measure of the contribution of system availability to the operating organization's mission. This change of focus probably will require a change in the readiness reporting rules, long wedded to counting "unavailable " days regardless of whether there was any event for which the system was needed. In this approach, the operating unit would plan the availability profile, based upon its campaign operation and training plans and the resources (training flying hours) that are allocated. The operating organizations most likely will have different combat readiness requirements dictating their tempo of operations and/or training. For example, the AEF component flying Afghanistan surveillance missions may require more flying hours than another component that is in a post-operation, stand-down status. Therefore, the first unit will require more maintenance support during its operational period than the second. Such differences in op tempo can be taken into account in the budgeting and budget execution processes and in the contractor's positioning of parts and technical support.

These "availability-at-the-gate" targets are the major objective for the whole team—operating unit, DSU, contractor team, and PM—and they need to constitute an important part of contract performance metrics. Yet the contractor's ability to influence system availability is limited. Therefore, the PM must devise metrics for contractor performance that reflect activities that the contractor *does* control. On the *availability* side of the ledger, the contractor manages the availability of repair parts and components. Therefore, customer wait time (the time between the order and its receipt at the DSU), the fill rate of DSU authorized stock of critical parts, the back order rate, component repair quality, and the quality of overhauled systems would be useful measures of performance.

COST METRICS   On the *cost* side, there should be an operating and support cost objective. Metrics supporting this objective would include component repair cycle time, component removal rate by the DSU, and inventory value. Shorter repair cycle times translate to a lower stockage requirement, reducing inventory costs. Low component-removal rates at the DSU reflect high component reliability, less demand for replacement components, and lower support costs. Such a metric would serve to incentivize the contractor to continually improve component reliability and training of technicians in diagnostic procedures if the contract is either for a fixed price per unit of use, e.g., flying hours, or contains share-in-savings terms. The inventory value metric is an incentive to stock the right amount of the right parts at the right places and aids in keeping inventory investment at the proper level to support the system availability objectives without excess stocks. Good performance requires the supply chain of vendors and repair activities to operate in concert to produce the needed results.

Adaptation to Unique Systems

While these cost and performance metrics are necessary to form an effective product support contract, each system has unique characteristics, and the environments in which the different services' DSUs function differ. The differences demand thoughtful work by the PM to fit the appropriate metrics to the particular system and environment. Army contracts may allow a clean break between the soldier-technicians' tasks of preventive maintenance, diagnostics, and component replacement on the system, and the contractor's tasks of component repair, system overhaul or major repair, and other outside-the-battle space functions.

One of the principal environmental requirements that affect Army and Marine Corps maintenance operations is the need to minimize the logistics battle space footprint. The Army and Marines require that tasks, such as component repair, that need not be performed in the land battle spaces should be sited either in the ISB or CONUS. Thus, in general only the on-system maintenance and repair tasks will be performed by soldiers and Marines.

On the other hand, as much as 60 percent of carrier-based aircraft components may be reparable by the naval technicians on board the carrier or ashore. The air wings enjoy a relatively clean environment, hospitable to component repair, in the carrier maintenance bays and shops. The major restrictions that limit the Navy's aircraft component repair tasks are likely to be space for the maintenance operations, inventory, and test equipment aboard the aircraft carrier.

Air Force maintenance policy has moved toward the Army end of the spectrum, as most back shops for component repair are not deployed to the main operating bases, in order to keep deployment requirements to a minimum. A regionalized component repair and supply system has allowed the AEFs to deploy with much smaller footprints than was the case during the Cold War.

Contractor Field Technicians

The fourth mechanism for managing risk is the assignment of the contractor's field service technicians to frequently visit the DSUs and operating units and see them in operation. They are the "eyes and ears" of the integration contractor and the PM. To the extent that these technicians coach and train the military technicians to improve their diagnostic and repair skills, maintenance of overall system availability should be improved. They can uncover problems with the system's performance, adequacy of diagnostic processes and equipment, tools, and repair parts management before these seriously affect availability. Instances of less than adequate performance can be identified and discussed in the performance reviews or brought to the PM for resolution with the organizations concerned.

Inventory Ownership

The second implementation issue has to do with the ownership of the inventory of components and consumable parts. Should the government own the inventory or should the contractor? The answer depends on the situation with each system. In the vast majority of cases, implementation of contractor-supported sustainment will involve systems already fielded, and the government owns the inventory at the time of implementation. The next section will argue that the inventory should continue under government ownership. In the cases of new system development in which the contractor not only produces the system but will also provide life-cycle support, it may be better for both the service and the contractor that the contractor own it. Let us turn first to the fielded (legacy) systems case.

Earlier in this chapter, I stated that the funding allocated to the PM would include WCF obligation authority for the management of inventory. Here I offer the reasons for the PMs' management of government-owned inventory of reparables and consumable parts.

In the late 1990s an unsolicited proposal by a major defense contractor to transform the Army's Apache helicopter system product support (outside the battle spaces) from organic to contract foundered on this issue, among others. On the government side was a belief that in order for the arrangement to work in the Army's interest, the contractor should buy the existing inventory. While this issue may have been simply a red herring designed to force the contractor to walk away, it points up the issue's importance to a successful implementation of contractor support for legacy systems. It is too much to expect a firm to invest scarce capital in an inventory of parts, the need for which is unknown. In fact, it is far better policy to have the service own the components and consumables parts inventory and to have the contractor manage that inventory as part of the support effort. There are several reasons.

The PM's mission in life-cycle support is to achieve a targeted system availability level within a relatively fixed budget. System usage is subject to unprogrammed deployments and wide swings in the customer units' op tempo during the budget execution year, creating unexpected resource demands. Therefore, the PM must program sufficient inventory to take account of surges in demand. The PM cannot operate on a policy that minimizes inventory, but rather must require a two-tier policy that includes, in addition to the operating stock, a "war reserve" of critical components and consumables. The war reserve inventory must also contain at least small quantities of all system-unique parts, even though some may experience no demands for years. This practice is common among firms like airlines, which have available-at-the-gate targets similar to those of military systems.

Service ownership of the inventory also increases the contractor's confidence that it can meet contract performance goals for availability. The contractor's responsibility to manage the inventory, recommending levels, positioning, and dealing with the many suppliers, certainly presents challenges, but they are manageable. Of particular importance will be the contractor's ability to ensure that the DSUs maintain their authorized inventory levels and perform their important roles in maintaining system availability. It should be the contractor's responsibility, in managing the parts and components supply chain, to assure timely delivery of needed items so as not to cause system downtime that exceeds the allowable standard. Certainly, contract incentives should recognize the critical role of inventory management.

Under the policy of service-owned inventory, reduction in the contractor's level of uncertainty should result in pricing that reflects a lower risk premium than if the contractor were required to own the inventory. The contractor also will thus avoid the liability for the personal property tax that is levied by many states on such property—no small savings given the multimillion-dollar inventories of complex aircraft and ship components. Removing this uncertainty may facilitate the formation of fixed-price contracts with reasonable risk premiums—potentially a benefit to both contractor and PM.

In the case of deciding on inventory ownership for a new system being produced and fielded, several factors may favor contractor ownership. First, the contractor has a clean slate; there is no inherited inventory with unknown reasons for stockage. Therefore, the contractor can use the testing period and initial fielding to gather experience regarding breadth and depth of stockage without having to make a large investment, especially since some tweaking of component designs may be required. The production line is the fallback if unexpected demands occur since the parts vendors have warm lines.

Secondly, by owning the inventory the contractor can exercise firm configuration management—ensuring that vendors' parts and components are tested appropriately and that design changes are reflected in issues to the DSUs and operating units. Since the contractor will be measured on how well it meets availability and cost targets, there will be great interest in assuring that only the approved parts and components are issued to match the particular platforms and components for which they are designed.

In addition, the contractor can better control the costs of distribution since there will be no requirement to use the DoD CONUS distribution infrastructure. Also the tax consequences can be mitigated and may be favorable. Personal property taxes can be minimized by locating inventory in locales with favorable tax treatment, and the contractor can depreciate owned inventory, thus adding to cash flow and lowering inventory costs. The service may also be able to finance the gradual buildup of inventory through adding a surcharge on each platform produced to cover the addition to inventory it will require.

Certainly, to the extent the above conditions do not work in favor of the contractor and the service, the government can take ownership and still preserve essential incentives for the integration contractor's performance.

IMPROVING WEAPONS SYSTEMS AND SUPPORT EQUIPMENT SUSTAINMENT: A SUMMARY

The improvements proposed in this and the preceding chapters can substantially enhance the performance of weapons system and support equipment sustainment in achieving our two logistics objectives: timely delivery of support to customers and a minimized logistics footprint in the battle spaces.

Timely Delivery of Support to Customers

The customers of the product support process are both intermediate and final customers. The latter are those who operate/employ the system for its

combat or support purposes; they expect the product support process to produce *maximum availability of the system for operational employment.* The
timely delivery standard for the final customer, therefore, might be characterized as "100 percent of systems available *when they must be employed.*" In
other words, when the air tasking order requires twelve sorties of F-15s, that
number can be generated. The brigade task force attacking toward Baghdad
during Operation Iraqi Freedom viewed timely delivery of support as having all its battlefield systems, including tanks, infantry fighting vehicles, command and control vehicles, and so on, ready for each engagement. For both
organizations, timely delivery means the ability to generate the combat power
designed into the force through the product support of their combat systems. It should not mean that all assigned F-15s or tanks are available all
the time. That's probably unachievable. That's why we say, "*when they must
be employed.*" Civilian airliners are expected to meet a contracted standard
for gate departures. Maintenance and repairs are scheduled, and the product support organization works to meet that "availability-at-the-gate" standard as close to 100 percent of the time as possible. Likewise, racecars are
expected to be available when the race starts and when it ends. So, too, with
combat and support systems. Between engagements, the owning organization and its DSU check and service the systems to ready them for the time
when they are to be employed—whether in combat or in training.

The proposed improvements to the product support processes will go far
toward achieving that standard of available-when-needed. The PM, who is
accountable for the support outside the battle spaces, with funding and authority to provide the necessary spares and technical assistance to the DSUs,
is the cornerstone of assuring timely delivery of sustainment resources to the
DSUs that support the PM's system. This PM, armed with authority and
funding, can cut through the numerous bureaucracies to concentrate on
achieving the availability objectives required of the units operating his/her
system in support of the campaign/training objectives.

Before campaign initiation, the PM, the integration contractor, the
DSUs, and the operating units analyze the likely needs for replacement components. They then position those components at the appropriate nodes in
the system supply chain and plan with the supply chain sources to ensure a
reliable supply of the components, including arranging for the establishment
of ISB and other repair centers if necessary. If the analysis of likely needs
turns out to require more resources than the PM has—not an abnormal

situation—the PM can describe the risk to the operating units and the operational chain of command. With the PM in charge of this support, there would be no more faceless individuals making financial and inventory decisions whose effects are not known until the operation encounters problems.

One example taken from the Army's experience in Operation Iraqi Freedom illustrates the disconnects between the present "faceless" functional logistics management and system-focused support. Among the many problems experienced by the Third Infantry Division in obtaining parts was replacing tank and Bradley fighting vehicle track and road wheels that were damaged by enemy action or wore out during the four weeks of intensive operations. When the division DSUs at last could order these items, the requisitions were passed through the theater materiel management center (MMC) in Kuwait to CONUS even though there were stocks of the items in storage in Kuwait. The reason? A "faceless" manager in the MMC had placed a "management hold" on these items, so the computer automatically passed the orders to the CONUS supply source. Only when someone who knew of the problem saw air pallets with track and road wheels on top of containers in the storage area and pointed them out to the MMC was the problem recognized. The functional layered process was made worse by the assignment of an MMC activated for the operation but with no experience in dealing with the high op tempo of organizations committed to combat.

Under the proposed system the PMs for M-1 tanks and Bradleys not only would know where stock was in the ISB and how much, but would have learned early in the operation of the growing need for track and road wheels and so shipped the items to the DSUs. No such problems apparently were experienced by the two newest systems of PM-led product support, the Navy's F-18 E/F and the Marines' medium tactical vehicle replacement (MTVR). Both systems were sustained at high levels of availability throughout the operation. Both also had integration contractors with field service technicians available.

Minimized Logistics Footprint in the Battle Spaces

Achieving both timely delivery of product support and a minimized footprint in the battle spaces is a tall order. The product support footprint in the battle spaces is made up of the systems support technicians in the operating unit (if any) and the DSUs, their system support equipment and life support (feeding, shelter, force protection, people, and equipment), and component inventory. The larger the number of technicians, the larger the footprint. Unless they can be confident that the weapons system support necessary to support the campaign plan is operating well, service component commanders have no choice but to insist upon more logistics resources, with the accompanying larger footprint, in spite of the added force-protection burden and casualty risks. If the product support processes cannot deliver available systems using the strategy of timely delivery with lean inventory and fewer technicians and test equipment, then inventories, technician numbers, and support gear in both the ISB and the battle space may grow back toward the just-in-case model.

The major concern, of course, is to minimize the product support footprint in the battle spaces. The proposal for PM-led product support outlined in this and the previous chapters affords major opportunities for keeping that footprint small for new systems and reducing it for legacy systems. These opportunities result from application of the principles discussed earlier. An accountable PM with adequate management and funding authority and a responsive, motivated integration contractor-subcontractor/vendor team, all equipped with a continuously shared knowledge capability, can produce the required footprint as well as timely support delivery results.

This team can ensure that the DSUs are supplied reliably with the necessary resources (replacement components, diagnostic aids, tools, and technical assistance) when needed, minimizing what has to be carried into the battle space. The team is incentivized to reduce component failure rates, thus reducing the depth of required parts stockage and eliminating the need to stock other components. Reducing customer wait time for parts further reduces the depth of required stockage. Improving the proficiency of DSU and operating unit technicians reduces the time required to diagnose faults and replace components over time, allowing reduction in technician staffing and its life-support elements. The continuously shared knowledge process is the glue that binds these elements together. It connects the DSU technicians faced with keeping systems operational with the resources that enable the PM's team to anticipate needs for replacement components, systems, or other resources. An effective knowledge process is the key ingredient to responsive military system supply/value chains just as it serves commercial systems in reducing cycle time and taking costs out of those chains.

Minimized Footprints through Product Support R&D

The longer-term pursuit of minimized footprint will require additional R&D effort. The process changes advanced here will streamline support and yield a smaller footprint than is practical at present. Further progress needs to focus on the footprint-influencing system attributes: principally improved reliability of components, ability to anticipate failures so as to make component replacements between engagements, and easier maintainability. Large footprint reductions may eventually come from the prospective conversion to fuel cell power packages, with their dramatically reduced bulk fuel requirement, and in the nearer term from the continued replacement of conventional ordnance with precision munitions, especially those not requiring chemical propellant or explosive warheads. One example illustrates such a footprint-saver aboard Navy surface combatants. Development of the rail gun concept would allow the stowage of more than *10,000* kinetic energy rounds in a vessel's magazines where only 1,500 of the new advanced (but with propellant and explosive warheads) gun system rounds are planned—a 7:1 advantage in targets per magazine, assuming the same target effects capability for both rounds. That advantage is possible because the rail gun projectile requires neither propellant nor an explosive warhead. The rail gun's electrical generation equipment can be accommodated in the presently available gun mount space.

THE EFFICIENCY OBJECTIVE

I have endeavored to make the case that adopting and implementing product support processes using the five supporting principles can produce *timely delivery of support* of weapons and support systems to the operating forces while *minimizing the product support footprint* in both the battle spaces and the ISBs. All the principles except coalition support are essential (it yields benefits but does not detract from the operation of the two major measures of effectiveness if not followed). The proposed changes to DoD's policies and procedures that were described above will facilitate the institutionalization of the principles and better assure the operational availability of systems that the combatant commanders are counting on. And implementing those policies and procedures will contribute to major resource savings, which can be plowed back into training, modernization, or further improvements to service members' quality of life.

Gains in Cost Visibility

Implementing the product support process improvements outlined in this and the previous chapter can generate significant resource savings. First, transferring accountability to the PM. A first order of business for a PM in charge of life-cycle support should be capturing all the funds flows, including payment to the PM's own staff, expenditures for contract repair, replacement components, and consumable parts for his system, and depot maintenance. Since the PM will be measured not only on operational availability of the system but also on management of the allotted resources, the PM will want to establish a baseline of costs in all the important categories. Given the terrible state of cost accounting in the DoD at present, this baseline establishment may not be feasible until the PM brings on the integration contractor (under the *maximum contracting of out-of-battle space support* principle) and develops the product support team (including its organic components). Costs become very visible when directly related to contract payments. The first year or so may be a struggle to simply collect, aggregate, and understand the operating and support costs of the system. That accountability should include the military technician force structure and its technical proficiency in the operating forces and DSUs on the presumption that, over time, maintenance personnel requirements are a variable cost, too—capable of being reduced as system reliability and maintainability improve and technicians' productivity increases. However, high system availability, especially in combat operations, depends on the assignment of trained technicians and leaders in appropriate numbers, a matter of as great concern to the operating forces as to the PM and the integration contractor.

It is almost axiomatic in management that once costs are known, they can be managed. Budgets can induce financial discipline, as will contractor incentives. One will see excessive inventory dry up; unnecessary maintenance, including that in DSUs, will diminish simply because it will now be very visible. One anecdote suggests reasons. When new (now "legacy") Army and Air Force systems were introduced, maintenance engineers conducted level-of-repair analyses to determine what tasks had to be done at depots and what could be done at intermediate and organizational levels. It became a standard (perhaps apocryphal) rule that the depot tasks should require at least the number of direct person-hours used for the system to be replaced, so that no depot jobs would be lost. All the better if the new, more complex system required *more* direct labor hours. It was said of one system that required, under this rule, about 100,000 depot maintenance person-hours for its periodic depot maintenance inductions that at least 50, 000 of those hours could be performed at the intermediate level rather than the depot, using the stands, tools, and test equipment authorized at the intermediate level. A contractor would make that change, working night shifts, if necessary, since that effort would raise the fleet operational availability and avoid the high costs of depot overhead. It is also reasonable to expect that those level-of-repair analyses would get a careful review by the integration contractor to find more efficient ways for organizing the tasks and taking advantage of modern testing and repair technology.

Sustainment Engineering for Cost Reduction

Because the PM and contractor would collect data on failure rates, component removal rates (including those with "no evidence of failure"), test equipment reliability, maintenance hours at DSUs as well as repair centers, and other similar data, sustainment engineering under the contractor can be focused on the high cost drivers. Here too the contractor would have a major incentive to drive down operating and support costs once the contract cost baseline was established. If the contractor owned the inventory, the integration contract could be changed to a firm-fixed price per operational use unit, e.g., flying hour, usage hour, or mile; then the contractor would have the incentive to pay for the improvements under a share-in-savings approach or through use of separately priced modifications within the fixed budget. The incentive for improvement can be made very lucrative; the benefit to the system is both higher availability, probably fewer DSU person-hours with an opportunity to reduce the military manpower associated with the system, and reduction in the inventory of components, with the associated smaller footprint and cost savings.

Cost Control through Better Knowledge

Policies to implement continuously shared knowledge not only will enable timely delivery of support and a minimized battle space footprint, but also will play a critical role in facilitating the achievement of cost savings. The knowledge system would give visibility to the critical information on maintenance and reliability to all parts of the supply chain, from operating unit to component vendor. Within the knowledge system a decision support process should track removal rates and person-hours by task, measuring them against standards and signaling deviations. Both the integration contractor and component vendors would be able to track those data on deviations as they occur and conduct early assessments of causes. For example, if the removal rate for a particular component were to rise unexpectedly in one organization, the integrator and perhaps the vendor could dispatch a field service representative to the organization to review the situation, analyze the components, and test equipment. If the cause was improper diagnosis, the technical representative could refresh the technicians' knowledge, repair the test set, or replace it. If the components were faulty, then the same process could find and fix the problem at either the repair center or the factory. Most importantly, the knowledge system communicates knowledge of the deviations so that appropriate actions can be taken by the contractors, who have a strong incentive to act quickly!

Another major efficiency benefit is the same outcome that contributes to the lower logistics footprint: a smaller inventory and storage requirement, both fixed and mobile, and fewer people to handle it, throughout the supply chain. This is the same large cost savings experienced by the best commercial firms over the last decade or so, once they learned to employ knowledge rather than large inventory holdings.

Contracted Incentivized Cost Control

Implementation of the policies and procedures to contract for product support outside the battle space probably is the main instrument for obtaining operations and support cost reductions in sustaining weapons and support systems. The areas of potential cost savings just described—better cost visibility, sustainment engineering efforts, use of continuously shared knowledge to reduce inventory—are premised on the service PMs' ability to engage the integration contractors under contract arrangements that incentivize cost reductions as well as system availability. Contracting for product support allows the services to structure much leaner oversight and management processes and organizations, with the attendant savings in overhead, in ways similar to industry's experience.

In the long term, DoD would no longer have to own inventory management organizations, distribution and maintenance depots, and ship-yards. The 21st-century generations of systems should not require those government-owned facilities; they could gradually be phased out as legacy systems are replaced by new systems. A faster attrition, as described earlier, might be achieved by including these activities in the next base-closure program, turning the real estate over to local development authorities with a provision for joint DoD and commercial use as long as necessary. As PMs brought on integration contractors, the depot maintenance and distribution activities located at those sites could continue in operation either as sub-contractors—as in some present depot partnership arrangements—or as organic work centers. In addition, the availability of the underutilized facilities at those sites may be attractive to the contractors, allowing them to lease some of the space to co-locate other functions, such as sustainment engineering, with the government subcontractor's repair activities, thus reducing the costs they would need to recover from the services. The great benefit to the services and DoD would be dramatic reductions in the yearly cost of the facilities' upkeep to only that required to sustain the diminishing organic activities.

Better Cost Control through Simplified Financial Management

The proposed set of policies and procedures to advance the *simplicity* principle surely will have a significant impact on cost containment and reduction. Implementing the transfer of life-cycle system responsibility with resources and appropriate authority to PMs simplifies the present dysfunctional management of product support, streamlining both processes and organizations and eliminating unneeded transactions and people. While the main purpose of the change, as we have said, is to centralize accountability in the PMs, the simplification of management relationships enables a coherent focus on system performance and costs. On the costs side, the services gain improved visibility of the current system operating and support costs in the initial business case, and a managerial cost-accounting system, employing activity-based cost analysis, that will track costs accurately after contracting for the support.

Better visibility allows better programming and budgeting and the end of the "slush fund" aura of the present use of working capital funds. If the services "buy" system operating hours, miles, or steaming days and then allocate them to the owning units, there will be no incentive for the kind of financial gamesmanship that the present financial management system promotes. There can be a clear separation between mission funding for systems and other legitimate funding needs, such as base support. While the operating force commanders' flexibility to shift funds might be impaired, they, their military departments, and DoD headquarters would have a better grasp of the real costs of operations and could gain much greater credibility with the congressional appropriation committees, the Government Accountability Office, and the services' own inspectors general.

The greater visibility of costs certainly will root out most of the more specious projects entered into by well-meaning but aggressive commanders who are determined to make some impact during their short tenures. Most organizations' experience supports the old saying that "if you can measure it, you can manage it." Managerial cost accounting in these complex activities puts the spotlight on deviations from budget or program and focuses managers' minds wonderfully, especially during the accompanying periodic review-and-analysis sessions with senior commanders.

Creating efficiencies in the product support processes, therefore, is a *result*, and not the primary objective, of the policies and procedures associated with institutionalizing the supporting principles. Controlling costs and rooting out unnecessary expenditures have always been desired goals; this book proposes the means of achieving them while focusing on effective sustainment of the weapons and support systems required to execute campaign plans. Making the necessary policy and procedure changes to produce timely delivery of support in operations and training while minimizing the logistics footprint of the product support processes will produce cost control and efficiencies in those processes—not quickly but enduringly—so that the programming and budgeting cycle can gradually reallocate the liberated resources to other defense needs.

CHAPTER 9

SUSTAINING THE PEOPLE IN OPERATIONS

THE TASK

We have traced the processes of force deployment and sustainment of the force's weapons and support systems. We turn now to the third important set of logistics processes: those required to sustain the people involved in the nation's military campaigns. We have learned from the nation's sometimes bitter experiences that the outcome of campaigns depends upon both our people's skill and competencies in employing weapon systems and their good health, high morale, and fighting spirit that allow them to endure the rigors of combat and other operations. The armed forces seldom will fight in benign environments. Our forces are nearly always exposed to diverse environmental extremes of climate, weather, and terrain as well as multiple diseases and, of course, multiple risks of death and injury from enemy action or from accidents. Campaigns can be long, drawn-out affairs alternating between periods of inactivity and periods of intense combat. People sustainment is essential.

People to be Supported

The job of logisticians and military medics is to sustain the people in the force and (increasingly) those civilians who are in some way attached to the force and require the partial or complete support given military members, e.g., the embedded journalists in Operation Iraqi Freedom. We should keep in mind the support required for contractors supporting the forces in the theater; civil servants deployed for various specialized functions—usually in the ISBs; members of approved nongovernmental organizations, who may even locate in the battle spaces; and local and third-country nationals who are employees in the ISBs. The land forces also have an obligation to provide life-sustaining support for both prisoners and noncombatants in the portions of the battle spaces they control. Our focus will be on the military members of the deployed force, but the process descriptions also apply to the civilians accompanying the force. We will conclude the chapter with a brief description of humanitarian assistance to the noncombatants and prisoners in the battle spaces.

Sustainment Objective: Healthy, Fit, High Morale

Understanding the complexities of the logisticians' mission to sustain people in the environment described above calls first for the understanding of requirements. One useful approach to that understanding is to use the term adopted by the Joint Staff to describe the medical support mission: "Force Health Protection." We shall broaden the term to encompass all the requirements associated with maintaining healthy, fit soldiers, sailors, airmen and women, and marines with high morale, ready for their missions. This approach is much like the objective we defined for sustaining weapons and support systems: *availability when needed.* The difference is that we plan for some systems not to be available at times, but we plan to sustain people in a healthy, fit posture *all the time.* We plan the actions necessary to restore to that posture those who become injured, ill, or unfit. This clinical way of looking at the objective helps us to describe the sustainment requirements in terms that show their relationship to the "healthy, fit, high morale" objective.

Basic People-Sustainment Requirements

The basic logistics (and medical) requirements for health and fitness are

- adequate nutrition and water intake
- clothing and shelter appropriate to the environment
- chemical-biological agent (chem-bio) protective clothing
- disease, illness, and accident prevention services and restorative care services.

For high morale the requirements are

- contact with "home" (including e-mail and telephone)
- recreation opportunities when operations permit

➤ opportunities to satisfy spiritual needs
➤ mortuary services.

The challenge is to provide these products and services where the forces operate—in battle spaces under combat conditions and in ISBs, as well as throughout the force projection period. The products and services must be adapted to each of these environments and must consider the different cultures of the services' operating-unit customers. The processes therefore will differ in some ways to fit the different environments and customers.

NUTRITION

Food services are designed to meet the different calorie and nutritional balance requirements of forces in their different environments in ways that minimize the food service footprint. Forces in fixed facilities such as air bases, staging areas in ISBs, and ships will have food preparation resources that allow the same diets they would have at home stations. Where resources are sparse, e.g., no refrigeration, food service teams will use heat-and-serve group rations. Land forces engaging in operations may subsist entirely for several days (or weeks) on combat rations—high-calorie, long-shelf-life, individually packaged meals. While the land forces in the battle spaces are the heaviest users of combat rations, the AEFs may also issue them for their base security and flight line personnel and for crews on long-duration sorties (tankers, bombers, airlifters). Likewise Navy vessels may keep a supply for emergency issue.

Combat Rations

Since land force members carry combat rations on their person, the rations need to be light and the packaging able to withstand the heat, cold, immersion, and other conditions the service member endures. The principal member of the current combat ration family is the meal ready-to-eat (MRE). By continually increasing the variety of foods and improving their similarity to the foods that these mostly young men and women in the forces recognize, the DoD tries to contribute to maintenance of morale as well.

Several types of combat rations have been developed to take account of mission and environment. A very concentrated ration known as the long-range patrol ration (LRP) was designed for those small units whose operations in enemy territory require high foot mobility and the need to eat on the run. A cold-weather combat ration contains higher calorie content to allow the body to produce the needed heat in frigid environments.

In addition, fresh fruits and other perishable items, such as milk or ice cream, are added when conditions permit. For example, apples and bananas can be stable for a day or two without refrigeration and can be included with normal ration issues as long as they can be transported to the DSUs for distribution to operating units within their limited shelf life.

There is a documented connection between the attractiveness of the combat ration to its consumer and the maintenance of the consumer's health. Simply, if the food is perceived as neither tasty nor familiar, the individual may not eat enough to sustain energy in periods of intense activity—thus the continual effort to change the meals to increase their appeal.

Combat rations are distributed to the land force consumers by the parent unit daily to minimize the weight they must carry. And, if the conditions permit, units try to feed a group ration at least once a day to contribute to both nutritional needs and morale by reducing the monotony of eating combat rations. The two or three meals per day per individual of combat rations are packaged so as to allow delivery to the platoon in boxes, to be distributed to platoon members at an appropriate time.

In this combat ration supply chain—a relatively simple process—the land force DSU delivers rations to the parent units in the periodic log pacs once to several times a day. The unit then breaks up the log pac for further distribution to its platoons. Navy and Air Force organizations normally issue combat rations as needed, e.g., at the beginning of a shift for security personnel.

Since rations have a reasonably predictable demand based upon the number of people, only a small inventory is maintained at the DSU, perhaps three days' supply. Daily issues come from that inventory (or occasionally by direct delivery) to units by truck, helicopter or airdrop (a normal delivery method for special operations teams).

Regular strength-reporting and inventory status reports allow the service component logistics organizations in the ISBs (or CONUS) to distribute the right amount of combat rations in the log pac deliveries to the DSUs. Menu variation to avoid boredom is managed through the distribution process. Although combat rations are "common supplies" managed by DLA, they are managed currently in the theater by each service component's theater logistics organization unless an executive agent is designated to respond to the requirements for distribution to all services' forces.

Managing the combat ration supply chain from the CONUS to the ISB is a matter of adjusting the flow of combat rations to theater from DLA-held operational and war reserve stocks. Since the manufacturing requirements are a very small part of the nation's food manufacturing capability, there are only a few small manufacturers. DLA has had to fund investment in these manufacturers to maintain an adequate production base to provide some ability to increase production to meet such surge requirements as encountered in Operations Desert Shield/Desert Storm and Iraqi Freedom. Thus DLA maintains a warm production base and an ability to quickly communicate to the few suppliers the changes in demand so that they can adjust their production and raw material and intermediate product intake. Also, in such cases of surge, a different interim combat ration was in the past necessary to allow feeding large numbers of people until field kitchens and group rations could be made available. Those interim rations can be packaged from high-volume products in the commercial market that are also not as expensive as the normal combat rations. In such situations the available combat rations would go to the land force elements requiring high caloric content. The interim ration is distributed to the large number of consumers who don't require the high-calorie rations until the food service process serving them can be converted to group feeding.

Group Rations

Group feeding is an opportunity to provide balanced, tasty meals to all service members, whether in the field, on board ships, or in garrison. However, these processes require a larger footprint for preparation, serving, and cleanup than the distribution of combat rations. All the services have trained food preparation personnel and encourage excellence in skill development through worldwide competitions both within the services and in civilian culinary competitions. The range of meals for group feeding runs from a type of heat-and-serve unitized group ration (UGR) to preparation of perishable foods as in any institutional or commercial kitchen. Heat-and-serve meals are packaged for long shelf life with minimum preparation in field kitchens or ship galleys and do not require refrigeration. Land forces have mobile field kitchens in nearly all organizations and employ them when operational conditions permit, by bringing either the mobile kitchens to the troops or the troops to the kitchen sites. Prepared meals are delivered short distances in insulated containers even though the risk of cold "hot food" is high. Navy and Air Force units also make use of the heat-and-serve rations as a backup to their preferred food preparation. Larger naval vessels have sufficient refrigeration to keep perishables for much of the time between shuttle-ship replenishments. The AEF relies on heat-and-serve rations until they can install refrigeration at operating bases or find local sources for daily resupply of perishables.

Like combat rations, DoD's heat-and-serve rations are developed to specifications, but they are similar enough to commercial institutional food packaging to enable DLA to use the commercial industrial base. The supply chain for this group-feeding process is similar to that for combat rations—but with important differences. It is rare for the land forces DSUs to carry inventory during mobile operations because of the extra transport resources required by the bulk of even the heat-and-serve products' concentrated packaging. They must rely upon log pacs to deliver these rations, which they must distribute promptly for consumption. However, during operational pauses, the DSUs can afford to stock a few days' worth of UGRs, which they may be able to supplement with fresh fruits and vegetables, providing the customer units with a change from the MREs. The AEFs and naval vessels are more capable of maintaining an inventory of UGRs.

Group Ration Supply Chain/Prime Vendors

Both combat rations and the heat-and-serve rations are managed in the traditional way by DLA's Defense Supply Center Philadelphia (DSCP). It maintains a national, and more recently regional, inventory. DSCP issues from inventory in response to customer DSU requisitions and then periodically orders from the industry suppliers to replenish inventory. Since both rations are military specific, albeit with some commercial parallel, such a process is appropriate. However, DSCP has transformed its supply chain management of its commercially available subsistence, both perishable and nonperishable, to a "prime vendor" concept. Prime vendors are commercial distributors that supply institutions; they take orders directly from military dining facilities of all services (including ships) around the world and deliver directly to dining facilities and ships.

One example indicates the effectiveness of using prime vendors. A Navy vessel transiting from the Baltic Sea to the Mediterranean placed its order with the European region vendor, arranging for delivery at several ports along the way. The distributor delivered all the items ordered; 95 percent were first priority, and the small balance were substitutes—a far better performance than ever attained before.

The prime vendor system eliminated a number of government middlemen in different organizations over which neither DSCP nor the dining facility customers had much influence. The prime vendor distributor has performance and cost objectives with incentives to meet or exceed them—a huge improvement in process accountability.

WATER

The second part of the health-fitness objective is the provision of water to deployed forces. As with food (subsistence), consumers' water requirements can be estimated accurately based on population served, with the consumption rates based on environment and experience for its various uses, e.g., drinking, food preparation and cleanup, bathing, medical treatment, and so on. Potable water can be produced with modern reverse osmosis purification technology and distributed in bulk from local production sites via tank truck or trailer. The alternative is to distribute commercial bottled water, which requires sizable general transportation resources because of its bulk but does not require the specialized water production and distribution equipment and operator's footprint—at least for drinking, food hydration, and "helmet" shaving and bathing. Bulk water must be supplied for land force laundry and shower services and for field hospital use. Ordering and distributing bottled water from ISBs to DSUs is handled much the same as with military rations, and prime vendors can be contracted to distribute to ISBs.

Water production and distribution capabilities are organic to vessels and traditionally have accompanied land forces into battle spaces in their DSUs. ISBs may rely on local water supplies, but usually require that water to go through the high-capacity water purification process, which is frequently a government-owned and contractor-operated (LOGCAP) service.

Ice

Ice is yet another necessity, especially in the hot climates in which many of the last decade's campaigns have been fought. Perhaps the most essential use for ice has been to cool bottled drinking water in order to bring its temperature down from the 100-degree-plus outside temperature of Southwest Asia to a more palatable 70 degrees. It is critically important that service members drink liberally in the hot climate to avoid ever-threatening dehydration. The cooler water has become nearly a necessity for them.

While ice machines are available on board ships and in AEF facility packages, supplying ice is a dilemma for the land force DSUs, especially during mobile operations. They are not equipped with ice-making equipment. Commercial sources in the battle spaces will not likely have high standards of potable water for ice making even if they have the equipment. The method employed in Iraq is to use the commercial ice to cool bottled water but carefully to dry the water bottles when they are issued, to minimize the chances of troops ingesting the melted ice. The alternative of providing a continuing supply of dry ice was used frequently in Vietnam. But it requires refrigerated storage for each unit if it is to last any time.

Clothing and Personal Equipment

Clothing and related personal equipment constitute the third component of people sustainment. Military personnel deploy to theaters of operation—battle spaces and ISBs—with their personal clothing and equipment, which likely includes a personal shelter and sleeping equipment. The logistics challenge, which begins with the military person's first line supervisor (e.g., Army/Marine squad leader, Navy section chief, Air Force team chief), is like the product support objective: keeping clothing and equipment serviceable and available. Clothing and equipment frequently are damaged, destroyed, or lost in operations, particularly by land forces. The test of this particular supply chain is its responsiveness in restoring an individual's lost or damaged personal clothing and equipment items—in the proper sizes.

Resupply to forward land force units is accomplished in response to orders for the specific items originated by the unit supply person, who receives the requirement from the individual's supervisor. The prudent unit supply person keeps a limited supply of frequently damaged or lost items if there is space—aboard vessels, at AEF bases, and perhaps a (very) few items in the land force unit supply trucks. Land force DSUs also hold a small inventory, including a few sized items in popular sizes. Otherwise the ISB, a CONUS distribution center, or a vendor must be the source—especially for unusual sizes.

Supply Chain

One example of how the clothing and personal equipment supply chain can work occurred during the staging in Saudi Arabia for Operation Desert Storm. A satellite-transmitted requirement for a pair of size-18 extra-wide desert boots came to the Army Materiel Command from its logistics support element in the theater, an order that originated, we were told, from the theater combatant commander, who had been told by a soldier that no one could find boots to fit him. A rapid inventory check of DSCP stock showed "zero" (customarily these sizes are made to order). The DSCP manager placed an urgent order with the boot manufacturer, with instructions to ship the boots to Charleston Air Force Base. The boots flew to Saudi Arabia only a couple days later and were on the soldier's feet in a few days. That pair of boots was one of many special orders that received dedicated order fulfillment treatment during the Gulf War. (In the next chapter we will explore the implications of such a rapid order fulfillment.)

This special-order example also provides insight into the supply chain relationships for these items. In fact, the Army engaged in the rapid introduction of a totally new desert boot only a few weeks after the initiation of the deployment, based on the theater commander's personal intervention in assessing the then-issued boot as unacceptable for the desert conditions. The R&D center at Natick, Massachusetts, working with several manufacturers, delivered several prototypes to the CENTCOM headquarters, where they were tested briefly. The commander expressed his preference; there being no reason not to accept it, an emergency contract was let and extended to include a couple million pairs. Deliveries began in a few weeks, and the combat forces were "re-booted" before the initiation of the land force attacks into Kuwait. This system acquisition probably set a record for time from requirement to fielding.

Prime Vendors

Many of the clothing items are migrating to prime vendor contracts, especially for initial issues of uniforms and for some personal equipment to initial-entry training centers of all the services. Such relationships are being extended to keeping shelves full and filling special orders for specialized clothing and equipment items normally issued at home stations. This is a variation on vendor shelf stocking, increasingly common in retail firms such as Wal-Mart. Further evaluation can eliminate the middlemen and keep DSCP managers in the role of establishing and policing the relationships— a brokering role that allows competitive commercial firms that possess these distribution competencies to bring them to defense logistics, enabling significant supply chain cost savings and support improvements.

NON-BATTLE CASUALTY PREVENTION

The third major leg in the triad of support for force health and fitness is the prevention of disease and injury to members of the forces. As we noted earlier, healthy, fit soldiers, sailors, airmen and women, and marines are the essential elements of successful campaign execution. Until very recently disease and non-battle injuries—not battle casualties—were the major cause of reduced effective strength in military forces. During Operation Iraqi Freedom, injury—but not disease—was a significant cause of casualties. While the task of planning and overseeing disease and injury prevention belongs to the services' medical departments, logisticians—and, most assuredly, unit leaders—play important roles in the processes necessary to keep the forces healthy and fit.

Disease Prevention

We have already discussed the provision of nutrition in subsistence, drinkable water to keep hydration at a healthy level, and clothing and shelter to protect service members from environmental extremes. All of these logistics products and services play major roles in the prevention of disease and non-battle injury casualties.

Veterinarian-medics have important tasks to perform: assuring food safety through inspections of perishables, certifying local sources as well as inspecting the products, and assuring the safe consumption of combat and group rations through product surveillance. Preventive medicine technicians similarly check water purification and distribution to assure safe drinking water. Logisticians plan for these surety checks to ward off the devastating illnesses that food and water-borne diseases can create.

Logisticians in charge of people support must be especially alert to these health risks, which are even more prevalent in the less-developed areas of the world where most modern campaigns are conducted. Such diseases run rampant in the populations of these countries, where food and water purity is far below U.S. standards. In addition, these populations have built up some immunities to diseases that U.S. personnel have never been exposed to; those without immunity can become violently ill when attacked. The Vietnam experiences of many who ate local food or ingested water are painful reminders of the immediate and delayed effects of these previously little-known diseases.

Injury Prevention

Injury prevention processes have become increasingly common as the awareness of workplace hazards has grown in civilian occupations. It used to be required to train for endurance fitness by running long distances in boots. (I recall the frequent seven-mile runs—"airborne shuffle"—during my time in an airborne infantry company.) We little realized the high rate of foot injuries that occurred—and the number of soldiers' and marines' healthy-fit-available days that units lost. Noncommissioned officers in these line units who experienced that and other physical-training injury-producing exercises—such as deep knee bends—became less and less able to physically exercise their enormous troop-leading responsibilities as a result of the long-term effects.

Training designed to avoid repetitive stress, heat, and other environmental exposure injuries has produced a much more fit and injury-free force, but attention to occupational safety to keep injury rates at a minimum is rightly a matter of intense command focus. Military occupations by their nature offer enough hazards, from aircraft carrier flight operations and underway replenishment to parachuting. Logistics organizations also have their share of potential injury-causing hazards and need the practiced eye of trained preventive care technicians to ensure that they recognize the hazards, design safe processes, and train their people to safely execute them.

Process and Product Design

The disease and non-battle injury prevention services operate in the battle spaces and ISBs as well as in CONUS wherever military forces are found. In both the battle spaces and ISBs their role is to forestall exposure from attack by harmful microbes or environmental extremes. In the CONUS their role includes influencing the design of products and processes, such as water production and distribution, maintenance of equipment, and training. Combat rations must have the required nutritional balance, shelf life, and packaging to perform their function of delivering nutrition to military members in the harsh environments in which they fight. Built-in disease prevention is critical.

Clothing design for those operating in extreme environmental conditions is only remotely similar to outdoor sports gear. Design and testing of clothing, shelter, and personal equipment must equip those who deploy to extreme environments to remain healthy and fit. Tradeoffs must be made to provide adequate environmental protection within the service member's ability to wear and carry the clothing and equipment or comfortably use it on the flight line or flight deck. This mandates a continuing search for lightweight, durable, breathable material that insulates from cold, cools when necessary, and dries out quickly. To complicate the task further, add the protective clothing and equipment necessary to defend against hostile fire and chem-bio threats—the super-environmental hazards.

CASUALTY CARE AND EVACUATION—RESTORATION TO HEALTH AND FITNESS

Prevention doesn't always work; combat casualties are likely results of any enemy engagement. Disease and non-battle injuries will occur (although they have been radically diminished in each successive campaign of the last two decades). Therefore, like the weapons systems and support equipment they operate, the service members who become casualties need a "repair" process to restore their health and fitness. Casualty care begins in all services with the units in the battle spaces and extends in a continuum of planned care with trained medical—and nonmedical—personnel participating to return the casualty to health and fitness as quickly as possible.

Since the most immediately available potential caregiver for a casualty is another squad/crew member or "buddy," the services train them in elementary lifesaving procedures. Not far away are the services' version of emergency medical technicians, the medics or corpsmen assigned to the combat units. They undergo demanding skill training designed to stabilize casualties and evacuate them into the hands of a physician. Each Army and Marine combat battalion is assigned a combat-casualty-trained physician (often trained in a large city emergency room to deal with gunshot trauma).

The physician at this level, a key player in the care continuum, is able to diagnose and stabilize the patient and decide if further evacuation to a hospital is necessary. Timely diagnosis and stabilization are critical to many patients' survival, so helicopter evacuation is used from land forces' engagement sites, forward aid stations, trauma team sites, and task force clearing stations to ARG vessels or airfields in the battle space, where the patients are transferred to Air Force intra-theater medical evacuation aircraft (perhaps rapidly reconfigured cargo aircraft returning from resupply missions). The patients then are transported to ISB hospitals, and perhaps on to CONUS or forward base hospitals, depending on the likely duration of recovery and the need for special treatment facilities. For example, it makes sense to retain patients at the ISB only if there is a reasonable chance of returning them to their units. Otherwise, stabilization and evacuation are ordered. The Navy process is similar, with casualties stabilized by the emergency medical technicians or physicians aboard the smaller vessels and helicopter evacuation to aircraft carrier or ARG vessels equipped for surgery and patient holding. Transfer to aircraft carriers allows further evacuation, if necessary, aboard the CODs shuttling to forward naval bases or to land ISBs for further evacuation to CONUS if necessary. Since AEF personnel (except forward air controllers and a few others operating with land forces) already may be located near ISB hospitals, their evacuation and treatment are less complicated than for casualties from either land or maritime forces.

The continuum of care extends to CONUS, where treatment and rehabilitation continue in station hospitals and the regional medical centers. For those permanently disabled, the continuum of care extends into the Veterans Administration hospitals or civilian facilities and clinics, once the patient is discharged from the service.

SUPPLYING THE CASUALTY PREVENTION AND CARE PROCESSES

The health protection processes provide the opportunity for unique supply chains for the acquisition and distribution of pharmaceutical and medical/surgical (P&MS) supplies.

Land Forces Distribution

Unlike the situation with other sustainment commodities, distribution of P&MS supplies for the land forces operates largely within the medical structure of land force battle space medical units. Air and ground ambulances are the transport means. Intra-theater transport carries P&MS supplies into Marine and Army task force landing zones and to combat-support hospitals in the battle spaces through the same distribution process as other supplies. Medical units of the task forces receive the P&MS supplies to replenish their stocks and distribute the supplies to the battalion aid stations via ambulance. The aid station's supplies are continuously replenished from the task force medical unit's inventory, allowing the aid stations to replenish the medical kits of the combat unit medical teams and maintain their operating level of supplies. Typically when casualties are evacuated to the task force holding facilities to await further air evacuation to hospitals, the returning ambulances pick up replenishment P&MS previously ordered. This battle space P&MS distribution process is perhaps the least changed of all sustainment processes. It has survived periodic attempts to amalgamate it with the other consumable processes, principally because the other processes cannot attain the service and responsiveness level of this dedicated system, which requires little or no common-user ground or air transport.

Deployed Naval and Aerospace Forces Distribution

This internal distribution process is unique to the land forces. The ARGs and CVBGs handle P&MS items like other consumables, restocking the limited inventory carried aboard their escort vessels from inventory aboard the ARG vessels and aircraft carriers. The ARGs are the ISB for MAGTFs ashore, accepting Marine and Navy (and frequently Army and Air Force) casualties brought in by helicopter and replenishing their task force P&MS stocks. Shuttle ships restock P&MS as well as other supplies in the ARGs and carriers, although the land ISB distribution center is also an available source, especially for emergency resupply.

The AEF base hospitals also are resupplied from the land ISB medical materiel distribution facilities, by ground transport when the base is close by or by air with other supplies as with the Army land forces in the battle spaces. When AEF elements are deployed into the land forces battle spaces, a field medical element accompanies them. That element's P&MS supplies are normally replenished along with other consumables through the intra-theater distribution system that serves the land forces.

CONUS Source: Prime Vendor

P&MS supply chain processes have undergone significant transformation in the last decade or so. P&MS supplies were the first commodity that DLA placed under prime vendor management. That process, which has gradually spread to other commercial or commercial-type supplies, converted DLA managers to managers of a service rather than managers of items. DLA contracted with the large commercial P&MS supply distributors whose customers are the civilian hospitals and pharmacies; their competitive processes transformed commercial supply chains by providing such extraordinary services as stocking hospital clinics as well as hospital and retail pharmacies, allowing large reductions in inventories. The prime vendor system allows similar treatment for military hospitals in CONUS. The prime vendors distribute P&MS supplies to the deployed forces through joint service regional medical materiel activities. DLA's role is to arrange the distributors' service through contract and oversight, embodying incentives and other terms that closely follow commercial practices. DLA can monitor the performance of the supply chain process through capturing images of orders to the distributors. Surge capability is less an issue for P&MS supplies since DoD, under most conditions, would require only a small portion of the vast resources available in the civilian health care system.

The military, of course, requires some items that are not in the civilian health care system. These limited-demand items can be managed directly with the vendors, and war reserve inventory and surge arrangements can be part of the acquisition.

Sustaining Morale

Logisticians have a major role in sustaining force morale, an essential ingredient in the sustainment of effective fighting strength. Health and fitness keep members of the forces physically ready; sustaining high morale in spite of the dangers of combat and nasty environmental conditions is essential to maintaining the crucial fighting spirit. The logisticians' role is to support the maintenance of high morale in operating units through the products and services distributed to them: mail, chaplains' supplies, recreational supplies and facilities, tasty food and beverages (e.g., beer and soda). Logisticians are also responsible for providing mortuary services, recovering the dead, processing remains for return to CONUS, and recovering and returning personal effects. Each of these logistics morale support tasks has its own unique set of processes.

Mail

Mail delivery, although evolving to a more e-mail-intensive personal correspondence mode in peacetime, still includes a considerable volume of correspondence, packages from family, and "adopt a soldier/sailor/marine/airman" community well-wishers' mail addressed to individual forces members. The mail-distribution chain also carries the unique clothing items made to order for individual members that are frequently mailed by the manufacturer or DLA distribution center to the member. One of the prerequisites of maintaining mail morale is the speed of service. Deployed service members understand that they cannot expect the same kind of two- to three-day service they are accustomed to at home stations, but morale can suffer if the service takes too long. This demand translates to a sizable part of the air cargo demand for strategic airlift into ISBs and thence into land force airfields/landing zones and by unit transport to the individual land force members. Naval forces members' mail competes for space aboard COD aircraft shuttling to the carrier battle group and for movement by helicopter from the carrier to the escort vessels. ARG and surface action group vessels get their mail from the shuttle ships. The ARG mailbags are included with resupply packages for the Marine task forces ashore in the battle spaces, unless mail has been redirected to the shore ISBs as in Operation Iraqi Freedom.

Sometimes packages and periodicals have to be separated from letter mail due to space/weight restrictions; these heavier items then travel by sea container to forward naval bases or land ISBs. At the forward naval bases, the containers are opened and tagged for the individual vessels and loaded aboard the combat logistics force shuttle ships for underway replenishment transfer to the CVBGs and ARGs—the afloat ISBs. Restrictions such as sending by air only first class mail can further lessen the load, with even a positive morale effect through a respite from incessant direct mail advertising.

Chaplain Support

Logisticians' roles in supporting chaplains' efforts to provide spiritual support are not inherently difficult but are critical. Responsive action to replenish land force chaplains' supplies of communion sets, books, or other equipment aids the chaplains' efforts in times of combat, when service members most need the chaplains' spiritual support. The logisticians' challenge is to recognize the need to integrate these resupply requirements into log pacs sent from ISBs to land force DSUs for delivery to chaplains with the task forces. These are small, unique requirements, easy to overlook in the press to assemble and move the log pacs from the distribution centers.

Recreational Support

Recreational equipment and facilities, along with the retail stores such as the services' exchanges, represent another method of keeping morale high. Aboard Navy vessels these are always present to help sailors and marines avoid boredom during off-duty time. For forces members in the land ISBs these facilities are established as soon as the TPFDD flow permits. Moving recreational log pacs from the ISBs to meet Army and Marine units in refit cycles is one way to meet this need. Mobile exchange stores, and even fast-food trucks or trailers, can be deployed to join the refitting units during their recovery periods. Like the other components of sustaining people, these services and products need to be part of the logistics planning that supports campaign planning; the windows for their employment are narrow and require quick reaction by logisticians to respond to commanders' ever-changing priorities.

Caring for the Dead

Mortuary services, usually visible only in major conflicts, are yet another of the unique reverse supply chains. The compassionate care of remains of fallen force members requires logisticians' constant attention. Sloppy completion of these tasks can harm morale, especially the morale of those, in all services, who must face direct engagement with the enemy. Careful, compassionate treatment builds the confidence of those most at risk that even if they are killed, their remains will be recovered and returned, with their personal effects, to their families. Mortuary affairs specialists often plan and operate these processes, as in Vietnam, under harsh and dangerous conditions. Normally combat units recover their own dead and turn them over to the support units with the personal effects. In some instances, however, the mortuary affairs teams must recover the remains.

Once recovered, remains in body bags and personal effects are transported to field mortuaries in the ISBs for preparation for shipment to CONUS. Proper identification, no easy task with some remains, is of paramount importance to preclude misidentification, with its sad consequences for families. Therefore, keeping identification tags and other personal effects with remains through processing is the practice. Transportation out of battle spaces to ISB and to CONUS is part of the same reverse logistics process as in recovering broken reparable components, although air shipment is the normal means.

HUMANITARIAN ASSISTANCE

The last section of our survey of the processes of sustaining people illustrates the breadth of logisticians' responsibilities. Most DoD campaigns of the 21st century will require distribution of humanitarian supplies and services to the populations in battle spaces (including prisoners of war) or locales of noncombat operations. Operation Iraqi Freedom once again has highlighted the critical importance of responsive, timely delivery of humanitarian supplies and services to the battle space population. The successful accomplishment of campaign objectives depends heavily on the effectiveness of the humanitarian support effort. The two major commodities provided by the U.S. Government are humanitarian rations, a specially designed set of foods for the particular locale, and water. In addition, PM&S supplies will be needed, as well as medical skills to augment those of the civilian populace. However, the most difficult requirements to estimate and plan are for reconstruction supplies to repair damage to essential facilities such as electrical power, water distribution, sewage, and communications. Planning for the stockage and distribution of these and other required items normally is part of the campaign planning process. DLA has handled the procurement of many of the items and distribution to the theater; the land force component normally stores and distributes the supplies, using the theater's operational lift and tactical or commercial transportation assets.

In coalition operations, several nations may participate in providing such support. When the security risks permit civilian agencies or nongovernmental organizations to operate in the affected areas, the military cuts back its role, especially in the distribution to the population. The combatant commander may still be required to act as the distributor to the civil agencies and NGOs.

CHAPTER 10

ASSESSING THE PROCESSES FOR SUSTAINING PEOPLE

In this chapter we will assess the processes for sustainment of people using the framework developed in chapter 1. We will begin with applying the principles and then examine how well the processes meet the two logistics objectives of timely delivery of sustainment and minimization of the logistics footprint in the battle spaces.

ACCOUNTABILITY FOR PROCESS PERFORMANCE

Accountability for performance of the operating unit and DSU parts of the supply chain is unambiguous. The operating units know who is responsible for bringing them food, water, medical supplies, clothing, and personal equipment and the morale supplies and services. And at the CONUS end of the supply chains, accountability for these supplies and services is clear.

Unlike the product support processes examined in chapters 7 and 8, accountability for performance of supply chains for sustaining people at the CONUS sourcing, buying, and distribution ends was transformed over the decade of the 1990s. DLA's major contribution to assuring accountability has been its prime vendor program, which has been extended to all of the people-sustainment commodities discussed in chapter 9,[1] albeit not completely covering all supply operations. The Defense Supply Center Philadelphia manages the prime vendor contracts on behalf of the customer organizations so that accountability for performance of timely delivery is visible and rewarded when it is achieved or penalized when it is below standards.

Filling the Accountability Void in the ISB

The remaining accountability void is at the ISB, where traditional service roles continue in play. These common commodities are stocked by each of

---

[1] Principally, food, bottled water, pharmaceutical and medical/surgical supplies, clothing and individual personal support equipment, and morale and religious supplies.

the service component commands' logistics organizations, making it difficult for the combatant commander to reallocate stocks in emergencies. The problem is lessened if one of the service component commands has been appointed the executive agent for that commodity. But that process is subject to the organizational problems discussed in chapter 5.

Filling the accountability void means overcoming the services' past objection to a joint theater logistics management organization (as described earlier) to manage the common supplies and services—which are the people-sustainment commodities and services (plus fuel, common munitions, and intra-theater transport). The management of the commodities (less munitions) would be an extension of DLA's CONUS management organization, detached for duty with the theater organization, but experienced in dealing with the prime vendors and others in the supply chain. This is an arrangement already practiced by the DLA's Defense Energy Support Center for bulk fuel management in the theater. The JTLM would take the management load off the service component command logistics organizations who are not experienced in managing these commodities (since DLA manages them outside the theater), allowing them to concentrate on the sustainment of their weapons and support systems while overseeing the overall logistics posture of their forces. Combatant commanders surely would prefer to have experienced management of these commodities, as well as the ability to react quickly to emergency requirements, rather than accept the traditional practices, with a pickup team for executive agency or completely decentralized service management.

CONTINUOUSLY SHARED KNOWLEDGE

The challenge of sustaining force members' health, fitness, and morale depends as heavily on continuously shared knowledge as do the force projection and weapons system sustainment processes. Those who operate distribution centers in the ISBs, ashore and afloat, should be able to keep track of the asset status of their customer task forces in all the people-support commodities, from food to whole blood. They can then adjust the flow of those commodities from the distribution centers through the intra-theater lift systems to the task forces. Regulating these flows avoids shortages of commodities critical to health and morale and avoids the buildup of inventories, with all their consequences for logistics footprint.

A New "Push-Pull" Process for Resupply

To achieve this objective, the services need to assure that the knowledge processes go beyond the traditional—and present—ordering and fulfillment process, the so-called pull system. Especially in the land forces' battle spaces, ordering can be delayed or shut down through communication failures or enemy action—as the land forces experienced during Operation Iraqi Freedom. Thus a "push-pull" process would allow the distribution center customer manager for each task force and the service component logistics command to program the distribution of periodic log pacs as "push" packages of sustainment supplies (such as food, water, medical items, batteries, fuel, munitions, and lubricants) that have fairly uniform consumption rates. By knowing the continuously changing asset status of those items in land force DSUs' inventories, the customer managers or DSUs can adjust the flows of those items. The DSUs and/or task force logisticians can then order items—the "pull" process—such as replacement clothing and different rations for periods of force reconstitution, and the ISB customer manager can have the distribution center include them in the periodic log pacs.

Individual Order Fulfillment

The ordering process also need not be hierarchical. Why shouldn't a squad leader be able to order replacement personal equipment for one of his squad members? With a Web-enabled "personal communicator" such as those used for text messaging, he could touch the appropriate icon for the blank order, put in the person's name, enter the name of the item, e.g., combat boots (stock number, size, and address would be added automatically to the order from the limited database in the personal communicator), and send it. The order would be routed simultaneously to the company supply sergeant, the DSU, the task force logistics staff, and, most importantly, their "customer manager" at the ISB distribution center. If neither the supply sergeant nor the DSU could fill the order, it would enter the distribution center's order fulfillment process; if the particular boot was on hand, an issue would be directed for the next log pac. Everyone included in the order process would be notified of the fill—all automatically—just like Amazon or L.L. Bean does. If the boot was an unusual size or type not stocked anywhere in the theater, the order process automatically would route it to DSCP's vendor; the fill and shipment could be tracked like a FedEx shipment by all the parties, from squad leader to the vendor's customer service desk.

The order fulfillment process would simultaneously adjust the distribution center's inventory and communicate the order with new status to the item's prime vendor, whose own order fulfillment system would determine whether a replenishment at the distribution center was required. If replenishment was required, the vendor would order that shipment and notify the distribution center and other nodes in the distribution process as well, and perhaps order the production of items to replenish its own inventory.

Several major benefits accrue from having the capability of sharing the service member's requirement for a clothing item with all those in the supply chain who influence the ability to satisfy the customer—first with the needed item and second with knowledge of the order and of its fulfillment. The ability to track the order fulfillment process on the Web helps the service member's morale and builds confidence in the task force leaders—from squad leader to commander—and in the logisticians regarding their ability to take care of the troops for whom they are responsible.

Each of the components of the supply chain in this example received relevant information and converted it through their IT processes to actionable knowledge. Two IT ingredients are necessary for continuously shared knowledge to facilitate people sustainment. First, business rules are necessary to convert information to action instructions to ship, to inform of status, to determine (given the relevant business rules) whether to replenish inventories, and so on. Second, continuous (or nearly so) data capture and information connectivity is required, to assure timely reaction to combat forces' needs.

The business rules, the continuous data capture, and connectivity are especially critical to the *distribution* part of order fulfillment. An example from Operation Iraqi Freedom illustrates the point. The RFID tags, interrogators, and mobility tracking system allowed logistics organizations in the ISB (Kuwait) and in the battle space to identify container location and consignee—a major improvement over the situation during Operation Desert Shield/Desert Storm. However, the logistics organizations could not identify the container contents in most cases because of the failure of the data capture process during loading.[2] Therefore the contents could be learned only when the container was opened. The technology—bar coding now, passive RFID in a couple years—is available; the business rules must require the information and mandate that loading facilities comply, as in commercial operations.

While the example used applies to perhaps the most difficult supply chain structures of the engaged land forces, the process should be the same aboard ships or on air bases. Empowering force members or their first-line supervisors to order personal items directly, as if to one of the Internet catalog distributors, and constructing the supply (or value) chain as described will enable responsive sustainment.

For other individual clothing or equipment items, similarly empowering the supervisor closest to the functional work—whether medic, food service sergeant, or chief petty officer—to use a Web-enabled system that informs all parties and implements order fulfillment will further facilitate effective sustainment processes. In addition, for those items with inventories aboard ship, on air bases, or with battle space task forces, creating automatic inventory reporting through bar coding or RFID tags can further engage the order fulfillment process, without much effort by the first-line managers. They and the distribution centers can get periodic timely updates of inventory status, which can trigger changes to the programmed flows of some commodities, such as food and water, and support replenishment for others based on business rules. Once again the necessary ingredients are (1) the business rules to convert information to actionable knowledge, (2) continuous data capture and connectivity of communication means.

Knowledge for Casualty Care

Another important role for continuously shared knowledge is its part in the casualty care process. Like the other logistics communities, the medics need continuously shared knowledge applied to their supporting supply chains for P&MS supplies and to the sustainment of medical transport and equipment. The medics also need continuously shared knowledge to support patient treatment. It has long been a health care objective to enable all the medics

---

[2] An important exception was the munitions containers whose contents were identifiable, which allowed the Army Support Command to selectively discharge the containers from the container ship rather than have to unload over 300 containers, assuring timely delivery of the munitions and a savings in footprint, since most of the containerized munitions were not needed.

in the casualty care process, from the platoon medic who first responds to the casualty throughout the processes to the CONUS hospital care team, to diagnose and measure vital signs, track treatment and evacuation status, and maintain an accurate timely record so that informed treatment can be accomplished and the status of the patient can be known by all authorized parties. The technology seems at last to be available; the challenge is to acquire the resources and institutionalize the processes that produce continuously shared knowledge about each force member's health and fitness, and about care status if the member becomes a casualty.

Telemedicine for nearly a decade has enabled remote diagnosis and treatment assistance, calling on clinical consultants' expertise for battle space treatment. Individual chip-embedded cards or ID tags can carry health and fitness data readable by all medics, from platoon to CONUS. There is no reason that the platoon medic, having put the casualty's tag or card in a reader, could not also identify the wound, treatment status, and evacuation request, transmitting it from the medic's personal communicator to all who need to know. That communication would give them the knowledge that Corporal Jones has a shrapnel wound, that the platoon medic has dressed it to stop the bleeding, and the patient needs evacuation from (automatically sent) GPS coordinates. On arrival at the pickup point, the air ambulance could activate Corporal Jones's RFID tag to automatically report his pickup, and later his drop-off, at the field medical facility. As in the example of the squad leader's combat boot order, all those with the need to know Corporal Jones's status could be informed automatically by the decision support process. Distribution of that knowledge could go partly through instant messaging to his leaders and the destination treatment center, causing it to prepare for his arrival and further treatment. The decision support process could note the field medic's action and characterization of the wound and possibly suggest the treatment supplies and equipment needed. The knowledge process could automatically post Corporal Jones's casualty status to the personnel database, report his status to his unit, create a replacement demand and casualty report, and generate a letter to designated next of kin.

Such a knowledge process can have powerful effects on preserving and restoring the fighting strength of the force and instilling confidence in force members that they will be well taken care of if injured, wounded, or ill. The morale effects are demonstrable.

CONTRACTOR SUPPORT FOR SUSTAINING PEOPLE

Most of the DLA activities responsible for these sustainment categories already have developed intensive partnerships with commercial firms for supply chain functions outside the battle space. Employment of contractors to take the place of military personnel is perhaps more widespread in this area than in either force projection or systems and equipment sustainment.

Contractors are involved intimately with people-sustainment operations in two significant ways. First, they are the prime vendors for many of the products needed to sustain people: food, bottled water, pharmaceutical and medical/surgical supplies, and some clothing and individual equipment. Second, through the LOGCAP-type contracts for services, firms can perform many of the base operating functions needed at land ISBs. Navy shuttle ships of the combat logistics force, like the strategic sealift vessels, are now operated by ship-operator firms under contract.

Prime Vendor Relationships

The prime vendor relationships for people sustainment are far easier to establish than are similar relationships for weapons systems parts. First, the products (such as heat-and-serve rations) are commercial or commercially similar, so no military specifications are necessary for most items. Second, the products have been DLA's responsibility to manage, and consumables are not encumbered with the political-cultural tentacles of depot/shipyard workers' jobs. Still, the culture change to move DLA's Defense Supply Center Philadelphia from managing (procuring, storing, filling orders, etc.) their million or so items to managing the suppliers of those items was not trivial. One part of its success can be attributed to the leaders who presented the change to prime vendors as a way for DSCP to improve its performance in spite of directed reductions in its workforce. And it took leadership courage and the vision of successive civil service and military leaders to plan, gain approval, and gain workforce cooperation for implementation. As with many commercial supply chain reengineering projects that are intelligently planned and implemented, DSCP's prime vendor projects have improved performance and saved a couple hundred million dollars of inventory. Defense became another (albeit large) customer of competitive distributors fully accustomed to constantly improving supply chain performance.

The existence of these already vigorously competing distribution channels for products needed by the forces was another asset in the conversion to the prime vendor system. (This asset does not exist in the consumable repair parts portion of DLA's present business because the parts were uniquely designed, in most cases, to be part of a weapons system or other equipment, as discussed in chapter 3.)

The fact that the people-sustainment commodities can fit into commercial distribution channels has opened the opportunity of transforming the DLA management structure from inventory managers to "brokers". DLA arranges through its contracts with these distributors for the customer organizations worldwide to order from the distributors. In effect DLA makes available to its DoD customers tailored catalogs of the products, whether food or medical or other supplies. The contracted catalog contains the terms and conditions for the customers. And DLA's supply centers monitor the process by receiving electronic copies of orders and shipment notices so that they can track the demands for the different products and the distributors' order fulfillment performance.

The brokering function puts DLA centers into the business milieu of seeking good value for DoD customers through the structure of pricing and delivery terms that affect the major performance metric, customer wait time, as well as meeting surge requirements and various government-required socioeconomic policies such as small-business participation. By managing the arrangement for providing these people-sustainment products through a commercial process, DLA's centers can foster competition among firms for this significant niche market and attain good value for both DoD customers and the taxpayer. DLA has achieved through the prime vendor program a combination of accountability for results and efficiency of resource use unobtainable in its former inventory management role. The prime vendor arrangements have become a model within DoD and the federal government of the proper role of government agencies—arranging for the needed products and services to be provided effectively and efficiently by accountable private sector firms motivated through business incentives—the revenues and profits to be made by delivering effective performance. Excellent performance is rewarded through award fees, shared savings, and/or a lengthened contract term. And through the longer term, e.g., three years with up to five- or ten-year options, firms are motivated to make investments in the processes that enable them to continually improve performance and/or reduce costs. The prime vendor concept has become a model of government-industry partnerships where both institutions share the benefits each could not obtain on its own.

Facility and Service Operations

In many ways the prime vendor relationships resemble the second major type of people-sustainment industry partnership—the ISB facility operations contract. A frequently used arrangement in the Vietnam War, this type of contracting relationship had fallen into disuse through the post-Vietnam period up until Operation Desert Shield in 1990. It was replaced by host nation support arrangements made with NATO partners in anticipation of Central European conflict. Since the forces planned to fight in Europe, it was logical to rely on the host nation structures to provide the facilities operation support and use of their infrastructure—a luxury not available in Southeast Asia. Although elements in all the services attempted to gain approval of contingency contract arrangements for areas outside Europe, their efforts were in vain.

Thus when Iraq invaded Kuwait in August 1990 and the President committed the United States to restoring Kuwait's sovereignty, the combatant commanders and services were not prepared for the facility operations tasks that accompanied the buildup of forces in Saudi Arabia. To their great credit, the services' component commands rose to the challenge through numerous ad hoc arrangements for contracting diverse services. The lesson was learned, and the terms LOGCAP, AFCAP, and NAVCAP came to identify the standby task-order-activated contracts for the host of base development and operations services needed by the forces building up and operating in ISBs. The Army's LOGCAP provides a useful example embodying a continuing requirement for a planning cell to work with Army component commands around the world, integrating their capabilities into theater contingency plans so that when an operation is directed, the contractor (on receipt of a task order) can gear up and move people and equipment to perform the various services the task order requires.

Such tasks in these omnibus contracts—tailored for each contingency—can include the full gamut of services: airport and seaport operations, local transportation, construction and maintenance of base camps, staging and equipment holding areas, distribution center operation, maintenance of equipment, and food service. These services and others, in whole or in part, are directed in the implementing task order. The service component commands no longer have to rely upon difficult-to-negotiate, detailed host nation support agreements (only the agreement to allow contractors to work and import equipment and people). Nor must the services keep the force units necessary in previous times for employment in these tasks. These units typically were in the reserve components, with the uncertain prospects of being called up for active duty when needed and released when no longer needed. Maintaining such units in the force structure also was costly; the need for them was temporary, but the costs of keeping them manned, trained, and equipped went on as long as they existed. It also is hard to justify the need for military units that do not operate in battle spaces when alternative providers—host nation and/or contractors—are available. The services, through these new contracts, no longer had to be buffeted by the inevitable political wrinkles of reserve call-ups and unnecessary disruptions to personal lives when initiating deployments. Better to reserve such consequences for justified use of the reserve components. Like the prime vendors, these contractors bring what some have called "products wrapped in services." They may operate dining facilities (as they have done in Bosnia, in Afghanistan, and lately in Kuwait and Iraq) and take responsibility for arranging with prime vendors and local vendors to provide the menus and feeding schedules directed by the supported units. Their performance since the first large undertaking in Bosnia and in subsequent smaller campaigns has been generally exceptional. Where performance lagged, appropriate oversight caused contractors to improve their operations to reach the agreed standard. The government always has the right to terminate these (like other) contracts if performance is not satisfactory. This drastic measure has been necessary in only a few cases. There is too much at stake in the large revenue streams (with practically no investment) for the contractors not to fix poor performance issues quickly.

Thus in two critical areas of people sustainment DoD has come increasingly to create industry partnerships, changing the logisticians' role from operating and managing the provision of most sustainment products and critical facility operations and maintenance services to arranging for contractors to perform the tasks: from doers to informed buyers of products wrapped in services. The transformation is not complete, but its progress certainly yields an example for the weapons system and equipment sustainment logisticians, who are racing at glacial speed to catch up.

ROLE OF COALITION PARTNERING IN SUSTAINMENT OF PEOPLE

The evolution of support to people has proceeded from the pre-19th-century practice of living off the land to the incorporation of the products of the industrial age that allowed, even necessitated, support of a campaign's forces from the nation's own sources, shipped over land and over ocean to force members. In the two world wars of the 20th century, coalition partners made available real estate and transport infrastructure, local products, and services to prepare land forces for combat; they also provided the facilities from which to launch air and naval strikes. The host nation support processes evolved to the point during the Cold War that "burden sharing" with allies became the totem of U.S. political leaders trying to maintain alliance commitments at least cost to U.S. taxpayers. From burden sharing we have evolved to developing coalition partnering as a way to take advantage of coalition partners' capabilities, to the benefit of all the nations contributing to the combined joint task force.

Opportunities for partnering in sustaining weapons systems and other equipment are limited. However, sustainment of people provides several possibilities in all the products and services we have discussed. Those opportunities come in the sourcing of supplies and services for delivery to battle space forces. A kind of "barter" arrangement would allow nations that could not contribute, inter- or intra-theater airlift to reimburse the United States through providing those goods and services it could, e.g., food, labor, local transportation, facilities, medical support, or use of recreation facilities. Nation-to-nation support agreements are the vehicle for constructing the support arrangements. Negotiating these agreements with likely coalition partners paves the way for implementing them quickly when a campaign is planned.

Combatant command or JTF logisticians and their service component command colleagues can improve the effectiveness of ISB-centered sustainment support by the artful combination of coalition partners' capabilities with LOGCAP/AFCAP/NAVCAP contracting, all to minimize the number of U.S. military personnel required for these support tasks. Such combinations of support providers can be planned and exercised by the United States and major coalition partners in each theater to prepare for the nearly inevitable surprises. The U.S. logistics community's experience with the multi-national (U.S.-sponsored) joint logistics exercises (LOGEX) during the Cold War period enabled close logistics cooperation in the campaigns of the 1990s. These exercises built up a reservoir of mutual understanding among participant nations, some of which later joined with the United States in Desert Storm and with NATO in the Bosnia-Kosovo campaigns. Similar exercises in the Pacific led to an ability to react quickly to the crisis in East Timor, where the Australians took the lead but the United States contributed much, including access to the LOGCAP contract.

SIMPLICITY IN PLANNING AND OPERATIONS OF PEOPLE SUSTAINMENT

Simplified Sourcing

In our assessment of these sustainment processes we can be encouraged by the progress in simplifying what had sometimes in the past been bureaucratically complex. The major change has come in the sourcing of most of the supplies, i.e., food, water, medical and surgical supplies, and clothing. The rapid development of the prime vendor system has brought a kind of accountability never before possible. But the simplification still has not reached all the way into the theater, and it will not until the combatant commanders decide they should exercise their prerogatives to manage the common supplies and services in their theaters, many of which are for people sustainment. As of this writing, DLA ships common supplies to both the Army and Air Force component commands and to Marine and Navy forces at the forward naval bases in the theaters. There is no theater-level management of the stocks; so if a number of containers of rations destined for the AEF were to be lost, it would take some time to determine if the Army could part with some of its stock.

Simplified Management of Theater Common Supply Support

Both services now must find warehousing—separate—for their theater reserves and operational stocks of these identical items. (An exception of late seems to be medical and surgical supplies, where a joint activity under the theater surgeon manages those stocks.)

DLA has managed these products for over forty years in the CONUS, as the operator of the sourcing end of the supply chain; but when it comes time to move out of CONUS, the services feel they must take control— with duplicate operations—in the theater. The obvious question is, why shouldn't the combatant commander arrange for DLA to manage the theater reserve and operational stocks of those items as part of the joint theater logistics management organization (JTLM)? Such an arrangement would give the combatant command, as well as the service component commands, visibility and responsive access to the supplies without having the burden of managing them. All the JTLM would need would be the funding that would come from the campaign directive. The physical task of inventory management could be contracted under the management of a team from DSCP (assigned to the JTLM), which holds the contracts with the prime vendors of most of the people-sustainment supplies.

The major simplification advantage lies in the continuity of management between peacetime and theater support. In the early days of Operation Enduring Freedom, an inexperienced Army element in Afghanistan took on the responsibility of managing the inventory (ordering, storing, and distributing) of food and did it badly. Rather than having to hand off inventory management to services' component commands not intimately familiar with prime vendor or local procurement relationships, the DLA team simply needs to relocate to the ISB, although much of the work can—and probably should—be done at the CONUS peacetime site. The precedent for DLA's management of common supplies and services in the theater as well as in CONUS is its management of bulk fuel, which its Defense Energy Support Center has managed for combatant commands for several years. The simplification advantage, to restate, lies in preserving management continuity in the time of great change that accompanies initiation of a theater campaign. Integrating DLA more deeply into the theater logistics planning, along with the service component commands' logisticians, will allow that organization to "do in war what it does in peace": support the forces with common supplies and services, e.g., distribution center operation and property reutilization. For the combatant command, DLA represents accountability, intimate knowledge of the supply chains, and leverage over the commercial firms that provide the products.

Simplified Food and Water Distribution through Technology

These process changes—improving theater management accountability, sharing supply chain knowledge, incorporating the resources of coalition partners, and extending DLA distribution and inventory management to the theater—go a long way to assuring timely delivery of people sustainment with minimum battle space footprint. Yet further opportunities remain to assure the achievement of those objectives and simplify the tasks of the DSUs and operating units in supporting their troops in the chaotic combat environment. Those opportunities arise through changing the nature of the food products and changing the technology of water production. Both commodities demand large portions of the theater's storage and transport resources. For example, bottled water consumed nearly 40 percent of the daily land transport resources during Operation Iraqi Freedom. While the MRE combat ration is an efficiently packaged way of providing nutrition, the services seek to provide variety similar to what their members consume at home station, but without the large footprint and complexity of distributing perishables.

Food preservation technology has evolved commercially and in limited government use to the point that DoD should commit resources to food irradiation or similar technology in order to design new unitized group rations that include meats, fruits, and vegetables. (We will explore this recommendation in greater depth in the section on minimizing the logistics footprint in the battle spaces.) Variety much greater than at present can be provided while retaining the simpler group-ration order fulfillment and inventory management system. The result for naval vessels and AEF bases would be to reduce the requirement for conventional perishable items and the refrigerated storage and transportation they demand—a benefit to organizations of all the services. Land force members would be able to enjoy nearly the same level of variety they have at home station. The DSUs and operating units would have no greater ration distribution requirements than at present.

Secondly, DoD should bring to maturity new technology that enables bulk water production in far smaller packages than the present reverse-osmosis water purification sets. The objective is to substitute the bulk water for part of the bottled water when the units are not engaged in mobile operations. More and smaller water production units would allow DSUs to move production closer to the consumers when operations permit and thus reduce the storage and transport demands, shrinking the footprint.

The longer term goal, which has received R&D resources, is to produce drinkable water as a by-product of fuel-cell electric power for vehicles and vessels. Incorporating these advances would both benefit the footprint reduction efforts and remove the need to centrally produce and distribute drinking and other small-quantity uses of water.

These two technology-enabled simplification measures—irradiated food and modernized water production—along with the process simplification measures—adding DLA elements to the joint theater logistics management organization to provide the theater a single source and a single inventory and distribution manager for the common supplies and services—can contribute to more effective delivery of health, fitness, and morale benefits to force members. There is enough near-chaos accompanying military operations so that efforts to remove the opportunities for human error in management and process design can help to insulate the troops from mistakes that would affect their health, fitness, and morale—critical ingredients in a campaign's success.

TIMELY DELIVERY TO CUSTOMERS

Unlike processes for sustaining weapons systems and support equipment, the timely delivery of people-sustainment products need not degrade unit readiness to fight—as long as delay does not exceed the DSUs' and operating units' stocks of the products. For example, most land forces in the battle spaces will keep a three-day supply of food and medical supplies, and the capability to purify small quantities of drinking water. Some units, such as special operations units, that are foot-mobile may not be able to carry more than a day or two of consumption. If the delayed delivery does not exceed those levels, health and fitness can be maintained. Air and naval forces typically have supplies that can last a much longer time.

Daily Delivery to Land Force DSUs

However, there is little question that health, fitness, and morale can suffer if the delays push the envelope of safety, and fighting capabilities will deteriorate if hydration, nutrition, and medical supplies fall short of needs. Therefore, the services must—and do—put a premium on timely delivery to keep

DSUs' operating stocks continually replenished to avoid the risks that result from delays. Thus the ordering and distribution processes should work on a near daily basis for land forces in the battle space, to ensure against the drying up of emergency stocks. Daily log pacs delivered from ISB to task force DSUs and distributed to their customer units should be the norm. Such an assured resupply program depends on the *continuously shared knowledge* principle. Part of the knowledge is the status of the customer units, whether a Marine reconnaissance platoon operating deep in enemy territory or a carrier battle group changing position. The capability for precise airdrop of a log pac to a Marine platoon at a mutually assigned time and place so as not to compromise its security depends on the many participants in the resupply operation sharing knowledge. Perhaps the airdrop must be made from an AEF airlifter operating from the land ISB, with the airdrop package built by the ISB distribution center on instructions from the MAGTF logistics staff and rigged by an Army aerial delivery unit. The mission may also require the joint forces air component command to commit a fighter escort. The ability to continuously update the knowledge content of the mission to include enemy-caused changes in time and place during the airlifter's flight has its payoff in successful resupply of the platoon, which, in turn, enables them to carry out their mission.

The complexity involved in arranging the timely delivery of resupply to carrier battle groups and amphibious ready groups may not be as great as in the above example, but the scale is huge. Timing the delivery of sustainment products to fit ongoing operations, coordinating the shuttle ships' sorties to the battle groups and ARGs, and then accomplishing the physical transfer of supplies are all major challenges.

Buffer Stocks to Mitigate Timely Delivery Risks

Enemy action, transport mechanical failure, and a variety of other factors that can influence the planned operation of the supply processes all pose delivery-delay risks that only buffer stocks can mitigate. These stocks need not approach the truly huge mountains of supplies seen in theaters up through Operation Desert Storm. But to sustain force members, no commander will—or should—accept a brittle transport-only supply chain between forces in the battle space and the CONUS. U.S. forces' experience in late 20th- and early 21st-century operations have demonstrated the risks of relying on improved but still imperfect resupply processes.

Timely delivery requires buffer stocks not only in consuming units, but in the ISBs. At the time of this writing there has been an effort to claim there is no need for ISBs, that resupply can go straight from the CONUS or permanent forward bases to the battle spaces. Such claims ignore the realities of the operation of supply chains, where no one in even the world-class commercial companies has found a way to defeat Murphy's Law: "If it can be screwed up, it will be!" For small operations, direct CONUS-battle space air resupply can work, but there should be a limited buffer within a couple hours' flight time of the committed force in the event supplies are lost, a programmed CONUS-based mission fails, or any number of events creates the need for emergency resupply.

As continuously shared knowledge processes improve, the levels of needed buffer stocks might well shrink, but even the best functioning knowledge processes and best managed order fulfillment processes can still be victimized; a readily available buffer can fill the gap to preserve health and fitness. The trick is to not let the most conservative logisticians (or commanders) buy so much "buffer insurance" as to defeat the next principle: *minimum logistics footprint.* Insurance, yes! Excessive risk avoidance, no!

The services—and the combatant commands' logistics processes—have a long way to go to reach the level of delivery responsiveness found in the best commercial practices.

There remains too little continuously shared knowledge, too much "heel-toe" echelonment of ordering and approving handoff-laden order fulfillment procedures. Until the services can enable the infantry squad leader or vessel supply chief to update his small unit's supply requirement and cause the relevant supply chain's responsive fulfillment action, the services cannot be confident that their units in combat will have timely delivery of health, fitness, and morale resources. Knowledge shared by capable, committed process managers is the key objective and the means to timely delivery.

MINIMIZING THE LOGISTICS FOOTPRINT OF PEOPLE-SUSTAINMENT PROCESSES

Building Trust in the Supply Chain

In assessing how the force projection and weapons system sustainment processes contribute to minimizing footprint, we saw how greater uncertainty about the reliability of the supply chain's timely delivery performance causes commanders to insist on a larger stockpile of supplies, with the accompanying larger footprint. Commanders and logisticians of all services try to manage the numerous and complex risks inherent in campaigns. The greatest fear, aside from being surprised by enemy action, is of running out of critical supplies or people when they are most needed. There is a similar fear about inadequacy of almost all critical resources, from communications to transport. The response is to get "more" so there is no chance of running out.

Of course, more supplies means more storage and more people and equipment to manage them. In turn, there is a greater *force-protection* requirement—more guards for the larger real estate requirement for storage and related support of the extra risk-avoiding stockage. The larger requirement for people and equipment can't help but hamper the operational agility of both ground and air forces in the battle spaces and create an additional source of friction for the host nations for ISBs. Thus the key to limiting footprint is to persuade commanders and (generally) risk-averting logisticians to trust that the system of supply chain management they have created will work for them. Eliciting that trust requires both the continuously shared knowledge capabilities outlined earlier and the demonstration in training exercises and day-to-day peacetime training that the processes are dependable.

Reducing the Field Feeding Footprint

One opportunity for footprint reduction is in the land forces' field feeding systems. Different types of combat rations are available in increasingly palatable variety. But troops become bored with eating just those rations, and the Army and Marine Corps have assigned field feeding capabilities to their combat units. But once they try to go beyond the heat-and-serve group rations, the footprint goes up because of the need for refrigeration, and the power to run it, so that they can prepare and serve perishable foods when combat conditions permit.

Shrinking Refrigeration

Technology has become increasingly available to permit carrying long-shelf-life perishables, such as poultry, meat, fresh fruits, and vegetables. In fact astronauts have for many years used products treated with low-dose irradiation, which destroys the microorganisms that cause these foods to spoil. (The author has eaten steak taken out of a heat-sealed wrapper and put on a grill. The steak had been irradiated about five years before. The meal was eaten in *1971*.) The problem with implementation beyond the astronauts has been the public fear of irradiated food—even though the astronauts have consumed it safely for decades. In fact the Army-operated DoD food research facility was forced to give up its low-dose nuclear reactor because of a political decision that reflected the fear. Gradually irradiation is creeping into imported spices to free them of the organisms that accompany them from their origins in Southeast Asia, and into chicken and beef (recently approved) as a means to counter *E. coli* bacteria, always a danger in hamburger and some other meat products. Encouraging developments substitute high-powered microwaves for irradiation to accomplish the objective of extending shelf life without refrigeration.

Adopting food irradiation or a substitute would go far to practically guarantee food safety in the far-off theaters of operation, allowing these treated perishables produced in the U.S. to be packed for units in the unitized group-ration configurations. Having these tasty familiar foods available would obviate the need for local procurement of possibly suspect perishables and the need for most refrigeration in the battle spaces. Such a capability would also improve the quality of food service on the AEF bases and onboard ships. Even for long deployments, the irradiated perishables, packed in ordinary storage spaces, could be treated like the combat rations in storage and distribution, with savings in refrigeration requirements for both services.

Improving Packaging for Perishables

The use of the new preservation technology would also be of great benefit to managing order fulfillment of field rations. Instead of ordering multiple individual products (and usually having many substitutes delivered), direct-support food service staffs could choose meals from the set of unitized group rations that would provide steak, shrimp, and other familiar, tasty, and nutritious entrees. Creating a web-based rations order fulfillment system for all services would approach the simplicity of ordering combat rations. The anachronistic ration order fulfillment process now in use could give way to one inspiring more trust in logisticians and commanders and facilitating a reliable supply chain that would give no incentive for having mountains of stored rations.

Providing food to sustain the health and fitness of force members is not simply a matter of supplying the product, food. Food preparation and distribution processes also can be improved to reduce the footprint they create. Both the Navy's and the Air Force's afloat and deployable food service activities are being modernized with commercial food-preparation equipment. The AEF's deployable kitchens and the galleys on naval vessels, while constrained for space, can take advantage of food-service preparation and storage technology being developed in the commercial sector, using equipment produced by the commercial manufacturers.

Reducing Power Generation

While the land forces' garrison dining facilities also use commercial equipment, their deployable field kitchens are designed to minimize the electric power requirements since the commercial-type equipment used by the AEF and Navy would require tactical generators and only add to their footprint and noise signature. Thus field stoves are equipped with fuel-fired burners. JP8 is readily available in the battle spaces and so offers an advantage. Since mobile electric power is needed for refrigeration, whether separate or mounted on a refrigerated container, distributing perishables to land forces becomes feasible only when they are refitting after engagements. Irradiated or similarly treated perishables, of course, would not need refrigeration; therefore such processes are important technologies for reducing the food preparation footprint while improving the quality of field feeding. Those preservation technologies, plus unitized group-ration packaging, precise product identification (i.e., stock number or commercial stock-keeping unit) of the contents of containers or air pallets, and order-tracking technologies, can contribute to significant footprint reduction while sustaining high levels of nutrition and morale.

While the new preservation technology can reduce the demand for refrigeration, the increased demand for ice (as noted in the previous chapter) will require both ice making and storage in all DSUs. The problem is greatest in the land forces' DSUs; both naval vessels and AEF bases will deploy ice-making and storage capabilities. DoD clearly needs to find technology that will permit sufficient production and distribution of ice or dry ice to land force units in order to, at least, cool bottled or canned beverages while the units are engaged in mobile operations in very hot climates. It may take both technology and process change to meet the requirement and to minimize the footprint of equipment and people that is created by meeting this need.

Reducing the Footprint of Casualty Care

Footprint reduction has been a continuous process for one other major contributor to the health and fitness of force members: casualty prevention and care. The services reached agreements after the end of the Cold War to change the single most critical factor in determining the size of the health care footprint, the evacuation policy. That policy tells the services how long they should plan to hold a patient in theater until the patient can return to duty. For example, with the evacuation policy at "thirty days" the services component medical commands would plan to retain patients in theater facilities if they could be expected to return to duty within thirty days. That means that the service must deploy medical units and facilities to the theater of operations sufficient to hold the projected number of casualties who would meet the criterion; patients whose conditions required a longer period of recuperation would be evacuated to CONUS and might not be returned to their parent units after recovery.

Evaluating Evacuation Policy

This issue has been hotly debated for many years. Those in favor of the longer periods (thirty-plus days) argued the need to preserve the strength of the command; evacuees would likely not return. These favoring the fifteen-day (or less) policy argued that less medical footprint would be required in theater—less to deploy, less to sustain. They also argued that since evacuees were still members of their services, they could be ordered back to the theater if necessary. The issue has largely been decided in favor of the fifteen-or-fewer-days policy and its significant reduction in medical force structure to be deployed (although no change in the total medical force structure). Combat lifesaver's training for non-medics in combat units, the higher level of training of the medics accompanying the ground combat units, and the provision of physician- and physician-assistant-led battlefield casualty treatment teams all contribute to the major objective in the battle space: to stabilize the patient and to evacuate that patient to a hospital outside the battle space, where more sophisticated treatment can be accomplished. Thus the casualty care resources—and footprint—needed in the battle space are principally for stabilize-and-medevac. There also is dispensary-type treatment for minor illnesses or injury, including a limited patient-holding capacity within the task forces. This resource is useful for getting service members back to their units after treatment. Combat support hospitals are in the force structure for deployment to land force battle spaces. However, their footprint and force-protection requirements suggest that, barring a critical shortage of air evacuation resources, such hospitals should locate in the ISBs.

Flexibly Applying Evacuation Policy

This reduced evacuation policy can also apply differently by service and by phase of operation. With a lot of casualties, the policy may be reduced to "five days" to allow the theater medical treatment personnel to concentrate on patient stabilization and medevac, keeping ISB beds available for patient stabilization alone even if patients could return to duty in the normal fifteen days. Resources available versus the unpredictable level of casualties will govern the adjustment of the policy.

While each of the services deploys medical forces to the theater, those forces will likely end up supporting all the services' casualties (as well as civil service and contractor personnel). Thus if an Army ISB hospital reaches capacity, the air medevac could go to either an AEF hospital or a Navy CVBG or ARG (or hospital ship if deployed). Joint operation also conserves footprint!

Campaigns since the end of the Cold War also have demonstrated the demands humanitarian medical support makes on battle space resources and footprint. Combat support hospitals treated perhaps more Iraqis than U.S. patients during Operation Iraqi Freedom. Such support must be provided to the battle space population until the indigenous medical system can be made functional. However, the load could be lessened through deliberate campaign planning to quickly reconstitute the indigenous system—with P&MS supplies and some equipment, medical personnel, and civil affairs administrators with language skills.

Providing Laundry and Shower Services

Laundry and bath services, essential to the health of force members, present few problems for naval force members afloat and for AEFs, where such facilities are included in deployable base infrastructure sets. However, they do present footprint management challenges for land forces elements in the battle spaces. Both kinds of services occupy space and require some shelter, a high-volume water source, and electrical power. However, equipment has been modernized to reduce laundry water consumption and to provide recirculation of waste water. In the next section we will see how these services fit into an overall set of processes to help revitalize units committed to campaign execution.

Resting and Refitting[3] Land Forces

In 21st-century campaigns, resting and refitting land combat forces will challenge logistics innovation in providing them the resources that maximize the health, fitness, and morale benefits in the time available for refitting. Our two objectives should be the parameters that guide the planning and execution of these operations. To produce timely delivery of the necessary services, rest-and-refit should be treated like a special operation, with a planned process and an organization with personnel, equipment and supplies, and the transport means to bring them to the rest-and-refit sites at the times designated by the combat commander. The process and organization should be constructed so that the combat unit can absorb the services in twenty-four to forty-eight hours, a likely period of pause in the combat operations. The process and organization can meet the objective of minimizing footprint by being inserted into the site for the operation and extracted at the end of the rest-and-refit period.

For example, the Army and Marines could organize field service detachments equipped with laundry and shower units, along with their own power and bulk water production, an individual clothing and equipment repair and replacement capability, unitized group rations with fresh fruits and vegetables, satellite phone banks, recreation resources, post exchange items, and beer and soda. A detachment might be sized to provide the services and supplies to a battalion-sized organization. It would be inserted by helicopter and augment the DSU's normal support, e.g., providing the rations to the DSU's food preparation teams.

Units would be rotated out of combat or other missions so they could draw replacement clothing and equipment, take showers, and launder clothes, in addition to eating better meals and getting sleep. Their systems

---

[3] The all-inclusive term "reconstituting" is also used.

would undergo an intensive "peak up" maintenance effort at the same time. While these refitting periods detract from the combat power available to the joint commander, the gain in health and fitness from even twenty-four hours' refitting can restore combat fitness in tired marines and soldiers (as well as the Navy and Air Force teams that accompany them). At the end of the rest-and-refit period, a rejuvenated task force would be available for future missions; the field service detachment would repack, and its helicopters would return and extract the detachment to prepare for its next operation.

This rest-and-refit proposal illustrates how the objective of minimizing the battle space logistics footprint can be achieved while providing service members with health, fitness, and morale resources. Reducing the land forces logistics footprint in the battle spaces is a useful tool to stimulate equipment improvements in order to minimize their space, weight, labor, noise, and power and water consumption demands. Such improvements will also be valuable modifications to AEF base modules and naval vessels.

Providing Shelter

The last part of our "footprint" assessment concerns the protection of the forces from the elements: shelter. Shelter footprint decisions are difficult tradeoffs. On the one hand, both most naval (afloat) and AEF personnel will have adequate shelter. The AEFs deploy modern base operations facilities, some from pre-positioned assets, some directly from storage locations. The issue is how soon to work these facility assets into the deployment flow. Since the destination of these modular sets is an ISB, CRAF or commercial vessels may minimize the competition for organic military lift.

Land forces (and accompanying Navy and AEF elements) will rely upon their individual shelters while in the battle spaces. However, when the battle space force protection task eases in the stabilization and security phase of the combat operation, the morale effects of having modern shelters, bathing, and dining facilities may be worth the force protection resources required to secure cantonment areas. This was the case in Bosnia with the NATO peace-keeping force and, more recently, operations in Iraq. Such experiences as the Bosnia operation persuaded the Army and Air Force to invest in these base camp sets to promote a healthy adaptation in the deployed environment when conditions permit. Health and sanitation are far easier to maintain in the base camp sets than with individual shelter arrangements.

CHAPTER 11

PROFESSIONAL DEVELOPMENT OF 21ST-CENTURY LOGISTICIANS

CHALLENGES

We have drawn a concrete picture of how defense logistics processes must function in order to yield timely delivery of support and a small footprint in the battle spaces in the 21st century. Transforming those force projection and sustainment processes cannot be done without competent and dedicated military and civil service logisticians to manage the changes and the processes. DoD must help them develop the new skill sets in performance-based service contracting and contract oversight, change management, knowledge management, and financial resource management, and the new technical skills that the new process designs require. They will continue to need the operational logistics skills developed and honed through the last several decades of experience in campaign support. Much of what this book discusses demands leadership skills—the ability to inspire colleagues, contractors, and customers to continuously improve their processes. It's a tall order. This chapter proposes a professional development strategy to enable 21st-century logisticians to fill the order.

At this writing we find a dedicated military workforce performing well in operating units and direct support logistics organizations in spite of an unprecedented operations tempo, the consequent shortage of training time, and the lack of the technology resources that are now common in the commercial sector. Yet military logisticians have professional development resources far superior to those of civil service logisticians. Improvements required in military professional development are concentrated in tasks of managing the product support and people support processes primarily outside the battle spaces—the same tasks that civil service logisticians face. In those tasks the services and defense commands and agencies have long intermingled military and civil service managers, a practice that brings the strengths of the military's direct customer experience together with the civil servants' provider experience and longer tenure.

GREATEST NEED: CIVILIAN LOGISTICIANS

The most challenging objective is improving the professional development of civil service logisticians. Since the late 1980s, the civil services logistics workforce has not benefited from continual refreshment at the entry level, as has the military. Many logistics civil servants are only a few years from retirement; the average age at this writing is about fifty. They have lived the last half of their careers under a workforce management strategy driven by the imperatives of budget drawdown, continuously faced with forced attrition reductions in force and with base closures or major cutbacks. Furthermore, reductions are normally made by seniority, with little regard for skill mix, due to the archaic civil service laws. Thus many people found themselves bumped into positions without the normal skills expected of those being hired for the positions.

Consequences of Management Practices

Such an environment conditions people to follow procedures, to keep a low profile, and not to push boldly to take advantage of the sweeping changes in logistics practices that have been embraced by industry. At just the time the Defense Science Board and other advisory groups familiar with the logistics changes in industry were practically pleading with DoD leadership to institute these changes but encountered a group of managers determined to hunker down and adopt a traditional bureaucratic attitude toward change, namely "this too will pass." Such an attitude is inimical to the demands of 21st-century defense logistics. It runs directly counter to the model of the logistics manager who manages suppliers of products and services and not, as today, the supplies or services themselves—the approach that this book advocates and that is occurring painfully slowly.

A viable development strategy for logistics professionals must rest within a viable human resources (HR) management system. The military largely has such a system that suits the needs of the services, joint commands, and agencies. DoD civil servants do not. Without the kind of reforms that the Bush administration demanded in 2002 for the new Department of Homeland Security (DHS), DoD will be unable to achieve the competent management level needed for the logistics processes described in earlier chapters. The characteristics of the DoD's logistics civil service workforce management system need to follow the commercial business model, which by and large has allowed talent to emerge to manage commercial ventures. Fortunately, DoD leadership persuaded the Congress in 2003 to extend to DoD the kind of human resources management authority given to DHS. That authority, contained in the Defense Authorization Act for FY 2004,[1] is the basis for DoD to develop the management process required by modern government organizations.

First Requirement: Civil Service Reform

A first principle is that most human resources management authority must belong to the managers responsible for the organizations' outputs. The HR staff should be a support staff to help line managers and assure fairness of treatment of employees. There are ample discrimination laws, governing hiring, termination, promotion, and other employment practices, that apply to industry so that more fairness rules for civil servants are unnecessary. Civil service leaders who manage to budgets should be able to interview and recommend hiring of people with needed skills, as well as promising entry-level people. Hiring approval, as in well-managed commercial and nonprofit firms, can be informed by the HR staff, but authority lies with higher level management.

A second needed reform is to eliminate the archaic idea that a government job is necessarily a job for life. The change in the retirement system over a decade ago from "defined benefit" to "defined contribution" allows portability of pension as in most commercial and nonprofit firms. To underscore the linkage between job holding and performance, DoD should be given the authority to use five-year employment contracts, renewable if performance and the needs of the organization require, but able to expire if the person is no longer needed. Such a category would eliminate much of the need for terminations and probably would motivate those who might need some external motivation. This contract for employees is analogous to the practice in the military of enlistment periods extending for noncommissioned officers throughout their careers and for officers only to the next promotion point. Enlisted members whose performance has slipped or who cannot adjust to new requirements simply get their honorable discharge at the end of

---

[1] U.S. Congress, *Defense Authorization Act for FY 2004*, PL 108-136, Title XI.

their current term of enlistment. Officers who fail to be selected to the next rank can be discharged. Such an arrangement, in the form of employment contracts, for civil servants would be far more responsive to the ever-changing demands of the defense logistics processes than the quasi-tenured status of civil servants today.

Terminations should be rare if hiring has been selective. When necessary, they should also follow good commercial practice; unless conduct related, they should be a matter of helping the person to find more appropriate employment. To be both legally fair and perceived so, the termination process must allow for the "due-course" exit, through the expiration of the employment contract, of those not able to fulfill the organization's expectations. "Due course" should include evaluation, counseling, and transfer, if feasible, to better match jobs and a person's abilities. But the staff must see that the organization will terminate those who cannot contribute, in order to make room in limited budgets for those who can.

Recognition of top performance through promotion and salary adjustment (as well as nonmonetary recognition means) is an important part of the HR system; it is a source of frustration to good government managers that they cannot use them as their commercial counterparts do. There should be no automatic "step" increases that simply reward longevity with little regard for performance, treating such increases as an employee's "right." Rather there should be adjustments in salary within a reasonable range, from zero (for the few who have not performed to expectations) to the top of the pay band for the position category, thus demonstrating that high performance results in higher pay. Pay compression relief also is required to better compete with industry and the nonprofit service firms.

The last major area of reform would further open up management's ability to reassign people. No longer can DoD tolerate a system that prevents managers from adjusting workforce assignments because of geographic constraints. The budget is constraint enough to prevent arbitrary assignment changes. If the work changes location, people must move or leave. Well-managed budgets can't tolerate redundant people.

THE 21ST CENTURY LOGISTICIAN—A NEW MODEL

The following discussion illustrates the kind of leaders, managers, and logistics specialists that the services and joint activities will need to manage the timely delivery of support with a minimal logistics battle space footprint. I also present thoughts on the professional development tasks that will enable logisticians to carry out those support tasks. This vision assumes implementation of the civil service reforms proposed above.

Military Logistician Development

We focus initially on the military logisticians and their roles in operating the direct support organizations that provide product support and people support in the battle spaces. Those roles evolve as technology changes but remain essentially unchanged in character.

Noncommissioned Officers

Noncommissioned officers of all services remain the backbone of the battle space delivery of support. They direct the product support, supply distribution, services, and transport efforts of the soldiers, sailors, airmen and women, and marines whom they lead. The commitment to minimize the logistics footprint while delivering effective support in the diverse and frequent campaigns in remote areas that we contemplate puts a premium on their technical skills, leadership, and management. They must understand the part of the logistics processes that support them and their customers. Their technical skills, including the ability to make effective use of the knowledge management system, need to be of a high order to train and oversee the work of their enlisted team members and to allow them to make good use of contractor expertise when necessary. These noncommissioned officers will continue to require continuously upgraded training and education to meet their customers' changing demands for both technical and man-agement skills.

Efforts to make the services more attractive as an occupation contribute by improving the retention of the most talented. However, the services need to give them the precious commodity of time and incentives to continuously improve skills. The Navy's long periods at sea allow their chiefs and technicians more off-shift time for skill improvement than is the case for the other services. The other services need to increase training hours—not necessarily institutional training—through hands-on, simulations, and other remote learning methods. Having system contractors assume routine garrison, base, and homeport maintenance tasks (periodic services, etc.) can make time for training. Working alongside contractor technicians can give apprentice military technicians some of the skills upgrade training necessary to improve their competencies.

Officer Development

The officer leaders of battle space logistics organizations develop their competencies through the variety of units and progression of positions to which they are assigned, as well as institutional training and graduate-level education. More learning, as in the case of noncommissioned officers, can be done through remote learning processes. Standards of competence should reflect the high demands of combat and humanitarian operations with small logistics footprints. The combination of frequent deployments and robust training exercises hones skills and helps these leaders to better oversee the professional development of their noncommissioned officers and enlisted technicians. One of the most important abilities they can bring to their logistics leadership responsibilities is solid customer awareness. And the best way to acquire the customer's perspective is to have experienced it—through an initial couple years' duty in combat organizations. Such an experience yields an acute appreciation for the customer's needs, especially the value to customers of timely delivery of support; it also gives the logistician far more credibility in dealings with combat organization leaders.

Joint Logistics Management Training

In addition to achieving competence in managing the battle space logistics processes, the officers must also prepare to play important roles in the joint logistics management organizations in theaters and in CONUS. In the regional combatant command theaters these officers manage the ISBs, the reception, staging, onward movement, and integration (RSOI) processes and organizations, and the distribution centers. Thus training in joint logistics should be a part of their institutional and remote learning experiences. However, officer logisticians will share these responsibilities with civil servants (and some noncommissioned officers) in the theater management organizations that are outside the battle spaces. Therefore, civil servants who have positions likely to involve them in the joint logistics management organizations also need the same kind of training. Both groups of logisticians should be familiar with how the organizations operate before being assigned, rather than be expected to learn "on-the-job," as has too often been the case in the past. Several years ago, the joint logistics commanders obtained agreement to jointly fund a short joint logistics course at the Army Logistics Management College. That course should continue, with the focus of preparing logisticians for the challenging duty outside their services.

Training for Coalition Logistics Operations

In earlier chapters we assessed logistics processes' fit with the principle of coalition operations. If, as this book suggests, coalition operations are likely to be a normal component of 21st-century campaigns, both military and civil service logisticians will need training and practice in working smoothly with allies. Much of this work likely will take place—like the joint logistics management tasks—in ISBs and naval battle spaces; but in humanitarian and peacekeeping operations such as Bosnia and Afghanistan, coalition operations characterize the whole campaign.

In chapter 5, we discussed the need for theater logistics planning to lay out agreed procedures for coalition logistics with coalition members' logistics planners.

The objective of this facet of logisticians' professional development should be the ability to develop these plans with the understanding of U.S. law and policies and coalition members' resources and constraints. There are two principal ways of providing such learning opportunities, and both should be pursued. The first is treatment in institutional training as part of the joint logistics course and the normal curricula of the service schools that logistics officers attend. It would also make sense to include civil service logisticians in these coalition logistics modules. In addition, such modules should also be available in the Web-based learning curricula, perhaps authored by the Industrial College of the armed forces.

The second component should be joint/coalition distributed logistics exercises using computer simulation drivers. Such exercises ought to be regularly engaged by the joint logistics management organizations, the logistics staffs of the combatant commanders, and coalition members' logistics staffs. They should resemble the JCS-sponsored LOGEX series run by the Army's Logistics Center[2] until 1991. As noted in chapter 10, those exercises brought

---

[2] The Logistics Center's current name is Combined Arms Support Command.

together European and Asian allies with their U.S. theater component and combatant command logistics staffs and organizations—active and reserve components—of all the services. These yearly exercises involved scenarios resembling contingency plans of the combatant commanders in Europe and the Pacific. During these exercises, officers and civil servants of participating nations learned to work together in the simulated but demanding environment approximating actual campaign logistics operations. Over a period of several years, allied and U.S. logisticians developed relationships that facilitated the coalition logistics of the Gulf War and the Balkans peacekeeping operations especially. Such training experiences demystify the complex business of working with coalition partners.

21st-Century Logistics Business Education

From their earliest entry into the services or DoD logistics organizations, military and civil service logisticians must prepare to be part of the logistics leadership of DoD. Since so much of the force projection and sustainment work is to be done by contractors, possessing the skills necessary to deal comfortably with business firms is a critical management ingredient. To achieve that comfort level, logistics managers, both officers and most civil service managers, should pursue graduate business education. An MBA from a graduate business school serves as the entry ticket to the ranks of professional logisticians. At those graduate schools, both military and civil service logisticians come to understand how businesses operate. The defense logisticians gain a healthy exposure to the major business functions: marketing, production, control, finance, human resources, and supply chain management. They learn through interaction with faculty and colleagues from business firms the culture of management and techniques such as activity-based costing, capital investment analysis, and service contracting methods—skills and knowledge immediately applicable to managing DoD logistics processes and organizations.

Logisticians in the Acquisition Workforce

Managing logistics processes outside the battle spaces requires that both civil service and military logisticians understand how to form and manage contracts—although not necessarily that they become contract specialists. Performance-based service contracting is just now coming into accepted use.

It will become the main contract vehicle used for logistics processes to "manage the suppliers" in each of the logistics domains. The unique contracting skills are common in the acquisition workforce. Therefore, it makes sense to include in that workforce both the civil service and the military logisticians engaged in managing suppliers of products and services. As members of the acquisition workforce, they will have better access to the training and certifications for contracting and resource management skills because of the mandates of the Defense Acquisition Workforce Improvement Act (DAWIA).

Development of Acquisition Logistics Competence

The present artificial distinction between "acquisition" and "logistics" must disappear. It is no longer relevant. Just as "logistics is information" reflects the rapid advances in supply chain management since the mid-1980s, so "logistics is acquisition" reflects the transformation from management of supplies to management of suppliers. The Defense Acquisition University (DAU), which recently inaugurated an acquisition logistics curriculum, will need to enlarge its offerings. Particularly helpful will be dozens to hundreds of case studies of using performance-based service contracts and managing suppliers. Such case studies yield the closest approximation to real-world experience for the students—especially valuable to them as a post-MBA experience. The experiences are occurring; resources to turn them into case studies need to be allocated.

Such a merger of the acquisition and the logistics communities will greatly benefit program management offices and their matrix support colleagues. Those now assigned to PM offices have dealt little with life-cycle support issues; they must add supply chain management skills to their repertoire of development and acquisition management skills—and make the not inconsiderable cultural change that accompanies life-cycle responsibility.

Therefore, acquisition and the related resource management skills must be added to the logistics process knowledge that military logisticians must have in addition to their deployment, product support, or people support process knowledge. These are competencies the officers share with civil service logisticians—essential abilities if DoD is to have effective support at reasonable costs. For logisticians to gain those competencies, professional development should include not only the institutional and remote learning opportunities and work experience, but also a year or two of industry experience with a logistics provider. That experience should follow the post-MBA institutional learning experience and precede an initial assignment in the "managing suppliers" role. The education, training, and early management experience will allow the logistician to profit from the industry experience. Parenthetically, DoD should invite defense contractors engaged in the three domains of logistics to place their managers with DoD management activities to contribute to their professional development and allow them to gain a better understanding of their defense customers.

Some of the officer and civil servant logisticians will acquire proficiency in a wide variety of logistics and resource management tasks and organizations. They will become the admirals and generals and civilian executives in charge of making the processes work. Others will specialize—as occurs today. They will manage the processes in battle spaces and ISBs, as well as in CONUS organizations. And the officers may continue after military service as civil servants, and both may continue after federal service as contractors, with all their experiences available to help assure the achievement of timely delivery of support with minimal footprint.

PROFESSIONAL DEVELOPMENT AND THE FIVE PRINCIPLES

One last important question in this focus on professional development is this: How does the recommended strategy help achieve the five principles we have centered upon as critical to achieving a responsive 21st-century defense logistics system?

First, *accountability*: The major facilitating step obviously is civil service reform, which we treated as a prerequisite for effective civil service professional development. Reform, coupled with incorporation of civil service logisticians into the acquisition workforce and the incentives of funded graduate business education and challenging job assignments, should facilitate the development of a climate where accountability is preeminent. Leadership of both logistics organizations and customer organizations will need to reinforce the expectation of accountability—just as in the military services.

Continuously shared knowledge should be part of the content of DoD institutions' logistics curricula; it certainly has that position in the graduate business education programs. Logisticians will be equipped through education and training to make use of the technology and knowledge processes— and will clamor for the availability of continuously shared knowledge because of their more intimate familiarity with best commercial practices. The higher level of integration with industry characteristic of 21st-century product support will make commercial knowledge processes the norm outside the battle spaces. Logisticians will become accustomed to making use of the constantly changing knowledge technology to oversee force projection and sustainment processes.

Contracted logistics support outside the battle spaces requires knowledge of commercial business principles and practices and of contract formation, administration skills, and program management skills that both military and civil service logisticians will acquire through graduate business education, assignments with industry, DAU-led acquisition workforce training and their own experience. Logisticians should be as well equipped to deal with industry partners in all logistics domains as their acquisition counterparts in development and acquisition of systems.

Exploiting the principle of *comparative advantage through coalition logistics* would become second nature to logisticians who learn about the processes in their institutional education and regularly engage in combatant command exercises (as well as operations). Through the increasing expertise of logisticians in coalition logistics doctrine, processes, and practice, the resources of coalition partners can be increasingly useful to the combatant commands.

Adhering to the *simplicity* principle should follow from the sum total of the professional development experiences proposed here. The increasing professionalism of logisticians, their knowledge of commercial practices, and their growing abilities to sort essential tasks from merely bureaucratic practices should lead to wider practice of simplified management, command and control, and funding arrangements. Civil servants' acceptance of more accountability through civil service reform should remove the present incentives to build complex procedures to avoid accountability. However, this principle will need a lot of attention in order to change the culture and gain acceptance.

The end result of implementing the proposed changes should be a far more effective corps of professional defense logisticians committed to the achievement of responsive, timely delivery of support with minimal battle space footprint in support of the nation's 21st-century campaigns and to the efficient use of resources assigned to them.

CHAPTER 12

A Way Ahead: Recommendations for 21st-Century Logistics

This book has painted a picture of 21st-century defense logistics processes that can produce force projection and force sustainment capabilities to achieve *timely delivery of support* with *minimum battle space footprint*. The processes support combatant commanders' campaigns and the operational training of the forces under the conditions projected for the next decade or two.

This chapter summarizes proposals for incorporating those processes into DoD practice. Since implementing them requires "change," innovative change management processes should be used, integrating the efforts of the stakeholders that must implement the changed processes. Change management skills are a necessary product of the professional development improvements described in chapter 11. They require, as a sine qua non, the firm support of DoD and service leadership, both operations (the customers) and logistics (the providers); they also require the support of the political leadership in the DoD and in the Congress. Leaders' firm support of transforming change has been key to industry's and government's past successful efforts; its absence usually brings disappointment.

This chapter presents the "way ahead" for each of the logistics domains, force projection and force sustainment, and in the latter, the product support and the people support processes.

Force Projection

The reinvigoration of joint deployment process doctrine development by Joint Forces Command deserves attention. I recommended in chapter 3 that it include several management improvements to better facilitate the timely delivery of forces.

Senior IPT for Deployment

DoD should establish a senior integrated process team, chaired by the Vice Chairman of the Joint Chiefs of Staff, to oversee the projection of forces to the combatant commander, approve TPFDD changes recommended by the combatant commander and force providing commands, and act as the final arbiter in disputes over priorities.

Reassignment of Installation/Depot Transportation Officers to TRANSCOM

DoD should direct that major installation and distribution depot transportation officers be transferred to TRANSCOM or its surface or air components in order to create a seamless transportation requirement-to-transport process. With their integration into the transportation operating organizations, the adoption of common standards, and better training and accountability, these offices could manage the ordering of transportation more effectively for their supported installations and allow TRANSCOM to better utilize scarce lift resources.

Deployment Management Capability for Combatant Commands

Chapter 3 concluded that TRANSCOM should be assigned the mission (and given the resources) to provide a theater reception and deployment management capability for each combatant command to manage intra-theater airlift and sealift and terminal operation resources. The mission should reflect TRANSCOM's and its component commands' management strengths in airlift and sealift, terminal management, and land movements control. This management team should fold into the proposed combatant command's joint theater logistics management organization. Likewise joint deployment doctrine should be changed to reflect this mission assignment. Such a change will facilitate the integration of strategic and theater lift management and intra-theater force projection integration with distribution. Common doctrine and procedures sanctioned by the Joint Chiefs of Staff would facilitate the employment of common processes for all combatant commands, making training simpler and allowing more focused use of continuously shared knowledge tools. As we noted in applying the *simplicity* principle in chapter

3, the establishment of the JTLM would clarify the complex management relationships, eliminate the often opaque "executive agent" concept, and provide a single funds management entity for all the theater common support functions. One should expect that simplified accountable management of the reception, staging, and onward movement processes would result in a far more effective operation in the next conflict than the Third Infantry Division reported it experienced in deploying to Kuwait in early 2003 in preparation for Operation Iraqi Freedom.

Deployment Decision Support System

Incorporating the already developed "intelligent agent" technology into the deployment management information architecture, as noted in chapter 3, will enable continuously shared knowledge to be available for all the participants in the force projection process. It will also facilitate tracking the continually changing task force organizations during force projection operations. Through the decision support system thus created (also developed in the 1998–2000 DARPA-led Advanced Logistics Project), decision making by combatant commanders, JFCOM, and the force-providing services, and TRANSCOM would benefit from the common operating picture and shared visibility of options, allowing better and faster coordination to adjust to changing conditions. Implementing this decision support system is less a matter of resources and more a challenge to fix accountability for its development. The services must be required to share modular force data with JF-COM to enable a viable TPFDD process. Responsibility, management, and funding should go to the deployment process owner.

Modernization of the DoD Activity Address Code Process

Investments in the deployment decision support system, equipment and force design changes, and new platforms will fall short of expectations if the foundational logistics processes are not modernized as well. Units that do not receive equipment or supplies shipped to them because the system cannot locate them in the theater will have impaired readiness for their combat missions. The DODAAC process is a prime candidate for upgrading to support the task force changes that are one of the hallmarks of 21st-century campaigns. I recommended in chapter 3 that DoD modernize the process and standardize its application among the services and Special Operations Command. A modernized DODAAC process and a uniform unit identification system that recognizes the need for rapid task force formation will improve the quality of knowledge, and most importantly the units' confidence that in the theater they will receive equipment and supplies they order. Chapter 3 pointed out that the RFID interrogators at all deployment and reception nodes would capture tag data containing the ULN and DODAAC of the deploying organization affixed to its equipment and carried by its personnel, and would provide these data to the knowledge system to enable tracking the organization's deployment status against its schedule.

Deployment Support Contracts

We recommended that the special operations and service components and the combatant commanders develop contractor support arrangements for all phases of force projection operations from pre-deployment equipment maintenance through theater assembly area reception. LOGCAP-type contracts that provide a small cadre of contractor planning personnel at both ends of the deployment process will help alleviate the continuity problems of military reassignments and civil servants who must focus on peacetime management. The contractors' access to skilled people and equipment needed for rapid employment will make the cadre a profitable investment when a campaign operation order is issued.

Contingency Planning for Coalition Deployment Support

In chapter 3 I recommended that the combatant commanders pursue a deliberate planning process and exercise program with likely coalition partners to develop specialized roles they might play in the event of contingencies. This planning and the staff exercises can be kept generic to develop procedures and a common basis of understanding. Further, the Joint Chiefs of Staff should reinstitute the LOGEX series of multinational exercises in a variety of geographic locales to develop applications of the principle of *comparative advantage*.

Necessary but Not Sufficient

None of the seven recommended process improvements requires a large re-source commitment. All would contribute to establishing critically needed management and decision support capabilities to assure the timely delivery of land and air forces into battle spaces and ISBs. These process improve-ments can improve the lift resources' efficiency of use, enabling the com-batant commander to gain maximum utilization of the allocated lift—not an inconsiderable achievement since it results in the projection of more com-bat power into the battle spaces for a given amount of airlift and sealift. More efficient use of lift resources can also be gained, as I recommended in chapter 3, by investments in force design improvements and equipment de-sign changes, both of which are being pursued by the services and are bear-ing fruit. Whether improvements are made through redesign of Army brigade combat teams and the introduction of the Stryker vehicle family or by re-design of Air Force and Marine Corps maintenance support concepts to avoid having to deploy most of their component repair capability, the ef-fects are the same: more combat power forward, especially in the early weeks of a campaign.

However useful these efforts are to increase the efficiency of the use of lift, they do not increase the lift capability to the level required for 21st-century timely force projection. To increase the velocity and mass of the forces projected into battle spaces, as chapter 4 maintains, will require more lift and more capable lift—both strategic and intra-theater. Here affordabil-ity is the major limiting parameter.

Investment in Strategic and Operational Lift
Strategic Platform R&D

Chapter 4 proposes an R&D investment program for strategic airlift and sealift that would produce transforming force projection capabilities in fif-teen to twenty years. DoD should also continue R&D programs to produce stand-off cargo delivery systems such as the UAV and parasail to comple-ment the strategic (as well as operational) platforms. These investments ought to produce capabilities to insert medium and heavy land forces close to po-tential engagement areas as early follow-on reinforcement of the lighter forcible-entry forces. In order to achieve strategic surprise and the operational effects of overwhelming force at the critical points, the lift platforms must be able to insert initial-entry forces from sea and land bases 1000–1200nm from landing zones and be able to approach stealthily. There must also be sufficient platforms to enable rapid reinforcement.

In the near term, platform investment should continue to be guided by the results of the mobility capabilities studies in order to keep platform requirements closely related to the national military strategy, with all its mobility force commitments. Within that context, C-17 production should continue, along with periodic technology upgrades to keep it productive over its expected life—similarly for the C-5. An Air Force proposed service-life extension program can keep the C-5 fleet an effective contributor over the next couple decades, by which time the proposed R&D investment program should produce a very large airlifter to replace it. Investment in modernizing the air tanker fleet is also necessary to facilitate strategic force deployment and theater air operations.

Modification of Pre-Positioning

Changes in defense strategy and operational concepts now demand rapid force projection for major combat operations in order to seize the initiative and swiftly defeat adversaries. While initial entry forces composed of Marines and airlifted Army light forces with maritime and air support can seize the initiative, heavier land forces deployed by sea are needed to maintain the momentum to defeat the adversary. Pre-positioning equipment sets for those heavier forces must continue a major emphasis on combat systems complemented by port opening and sustainment capabilities. That is about the only way, for the next several decades, that combatant commanders in the likely areas of conflict can employ the heavier land forces to meet the rapid decisive operations goals. Deploying them from CONUS simply would take too long. Pre-positioning complemented by high-speed shallow-draft theater support vessels to access austere ports will complement both the strategic airlift force as it projects more lighter weight Army land forces and the amphibious ready groups as they project Marine air-ground task forces into battle spaces, giving both kinds of forces adequate initial sustainment. Pre-positioned munitions also enable AEFs and Navy/

Marine aircraft to sustain necessary sortie rates early in a campaign. Continuing to convert pre-positioning from ashore to afloat will provide more flexibility and lessen the political and long-term resource costs of this capability.

Acquisition of Intra-Theater Lift

The operational component of force projection platforms—intra-theater airlift and sealift—should be continuously improved through the acquisition of high-speed theater support vessels for the Army and Marine Corps, the V-22 for the Marines, SOCOM, and the Air Force, and range and capability improvements for cargo helicopters of all the services. DoD also should make R&D investments in advanced tactical transport to eventually replace the C-130. Efforts should be focused on both a fixed-wing/VSTOL and a rotary-wing model, both with the general cargo configuration of the C-130, but capable of delivering twenty tons of cargo into the land forces battle space landing zones. DoD also should invest in a cargo-delivery UAV for use by both strategic and operational airlift and sealift.

The resulting complement of force projection means, along with the process improvements proposed above, would continue to undergird the national military strategy by providing to allies and potential adversaries convincing evidence of the nation's capability to project combat power anywhere, quickly, with decisive effect.

FORCE SUSTAINMENT

This book makes five major recommendations to build a force sustainment capability that will support rapid decisive operations by joint or combined task forces:

1. Implement PM-led contractor support for weapons and support systems
2. Invest in continuously shared knowledge for sustainment operations
3. Transform distribution to minimize the battle space logistics footprint
4. Provide a joint theater logistics management organization for each area-based combatant commander
5. Expand the prime vendor arrangement for people sustainment

Implement PM-Led Life-Cycle Support for Weapons and Support Systems

Ready and durable weapons and support systems operated by well-trained crews are critical to achieving campaign objectives in *rapid decisive operations*. Therefore, the most important force sustainment recommendation that this book makes is to transform the processes for sustainment of the nation's weapons and support systems. I strongly recommend, based on the evidence and analyses in chapters 7 and 8, that DoD implement its policy of PM responsibility for system life-cycle support reiterated in May 2003 in DOD Instruction 5000.1 by directing the services to give the PMs the necessary authority and funding that must accompany that responsibility if it is to mean anything. The DoD leadership in two administrations recognized the dysfunctional nature and poor management performance of the present stovepiped management process, with its lack of accountability and its complex responsibility and funding assignments, and they changed the policy. It is time to exercise that leadership again and require that the services implement it for the large number of presently fielded systems on which combatant commanders depend for executing rapid decisive operations. The services should first convert the most critical weapons systems in order to achieve the maximum benefits in combat effectiveness at the earliest time.

Provide System Life-Cycle Management Funds to the PMs

Progress in implementation is difficult to achieve—a fact that underscores the barriers to change that face this performance-based logistics program. Those barriers include the financial processes of DoD that obscure the costs of operating the organic product support processes. Funds, as we noted in chapter 8, are split between the owning commands, the service headquarters, its logistics commands, the PM, and other activities. DoD should remove this barrier by giving the PMs the funds to achieve the systems' fleet-wide availability objectives. This is the first step in giving PMs real authority. This action would both simplify the terribly confused product support funding arrangements and fix accountability for system support outside the battle spaces. Giving PMs funds management authority would also remove much of the financial accounting burden from the operating forces and the DSUs. In parallel, PMs must establish financial controls for their O&M and working capital funds linked to system use metrics such as flying hours and steaming days, with target budgets for the typical system in each operational tempo category and, therefore, for the system operating units and DSUs.

Convert to Contractor Life-Cycle Support

The next step goes to the principle described in chapter 7, instituting contractor life-cycle support outside the battle spaces. Recall from chapter 7 the principal reasons for moving from organic to contractor support: a higher level of systems technical knowledge, better accountability, a better capability to integrate product improvements with product support, and better workforce flexibility. The fastest route to accomplishing this step is by contracted major system modifications or system life extension programs. The contract for either should have an initial contractor support period to confirm the viability of the work and to develop a cost baseline. The contract should then convert to the same type of performance-based long-term contract used for newly fielded systems, e.g., C-17, F-18 E/F, and MTVR. An integration contractor, as described in chapter 7, should be designated to pull together both commercial firms and government entities as subcontractors.

It may be necessary to operate the modernized part of the fleet under the contractor mode but keep the unmodernized part of the fleet under traditional organic support, incorporating it into the contractor mode as it is modernized. Or it may be necessary to migrate some systems in pieces, i.e., contractor life-cycle support for subsystems or for groups of subsystems. Each system will be unique.

Performance Agreements and Performance-Based Contracts

Core components of the PM's life-cycle management will be performance agreements with the operating force customers and the performance-based service contract with the integration contractor for the system.

PMs construct performance agreements with customer organizations that will help to define the parameters of the industry contracts. They should embody the expected results, primarily system availability, based on the service-directed operational tempo level of resources. The performance contracts with integration contractors must include not only the particular performance metrics for the system, linked to incentives and penalties, but also other unique service contracting facets, to include the involvement of government entities as subcontractors. It has been done before, but not often. Government subcontractors could be parts of maintenance depots or shipyards performing platform disassembly, repair of components and reassembly, and software maintenance on legacy systems. The government's investment in a trained work force, equipment, and facilities would be especially useful when dealing with legacy systems incorporating old technology that industry no longer uses.

Writing the metrics and incentives for performance-based contracts is still a new venture in DoD. Significant training and "integrated process team" (IPT) work has begun in such areas as preparing the business case analyses (BCA) as the basis for the performance-based service contracts, but more learning and experience challenges lay ahead. In order to do adequate BCAs, the teams need the as-is costs and process descriptions—the former element obscured by the lack of readily available financial management information. More model IPT organizations, BCAs, performance agreements, and contract language modules are needed, and the services should allocate the resources to train the PMs and staffs for this new approach to product support.

Rationalize Organic Product Support Infrastructure

A major consequence of the conversion from organic to contractor life-cycle support is the impact on DoD's product support infrastructure, primarily the depots and shipyards. Parts of these facilities contain valuable components such as engine test cells, modern machining centers, and software engineering and test facilities. In addition, the growth of partnering between contractors and depots and shipyards has proven to be valuable to both parties. Yet rationalization is necessary and inevitable. The solution suggested in chapter 7 was for the BRAC commission to recommend transferring these facilities to local development authorities, but give DoD the ability to lease back for appropriate periods the components that are needed.

This course of action recognizes the considerable public investment in some of the facilities, the indemnification (primarily environmental) value for contractors in using government facilities, and the unique capabilities some possess that are not commercially available. But it also recognizes the wisdom of divesting real estate holdings and facilities not needed at present or in the future, of which there remain a great many. The action, in effect, transfers the excess parts of the facilities to the local communities, which can then make productive use of them, and it allows the remaining DoD activities to be tenants without responsibilities for managing the whole facility, paying only their fair share of costs.

Invest in Continuously Shared Knowledge for Sustainment

The major improvements in accountability brought by the conversion of management of weapons and support systems to PM-led life-cycle sustainment with contractor support will go a long way to enabling timely delivery of support to the forces with minimum battle space footprint. These improvements are a necessary but not a sufficient condition for achieving those objectives. The second major proposal for 21st-century sustainment is to evolve the logistics information systems to achieve continuously shared knowledge. We examined the characteristics of the knowledge process in chapter 7 for product support and chapter 10 for people support. There are many common ingredients between them; indeed at the customer organization level they converge into one input and tracking process that serves the customer units' need for knowledge of the status of the availability—past and projected—of its systems and its near-term capability to sustain itself with critical consumable supplies, e.g., fuel, food, water, munitions, and medical items.

As we noted earlier, the continuously shared knowledge system necessary to 21st-century sustainment would include all the stakeholders in the supply chains supporting both weapons/support systems and common supply commodities. It should reach from the rifle squad leader who sees that Private Jones needs a new pair of size 18 boots or the chief petty officer crew chief of an F/A-18 who discovers an avionics fault. The system should include their parent customer organizations, their DSUs, the ISB distribution centers, the F/A-18 system PM and integration contractor and its ISB avionics repair center, the prime vendor for boots, the DLA prime vendor manager, and the vendors for both items.

Establish an Enterprise Resource Planning System

The continuously shared knowledge system could be an "enterprise resource planning system." This system would bind all the participants together through Web-based processes with order entry inputs and failure data reporting through autonomic component failure diagnostics. It would have point-and-click, drop-down menus for other order entry and tracking, and queries. It would employ battle space wireless, wideband communications through satellites and terrestrial means to facilitate order fulfillment and query. The knowledge system should also feature RFID-enabled asset tracking and intelligent agent-enabled supply chain decision support processes. These are the evolving features of commercial world-class product support and distribution enterprises. The technology is available. With this continuously shared knowledge system in operation, both the soldier or marine who needs the size 18 boot and the F/A-18 crew chief who needs the new avionics component can get timely delivery, and their units will gain the contributions to their combat missions of a combat-ready soldier/marine and F/A-18. Because of the rapid flow of information, all the concerned participants will have the knowledge they need to move the boots and avionics component to the customers quickly. Knowledge will preclude the need for large inventories, repetitive ordering, and multiple opportunities for the items to go astray on their way to the customers. Failure to invest in continuously shared knowledge will force logisticians into maintaining larger inventories, redundant processes to mitigate risks, and, inevitably, a larger battle space footprint to assure uninterrupted product and people support.

Transform Distribution to Minimize the Battle Space Logistics Footprint

I recommended in chapter 5 adopting two process-doctrine changes that could best exploit the continuously shared knowledge investment: using log pacs and cross-docking/cross-decking the log pacs by DSUs. The log pacs should be built at the ISB distribution centers, ashore or afloat, for land force units no larger than battalions and for individual naval vessels. Because of the added risk in eliminating the intermediate echelons of supply, each land force DSU should have a liaison team at the distribution center to assure good communication of requirements and status and to represent the DSU and its customer units to the distribution and repair centers and transport organizations. The technology of continuously shared knowledge may work well; but as we old logisticians found in Vietnam and other conflicts, for assuring timely, accurate log pac distribution to their DSUs, there is no substitute for the personal interest that a liaison team can bring to the preparation and shipment of the log pacs.

Land force log pacs would be transported by aircraft, truck, or vessel to the brigade/regiment task force DSU and cross-docked for truck/helicopter lift to the battalions. The DSU would add (or remove) items as necessary to reflect the latest requirement of the customer organization. Naval vessel log pacs would be assembled for loading on the combat logistics force shuttle ships at forward naval bases and transferred to station ships (distribution DSUs) for transfer to the customer vessels. To improve the transportability of the supplies, chapter 5 recommends greatly increased acquisition of standard-sized intermodal ISO[1] containers. Containers such as "quad cons" used successfully by the Marines and PLS flatracks used by the Army are examples. The containers should fit the strategic, operational, and tactical airlift— C-17s to medium helicopters—and vessels. The containers should be equipped, as noted in chapter 5, with GPS-RFID transponders to facilitate tracking the container and its supplies and returning the empty containers for reuse.

Adopting log pacs and cross-docking by land forces will enable removal of intermediate echelons of inventory and ground convoys from the ISB to the brigade/regiment task forces, thus reducing the battle space force protection requirements of the logistics "tail."

Provide a Joint Theater Logistics Management Organization for Each Combatant Commander

I made the case for the JTLM organizations in chapters 5 through 10. Each geographic area combatant commander needs an operational organization to manage the common theater logistics resources and processes. The JTLM would manage the operations of the APOD and SPOD, the operational airlift and sealift and their terminals, the theater common supply stocks and distribution centers, real estate allocation to service component commands in the ISB locations, and ISB base operations outside the service component areas. It would provide the framework to plug in the TRANSCOM theater element and the DLA commodity prime vendor management teams. **It would not manage all support.** The service component commands have

---

[1] Conforming to the International Standards Organization sea container dimensions, generally eight feet high, eight feet wide and forty feet long. Also applies to smaller modules that add to those dimensions, e.g., two 8' × 8' × 20' containers.

logistics management organizations to take care of their ISB tasks such as receiving and staging their forces for onward movement and managing product support functions such as repair centers for their weapons and support systems.

This issue has too long been the proverbial "tin can" that repeatedly is kicked down the road, ostensibly because of service fears that this joint logistics organization would put them on the slippery slope toward one joint logistics command for all DoD logistics. With the decisions by DoD on PM-led life-cycle system support, the idea of a single, huge logistics command should be dead. It is time for the logistics leadership of the services, the Joint Staff, and the Office of the Secretary of Defense to get together and create the JTLM organizations. Each of the large regional combatant commands' organizations should be established with a core of thirty to forty military and civil service personnel for normal operational planning (as a complement to the combatant command J4 staffs' logistics campaign planning elements), coordination with potential host nations, and exercise planning. Each would serve as the framework organization to integrate the TRANSCOM and DLA elements that would manage transport, distribution, and theater stocks of common supplies. The JTLM organization would also contract with one or more service firms for LOGCAP-like support, working with the contractors' planning elements to prepare for the multiple ISB services needed to support the forces and their ISB stationed elements in likely operational scenarios.

The Secretary of Defense's campaign operations order would initiate the process to flesh out the JTLM to its operational strength. In addition to the TRANSCOM and DLA elements and the LOGCAP contractors, the services should be tasked with appropriate augmentation, much of which should come from reserve component organizations missioned to augment the JTLMs and train with them.

Establishing the JTLM organizations is but one piece of the structure to provide the combatant commanders with a joint common supply and services management capability. The structure needs common doctrine and procedures, especially that associated with the standard continuously shared knowledge system described earlier. Those common procedures and the knowledge system are the bases of training needed to prepare the organizations for their vital role in campaign execution. The single standard doctrine, set of procedures, and knowledge system will allow the people who become experienced with one combatant command's organization to move easily to another. Procedural standardization is particularly important for the reserve component personnel and the augmentation elements of TRANSCOM and DLA, who may serve in a couple JTLM organizations within a short period of time, e.g., moving from a European Command Balkans operation to a Central Command operation in Afghanistan.

Expand Prime Vendor for People Sustainment

Chapters 7, 8, and 10 underscored the critical importance of improving sustainment of forces through instituting better accountability. The fifth building block for 21st-century sustainment is to continue the great progress that has been made in DLA's management of people sustainment commodities— food, water, pharmaceutical and medical supplies, and individual clothing and equipment—through the prime vendor program. DLA has moved from being a middleman in the supply chains for those commodities to being a facilitator that satisfies the forces' needs from vendors or commercial distributors. There is work yet to be done, but the momentum and progress are evident. DLA has brought a similar management approach to the major commodity contributor to system sustainment, bulk fuel, oil, and lubricants. For DLA the "way ahead" should be to complete the transition of management of these and other commercial commodities such as construction, housekeeping, and industrial materiel to the prime vendor program, through which DLA can manage suppliers rather than supplies.

Invest for a Small Battle Space Footprint

The five building blocks for 21st-century sustainment contain only *one* that requires modest investment, implementing continuously shared knowledge. However, to realize the goal of minimizing the battle space logistics footprint in supporting effects-based operations, other significant investments must be carried out.

I proposed that DoD invest in force projection platforms and in continuously shared knowledge systems for both force projection and sustainment. The knowledge systems and platforms will improve DoD's capability for rapid and timely delivery of forces and support. A companion investment program, already underway, should be focused on reducing sustainment requirements that drive the size of the logistics footprint in the battle spaces. Several that were noted in chapter 8 are repeated here for emphasis.

Reducing bulk fuel requirements, especially the fuel that must be moved by ground and air transport to land forces, should be a high priority. Therefore, investing in the development of hybrid engines that potentially can halve the fuel consumption of land combat and support systems could make a major near-term cut in the footprint. Investing in fuel cell technology offers even greater potential reductions in battle space footprint, dramatically reducing the bulk fuel requirements to power both vehicles and power-generation equipment. Fuel cell technology potentially could also be an important potable water source—a by-product of its power-production function—greatly reducing the need for water production and distribution and doubling its contribution to footprint shrinkage. Since great commercial interest in both technologies already exists, DoD should find ways to leverage promising developments by acquiring and testing prototypes.

We also noted the tremendous footprint reduction potential of rail gun technology, eliminating propellant and land munitions warheads in the class of large-caliber direct- and indirect-fire weapons of all services. That technology has been disappointingly slow to develop but appears to be close enough to warrant greater effort in packaging the huge impulse-power requirements that are called for. In the meantime, continuing with the well-advanced transition to precision munitions will further shrink the current footprint for bombs and missiles storage and movement.

Another high-priority area of investment is in what can be termed the "Boeing Triple 7" model of product support—equipping critical components of systems with sensors that can warn of impending failure so that component replacements can be planned to preclude failures "at the gate," i.e., when the system has a mission tasking. While this technology investment certainly will not preclude all surprise failures, it should make them rarer. The ISB repair centers can assemble the repair packages for systems in the battle spaces (ashore and afloat) based on the sensor warnings and forward them in log pacs so that work can be accomplished between engagements. Major weapons and support systems benefit similarly when most component replacements can be planned to minimize the effects on scheduled operational sortie generation.

Both high-bulk commodities and bulk POL distribution can be significantly improved with modest investment. The experience in Operation Iraqi

Freedom of selectively discharging RFID-tagged munitions containers from a chartered container vessel to replenish limited stocks in the ammunition support areas in the ISB should be extended to the other bulk commodities. Chapter 5 described how container vessels with subsistence, bottled water, chem-bio protective suits, construction supplies, barrier materials, tires, and packaged POL products could remain at sea until called forward to discharge the needed containers. This concept could be extended to include war reserve equipment such as containerized facility packages, field hospital sets, airfield sets, and other containerizable replacement equipment, as well as major combat equipment on board roll-on/roll-off vessels. The investment is the cost of the chartered vessels operating at sea during the period of the campaign.

Bulk POL distribution, as noted in chapter 5, remains a problem for the land forces and for Air Force and Marine aviation elements that may operate out of expeditionary fields in the land force battle spaces. Development of more easily constructed pipelines and temporary storage facilities would improve the effectiveness of the distribution system. Securing such installations is problematic, but would be helped by (1) embedded sensor technology to identify break points in the pipelines, (2) rapid shutoff mechanisms, and (3) fast repair techniques.

The assessment of people sustainment processes in chapter 10 covered the major contribution that preserving the shelf life of perishable foods makes to minimizing the food service footprint in battle spaces through drastically reduced refrigeration and its power-generation requirements. With the Food and Drug Administration's approval several years ago of irradiation techniques, there should be no major barrier to adding perishables to group rations, following prototype evaluation. There is nothing like a barbecued steak dinner to improve morale as well as provide needed nutrition. Water production and distribution should be improved for land forces with smaller packages of water production, operated closer to consumers—also a modest development resource requirement.

Taken together, these R&D and acquisition investments in bulk commodity distribution, hybrid engine and fuel cell power generation, rail gun power packaging, irradiated foods, modernized water production, and the prognostics sensors for components would dramatically lessen the battle space logistics footprint for all services. They also would shrink the ISB footprints, lessening the large impact of U.S. forces in sometimes politically fragile nations.

TRANSFORMING THE LOGISTICS WORKFORCE

The contributions of all the process improvements and technology investments laid out in this chapter rest on the assumption that the people who manage them are knowledgeable and committed to the high standards necessary to project and sustain 21st-century American forces. A high-quality workforce is not a foregone conclusion. Much work and some resources, as noted in chapter 11, are necessary.

Instituting Focused Skill Development for Military Logisticians

The military component, because of the military personnel system, adapts to new requirements more readily than the present seniority-based civil service workforce (although there obviously are individual exceptions). Since they are focused on battle space sustainment and force projection tasks, the military logisticians live with their customers. The military component of the logistics workforce does need better skills, as well as better personnel retention for the highly skilled people. Two principal areas demand attention if the process improvements and technology investments that this book recommends are to pay off in meeting the timely delivery of support and footprint minimization objectives: (1) weapons system diagnosis and repair skills for the military technicians in the battle spaces and (2) skills in acquisition, including contract formation and management.

Skill development and maintenance for military technicians should be a performance metric for the contracted life-cycle support for systems. The system training process for new technicians and skill upgrading of experienced technicians should be the integration contractor's responsibility. Those technicians should have a performance standard that seldom requires them to reach back to the ISB from the battle space for diagnostic and repair assistance.

The second priority area is helping military logisticians become proficient in acquisition management—the contracting, financial, negotiating, and decision skills necessary to contract successfully with host nations as well as U.S. firms—mainly for services. At a higher level, military PMs need those skills to manage their systems. Since it is likely that the services might place logisticians into PM positions as implementation of PM-led life-cycle support evolves, acquisition training should become part of logisticians' core professional development. Such training becomes even more critical as more force projection and sustainment processes are competitively sourced. The skills to structure and manage these performance-based service contracts ought to become an essential part of military logisticians' expertise to assure effective support.

Transforming the Civilian Logistician Workforce

I made the strong case in chapter 11 for a true transformation of the civilian logistician workforce, who themselves are becoming managers of suppliers rather than of supplies. The only way this can succeed in producing competent, decisive managers is if the civil service undergoes transformation. The current civil service personnel system is so dysfunctional as to stultify all but a relatively few who succeed in spite of the system. The civil service system, at least in DoD, needs to undergo the far-reaching changes noted in the *Report of the National Commission on the Public Service* (Volcker Commission) in January 2003 and now authorized in the FY2004 Defense Authorization Act. Among those changes should be the substitution of a half dozen pay bands for the 150 civil service GS grades and the ability to use employment contracts at all levels. Hiring and termination provisions should be comparable to those used by the best commercial firms and nonprofit organizations. With that transformation, DoD can proceed with serious investment in professional development of its civil service logisticians.

Professional development should parallel that of military logisticians, including subsidized graduate management education—including acquisition, financial, and human resource management competencies. Civil service logisticians should learn with their military colleagues, taking rotational assignments in ISBs, PM offices, and service and joint logistics organizations to manage prime vendor and product support contracts and develop proficiency in acquisition planning, contract formation, and oversight.

Achieving this vision of professional military and civilian logisticians will be key to achieving the objectives of this book's view of 21st-century logistics: the *timely delivery of sustainment and forces with minimum battle space footprint*. Competent, energetic, and dedicated **people** will manage this streamlined logistics system in support of the combatant commands who must fight the nation's campaigns. The process changes, especially contracted life-cycle product support and robust prime vendors for people support, plus the investment in a continuously shared knowledge system proposed in this book, will give them the essential tools to realize those objectives.

GAINING EFFICIENCIES THROUGH BETTER PROCESSES

Many, if not most, of the major studies over the last decade that sought logistics improvements—or "revolution" or "transformation," whatever the term of art at the time—were focused on reducing the huge costs of the DoD logistics system. One of the favorite objectives of those studies was to find the "low-hanging fruit." However, for a number of reasons, not much "fruit" was "low hanging." Even though there has been—and still is— major opportunity for savings in life-cycle system costs and other logistics functions, these savings can come only from transforming the DoD process of force projection and sustainment to produce more **effective** ways to support campaigns. Therefore, the focus of this book has been on the effectiveness side—achieving timely delivery of forces and sustainment with minimum footprint—rather than on cutting costs. However, it is abundantly clear that the process changes and investments proposed here will have major payoffs in a more efficient system. DoD can rid itself of anachronistic facilities and redundant workers by introducing competitive sourcing for product support and prime vendor commodity support. Substituting *knowledge* for large inventories and the related distribution facilities, people, and supporters of people will yield additional savings. One of the major opportunities for logistics savings will be the opportunity to tailor the military direct logistics support organizations to take advantage of the benefits of contracted product support. Several hundred thousand military personnel are involved in those tasks in all the services. Many of those positions can be converted to the kinds of organizations demanded by the nation's 21st-century campaign requirements without as much increase in strength as would otherwise be necessary. The introductory chapter of this book noted that the major cost of defense logistics—about 70 percent—is tied up in product support. At best these process changes will mitigate some of the yearly increases brought about by the sheer number of aging systems being operated at high tempo. But even though modest, the savings will contribute to a more efficient defense establishment—as well as the most effective one in the world.

APPENDIX A:
DEFENSE LOGISTICS COSTS

This appendix summarizes what has become a definitive method of calculating the costs of defense logistics. Its source is Department of Defense, *Product Support for the 21st Century, A Report of the Product Support Reengineering Implementation Team*, Appendix D, July 1999. Actual data were available only through FY 1997. Data for future years were derived from the Future Years Defense Program (FYDP). Thus they are programmed or expected costs—the best estimates that can be attained in the absence of a DoD cost accounting system.

The methodology to determine the costs is included in the first part of the appendix; the remaining sections present the product support cost analysis. "Product support" is the term used to describe the maintenance, repair, overhaul, improvement, and other kinds of support provided for DoD weapons and support systems and equipment.

LOGISTICS COSTS BASELINE

Logistics costs are those costs incurred in maintenance, supply, distribution, and transportation for the purposes of this appendix (and its source). Its components are:

> ▸ resources in logistics programs in the Future Years Defense Program (FYDP)
> ▸ purchases from the Defense Working Capital Funds (DWCF) that are not included in logistics programs
> ▸ costs of active military and civilian logisticians not reflected in logistics programs or DWCF purchases
> ▸ costs of reserve logisticians not reflected in logistics programs or DWCF purchases.

Resources in Logistics Programs

The FYDP database displayed the following costs associated with the logistics programs for fiscal year (FY) 2003 ($ in millions, projected in 1999):

Military personnel (MILPERS):	6,230
Operations and maintenance (O&M):	14,570
Revolving and management:	381
Total:	21,181

DWCF Purchases Not in Logistics Programs

In this component are the revenues shown in the FY 2003 DWCF business plans coming from DoD appropriated accounts that are reported by the supply (including distribution), maintenance, and transportation business areas ($ in millions):

Business Area:	
Supply:	23,494
Maintenance:	7,610
Transportation:	4,455
Total:	35,559

However, approximately 25% of the above O&M costs (3,643) is included in these revenues, giving a net DWCF cost of 31,917 as not included in the logistics programs.

Costs of Active Military and Civilian Logisticians Not in Logistics Programs or DWCF

The Defense Manpower Data Center database, which links personnel to programs in the DoD budget, identifies personnel that have logistics job codes. The database showed 585,045 civilians and active duty personnel who were not in the logistics programs or DWCF in the baseline year (1997). Since the manpower database contains only current year information, the ratio of civilians and active duty military not in logistics programs or the DWCF in 1997 to total manpower not in logistics programs or DWCF (1,793,822) was computed (0.33) and applied to the projected total manpower not in logistics programs or DWCF in the FYDP. The result was a projected 539,921 civilians and active-duty military for FY 03. At the projected cost per man-year of $59,650, the total projected costs of this component came to $32,206 million for FY 03.

Costs of Reserve Logisticians Not in Logistics Programs or DWCF

Similarly the FY 97 data showed 302,651 reserve logisticians not in logistics programs of DWCF, out of a total of 882,374 reservists, making a ratio of 0.34, which when applied to the projected FYDP reservist total for FY 03 shows 272,588 reserve logisticians not in logistics programs or the DWCF. At the projected cost per man-year of $11,930, the total costs of reservist logisticians are $3,252 million.

Logistics Costs Summary

Below is the summary of the above cost analysis ($ in millions)

Directly funded logistics programs:	21,181
DWCF purchases not in logistics programs:	31,917
Active military and civilian logisticians:	32,206
Reserve logisticians:	3,252
Total:	88,556

Note: An updated analysis using FY 2000 data showed the FY 03 costs at $88,537 million—the cost to be used in computing the product support costs component of this total. Each of the above cost elements to be used in the product support cost analysis also reflects the FY 2000 data.

As a matter of interest, the operations in Afghanistan and Iraq drove the actual logistics costs for FY 2003 to $125.1 billion.

PRODUCT SUPPORT COSTS

Since the purpose of the Appendix is to illuminate the types and magnitude of product support costs, FY 2003 projected data were selected. This analysis categorizes product support as "national"—those resources that do not deploy, such as depots and shipyards—and "operational"—those resources that do deploy, such as the military maintenance personnel and their equipment. The table below shows the components of product support costs ($ in millions). Explanatory notes are keyed to each of the components.

Cost Component	National	Operational	Other Logistics	Total
1. Logistics programs	9,094	5,273	7,400	21,767
2. DWCF	25,362		6,520	31,882
3. Logistics manpower	1,397	23,665	9,837	34,889
Total	35,853	28,938	23,757	88,538
Total Product Support: 64,791 (national plus operational)				

Explanatory Notes

1. Directly funded logistics programs: Reflects analysis of each program element and classification in one of the two product support categories or as "other logistics." The division between product support and other logistics was made based on the FY 97 ratio of (a) sales of service inventory control points plus DLA hardware centers and fuel that were assumed to be product support materiel to (b) total materiel sales. The ratio was 88% product support and 12% other logistics (clothing, medical, subsistence).

2. DWCF purchases (not in the logistics programs): The analysis covered the four activity groups: supply, distribution, maintenance, and transportation. The supply and distribution activity groups are divided 88% and 12% between national product support and other logistics respectively. The maintenance activity group is all national-level product support. The transportation activity group is considered strategic lift and is placed in other logistics. The cost of moving materiel in support of weapon systems or support equipment is considered second-destination transportation and is a directly funded logistics program.

3. Manpower costs not included in logistics programs or in the DWCF: These logistics manpower costs were allocated between the two product support categories and other logistics based on an analysis of each of the eleven major force programs and employed the 88-12% ratio to allocate between product support and other logistics. The result shows the $23.7 billion costs of DoD's deployable maintenance and supply personnel responsible for the support of weapons systems and equipment.

4. As of 2004, the analytical approach to estimating logistics costs changed since the Office of the Secretary of Defense no longer required the services to forecast their working capital fund operations. The new approach relies much more on manpower data.

Appendix B:
Abbreviations and Acronyms

AEF	Air Expeditionary Force
AFCAP	Air Force Contractor Augmentation Program
AIT	automated identification technology
ALP	Advanced Logistics Project
AMC	Air Mobility Command
APOD	airport of debarkation
APOE	airport of embarkation
ARG	amphibious ready group
ATACMS	Army Tactical Missile System
BCA	business case analysis
BRAC	base realignment and closure
C2	command and control
CCP	container consolidation point
CENTCOM	Central Command
CJTF	combined joint task force
CLS	contractor logistics support
COD	carrier-on-board delivery
CONUS	continental U.S.
CRAF	Civil Reserve Air Fleet
CVBG	carrier battle group
CSSD	combat service support detachments
DARPA	Defense Advanced Research Projects Agency
DAU	Defense Acquisition University
DAWIA	Defense Acquisition Workforce Improvement Act
DESC	Defense Energy Support Center
DHS	Department of Homeland Security
DoD	Department of Defense
DODAAC	DoD activity address code

DODIC	DoD identification code
DSCP	Defense Supply Center Philadelphia
DSC	defense support centers
DSU	direct support logistics organizations
DWCF	Defense Working Capital Funds
EWG	execute working group
FFD	forward floating depot
FY	fiscal year
FYDP	Future Years Defense Program
GAO	General Accounting Office
GAO	Government Accountability Office
GPS	Global Positioning System
HR	human resources
HULA	hybrid ultra-large airlifter
INMARSAT	international maritime satellite
IPD	issue priority designators
IPT	integrated process team
ISB	intermediate staging or support base
ISO	International Standards Organization
JCS	Joint Chiefs of Staff
JFCOM	Joint Forces Command
JLOTS	Joint Logistics Over-the-Shore
JMC	Joint Munitions Command
JOPES	Joint Operational Planning and Execution System
JPAG	joint planning advisory group
JTF	joint task force
LSE	logistics support element
JTLM	Joint Theater Logistics Management
LMSR	large, medium-speed, roll-on/roll-off
LOC	line of communication
LOGCAP	Logistics Contractor Augmentation Program
LOGEX	logistics exercises
LRP	long-range patrol ration
LST	landing ship tank
LSV	logistics support vessel

MAGTF	Marine air-ground task force
MARAD	Maritime Administration
MCS	Mobility Capabilities Study
MEU	Marine expeditionary unit
MLRS	Multiple Launch Rocket Systems
MMC	materiel management center
MOB	mobile off-shore base
MOG	maximum [aircraft] on ground
MRE	meal ready-to-eat
MRS	mobility requirements study
MSC	Military Sealift Command
MSE	mobile subscriber equipment
MTMC	Military Traffic Management Command (changed to SDDC in 2003)
MTS	movements tracking system
MTVR	medium tactical vehicle replacement
NAVCAP	Navy Contractor Augmentation Program
NGO	nongovernment organization
O&M	operations and maintenance
OEM	original equipment manufacturers
OSD	Office of the Secretary of Defense
P&MS	pharmaceutical and medical/surgical
PACOM	Pacific Command
PDA	personal data assistant
PEO	program executive officer
PLS	palletized load system
PM	program manager
POMCUS	pre-positioned equipment configured to unit sets
RDT&E	research, development, test, and evaluation
RFID	radio frequency identification
RFP	request for proposal
RSOI	reception, staging, onward movement, and integration
SARSS	standard Army retail supply systems
SDDC	Strategic Deployment and Distribution Command
SEDRE	Sea Emergency Deployment Readiness Exercise

SIMA	shore intermediate maintenance activities
SKU	stock keeping unit
SPOD	seaport of debarkation
SPOE	seaport of embarkation
STANAG	[NATO] Standardization Agreements
TACC	Tanker and Airlift Control Center
TPFDD	Time Phased Force Deployment Data
TRANSCOM	Transportation Command
TSV	theater support vessel
UAV	unmanned aerial vehicle
UGR	unitized group ration
UIC	unit identification code
ULLS	unit-level logistics systems
ULN	unit line number
VISA	Voluntary Intermodal Sealift Agreement
VSTOL	vertical and short takeoff and landing
WCF	working capital fund

INDEX

access denial, 101–2
accountability, 15
  C2 meetings requiring, 64
  contractor support for, 198–200
  defense organizations fixing, 15
  DLA contribution assuring, 266
  DoD leadership with, 39
  improving, 20–21
  ISB filling void of, 266–67
  ISB operations improving, 77
  PM transferring, 242
  PM-led contractor supported systems
    with, 177–82
  process performance with, 12, 37–48,
    266–67
  product support with, 174–82
  professional development with, 299
  resources lacking with, 175
  responsibility fixed for, 39
  senior integrated process team improv-
    ing, 69
  unit of command having, 38
accountability barriers, 180–82
acquisition management, 318
acquisition workforce
  contracting skills in, 298
  logisticians in, 297–98
actionable knowledge
  continuously shared knowledge with,
    182
  as information, 7
  role of, 13
active force structure, 60
administrative lead time
  engineering drawings in, 158
  as incompatible, 185
administrative loading, 30–31

Advanced Logistics Project. *See* ALP
AEF (Aerospace Expeditionary Force), 28,
  50, 71, 129
  elements of, 34
  heat-and-serve rations for, 252
  main operating bases required for, 132
aerial refueling
  strategic deployment with, 32
  tanker fleet using, 83–84
Aerospace Expeditionary Force. *See* AEF
Afghanistan campaign, 77
air cargo industry
  commercial versions for, 84
  strategic airlift from, 262
air component, 122
air delivery systems
  options for, 125
  as useful, 85
Air Force, 186, 187, 195, 242, 254, 305,
  307, 317
  approach of, 169
  combat rations issued for, 250
  depot facility investment for, 210
  maintenance policy for, 234
Air Logistics Centers, 180
Air Mobility Command. *See* AMC
air space control, 140
air superiority, 71
air tanker fleet, 306
airborne force, 4–5
aircraft
  as carrier-based, 234
  crew chief for, 146
  land force log pacs delivered by, 313
  making available, 81
  as technicians, 190–91
  updating, 83

GEN. WILLIAM G. T. TUTTLE JR., USA (Ret.) has written previously about logistics matters for *Army Logistician, National Defense Transportation Journal,* and *Transportation Research Quarterly.* He began his nearly 34 years in the Army as an airborne infantry platoon leader and ended as the Army's senior logistician, commanding the U.S. Army Materiel Command during Operations Just Cause, Desert Shield, and Desert Storm. He served in logistics assignments in Korea; with the Ninth Infantry Division in Vietnam; and had tours as the Division G4, Supply and Transport battalion commander, and DISCOM commander in the Third Armored Division in Germany during the Cold War. He also commanded the eastern region of the Army's port and traffic management command, its operational testing and evaluation organization, and the Army Logistics Center, the predecessor to the Combined Arms and Support Command.

Following his retirement from the Army, General Tuttle served for nine years as the President/CEO of LMI, a not-for-profit government consulting organization. He currently chairs the Board of Visitors of Defense Acquisition University and recently chaired a Defense Science Board Task Force on Mobility. He also holds two appointments for 2004–2005: as the President's Professor of Logistics at the University of Alaska, Anchorage, and as an Executive Fellow of the Institute for Defense and Business of the University of North Carolina. General Tuttle also consults with several defense firms and is a director/trustee of others. He resides with his wife, Helen, in Fairfax County, Virginia—close to their three grown children and three grandchildren.

THE NAVAL INSTITUTE PRESS is the book-publishing arm of the U.S. Naval Institute, a private, nonprofit, membership society for sea service professionals and others who share an interest in naval and maritime affairs. Established in 1873 at the U.S. Naval Academy in Annapolis, Maryland, where its offices remain today, the Naval Institute has members worldwide.

Members of the Naval Institute support the education programs of the society, receive the influential monthly magazine *Proceedings*, and discounts on fine nautical prints, ship and aircraft photos. They also have access to the transcripts of the Institute's Oral History Program and get discounted admission to any of the Institute-sponsored seminars offered around the country. Discounts are also available to the colorful bimonthly magazine *Naval History*.

The Naval Institute's book-publishing program, begun in 1898 with basic guides to naval practices, has broadened its scope to include books of more general interest. Now the Naval Institute Press publishes about one hundred titles each year, ranging from how-to books on boating and navigation to battle histories, biographies, ship and aircraft guides, and novels. Institute members receive significant discounts on the Press's more than eight hundred books in print.

Full-time students are eligible for special half-price membership rates. Life memberships are also available.

For a free catalog describing Naval Institute Press books currently available, and for further information about joining the U.S. Naval Institute, please write to:

Customer Service
U.S. Naval Institute
291 Wood Road
Annapolis, MD 21402-5034
Telephone: (800) 233-8764
Fax: (410) 269-7940
Web address: www.navalinstitute.org